DARYL JACKSON

ARCHITECTURE FOLIO

DARYL JACKSON

ARCHITECTURE FOLIO

images
Publishing

Published in Australia in 2007 by
The Images Publishing Group Pty Ltd
ABN 89 059 734 431
6 Bastow Place, Mulgrave, Victoria 3170, Australia
Tel: +61 3 9561 5544 Fax: +61 3 9561 4860
books@images.com.au
www.imagespublishing.com

The Images Publishing Group Reference Number: 346

National Library of Australia Cataloguing-in-Publication entry:

Daryl Jackson.

ISBN 1 86470 049 1
ISBN 978 186470 049 7

1. Jackson, Daryl, 1937– . 2. Architecture, Modern – 20th century.
3. Architecture, Modern – 20th century – Australia – Pictorial works.
(Series: Millennium (Mulgrave, Vic.)).

720.92

Designed by Daryl Jackson Pty Ltd

Production by The Graphic Image Studio Pty Ltd, Mulgrave, Australia
www.tgis.com.au

Digital production by Splitting Image Colour Studio Pty Ltd, Australia

Printed by Everbest Printing Co. Ltd. in Hong Kong/China

CONTENTS

The intent of this introduction is to discuss the process of design and the architectural ideas that underpin the work of Daryl Jackson and his colleagues.

In addition, it addresses the challenges encountered by architects in a new millennium as visionary Modernism attempts to address the energies of a globally informed, urbanised and technologically driven world. How do the ideas of architecture as a culturally expressive exploratory medium persist as far reaching geo-political changes occur, affecting both the identity and memory of people everywhere?

In a modern, dramatically expanded, globally interactive world of symbolic and intellectual exchange, architecture is always in a state of progression and self-assessment. Renewal is obligatory. Sometimes the leap forward is revolutionary, but more often than not there is an evolutionary sequence to the internal argument attached, as individuals profess and progress.

Daryl Jackson is an Australian-born international architect. His work is principally found in Australia's four east coast capital cities: Melbourne, Sydney, Brisbane and Canberra. Projects are also located in Shanghai, Qingdao, Hanoi, Berlin and London.

JACKSON ARCHITECTURE FOLIO

The 23 projects presented in this book represent a pattern of thinking and design authorship.

Time, evolutionary progression, shifting demands, the availability of finance (public or private), and even the vagaries of how competitions are decided, have an impact on the careers of those involved.

Analysis indicates a consistent attitude and recurring ways of doing things, but also of evolutionary direction; as other ideas are discovered, a receptive form of consciousness is always in a conditional state, ready to be extended.

In creative terms, ideas exist in a continuum. They naturally overlap and germinate, when further intuition, instinct and opportunity coalesce with a will to form. Relevant ideas established in one project may also transmit to another.

One constant is the attention paid to design, and to the compositional structuring shared by the principals of the practice in each city. A healthy collaboration, respect and philosophical connection amongst team members in associated international offices is also a constant theme.

As the national Design Principal, Jackson sees his roles (and those of other design leaders) as not unlike those of a film director: working on the plot, lining up the cameras, producing and editing to generate the desired result. To do so is demanding on all the participants who customarily work within a collegiate, the dedicated forum for idea-making. Each project is unified through Jackson's direct design involvement, expressive of his partisanship or position. There is also an acknowledgement of the high-energy talent and co-professionalism of other designers required to bring it all about. This is not that different from movie making, where a host of talents are brought together in the process, with the plot remaining apparent and intact.

Form-finding, the visionary structuring of architecture as idea, is central to the object, with surfaces and shapes seen in light and experienced through the tectonics of construction. There is a consistent concern or preoccupation with abstraction, geometric construct, materials assembly, organising perception and spatial experience. In addition, the culture and associative meaning we attach to design become key conditions that signal the authorisation, desired identity, and memorability needed to provoke recognition.

Generally this type of architecture is produced in modern democracies where freedom of artistic or architectural will is matched by the trio of publicly controlled decisions of planning authority agencies, client design appreciation and construction economics.

One truth is that laws of uncertainty and chance emerge and choices have to be made. Urban planning controls, heritage values, public and community interests, even political intrigue, become a vexatious bed upon which design, as a process, is founded and measured. Notwithstanding these conditions, design as art is still expected to stand or fall on the double-edged sword of talent and conviction. This is why projects may not live beyond the drawing stage.

Two projects in Malaysia were not built because the volatile Asian economy had collapsed. Others have been recalled from the bottom drawer, as unsuccessful competition entries.

None of this invalidates the underlying ideas that customarily precipitate the form-making and the architectural ideals, or even underpin the preferences given to particular visionary intent at the time of their design.

The following projects differ because they exist in a continuum of progress and changing conditions across circumstances that range from a big-city, publicly funded object, to the finesse of a private interior. There are more divergent exploratory definitions and expressions occurring in global architectural structures than an original convergent European modernism may have thought possible. And, it has to be remembered: ideas of a universal kind are continually under challenge by attitudes about regional applicability and individual interpretation. What applies in London or Berlin may not be accomplished in northern Queensland or western China. A school in an emerging Hanoi has to be built in an economy that is not rich by Western standards, and by a technology that, in order to make the project achievable, uses available skills and vernacular systems.

Modern architecture progresses across multiple strands of thought on many fronts: local culture and site-specific identity; regional and global policy settings and issues; landscape and urban form connections, and the obligations of environmentally sustainable development.

Influences in a communication-oriented and urban-informed intellectual system are bound to be varied and subjectively established, meaning they are ingested and emerge from within the authorship. Other influences are brought into focus from more divergent general sources. Both are transformed by the 'free will' consciousness and debate applied to interactive design propositions, means of production, and ultimate resolution as objects.

Some of this work is attached, by definition, to particular urban or landscape locations where strict planning rules apply; design is therefore an act of demand intervention, or transformation. Others are not anchored by such sensibility and may readily transcend previous preconceptions.

Even so, intellectual substance and the dialectics attached to cultural understanding within the city or region in which we are working may also be critical to discovering the architectural expression, reason or identity!

This work is characterised by an approach that values ideas about architecture as instinctive and form-driven, yet intellectually resolved. There is the gravitas of serious endeavour, research and debate, as well as the ability to move freely to determine particular identity and memorability. Sculptural in shape, buildings may literally be light or heavy, playful, spirited, or severe. There are circumstances where the natural is opposed by the urban; others where one generation of pre-existing urbanism has to be confronted and challenged by the juxtaposition of the new.

Hopefully there are detectable common threads discernible in all projects.

Generally there is a desire for modernist principles to prevail alongside a central coordinating idea about circulation and movement, the clustering of dependent activities, and a need to prescribe for public place-making that people will enjoy and remember.

This approach is readily apparent in the compositional idea for the Wesley Preparatory School where a centrally located 'living' room welcomes all students each day and becomes a focal point of exchange between home and school.

Customarily, overt symbolism is restrained, even though structure is expressed and exploited as metaphor in examples of sports architecture such as the Brisbane Cricket Ground, and in Melbourne's Docklands Stadium, where the long span roof structures are developed in the form of bow-shaped trusses: one above, to hold the flying, opening roof, the other with a similar profile, but reversed to support the fixed roof. These sweeping graceful forms add drama to the event, the dynamic of the curve avoiding the rectilinear.

In making the bow form legible in the section against the sky, the obvious architectural connection allows the plan form ellipse of the field to repeat as a key element of the vertical figuration.

This expressive engagement of structure and form also creates anthropomorphic reference; the muscularity, tensile strength and poetry of welded steel elements are meant to register, deploying minimal structure for maximum effect.

New buildings in existing cities require sensitivity. There should be no preserved or embodied meaning by replicating the past in order to redefine and create the future.

Of course the idea of intervening in the past to build the future is not new. Cities have continued to be rebuilt throughout history. However by employing the new to further inform the essence of an inherently enriched historic site condition, a new appreciation emerges as a key ingredient for the future. Intervention, as well as significant transformation is required, allowing historic or valued buildings to be optimistically investigated and understood for their importance in the modern city.

The destructive demolition of the past may not be necessary. Valued renewal is necessary to signify the past, with demanding new modern architecture part of the evolving present, deployed as new history.

Projects such as Georges department store, the Conservatorium of Music in Sydney and Melbourne's Immigration Museum are characteristic examples of respect for the existing. In these examples the new elements overlaying the existing become a palimpsest, breathing new life into historically changing conditions. New formations are added by carefully controlled expressive, sharp edge structure and skin, ensuring new definition and contrasting imagery.

In each case, careful reinterpretation, restoration and conservation of the existing historic buildings is not compromised. This case for urbanism prompts useful change in ideas, allowing new solutions to be formed, debated, adopted or rejected.

3. URBANISM AND IDENTITY

Dynamic and changing forms of urbanism are currently being debated within the polis, at the same time as architects set about building them. Forty-kilometre transport networks, incorporating public and private buildings, connect historic or existing urban centres and 500-kilometre freeways connect the cities in ways never before imagined.

Yet, suburban, inner urban, and city centre complexes exist as discrete typological forms, each demanding new layers of connection to establish their newfound formal identity and sense of place.

Such circumstances continue to affect particular built settings, with the new deployed to offer both abstract ideas and specific analogue.

Within this series of projects, two buildings, Swinburne University's Graduate School of Management and the Victorian County Court in central Melbourne, work their way into their respective street grids to form hard-edge modern figures on important street corners. The slicing, 'cut edge' profiling of the Court entrance portico is a gesture of urban affirmation that symbolises and emphasises a new presence. The street edges are additionally met by a punched masonry mass. A lighter folded skin tower of etched zinc is set back and poised above the complex to appear as a strong renewing form in this sector of the city.

These ideas are readily apparent in other projects, particularly the Mukim Tebrau scheme in Malaysia where an urban plinth of new building defines a low-rise courtyard form, from which a luminous circular tower creates a powerful and focal figurative image, identifying this newly created micro modern city.

Another new city edge structure is a project for Aoshan, China. A ground figure of three axial parks and canals draws the foreshore together with the site interior to provide a strong, compelling and clear public framework. A range of smaller, more intricately formed precincts are developed over time, each based on distinctive housing typology and form.

4. TOPOGRAPHY AND GEOGRAPHY

Climate, topography, landscape – principally the orientation to sun, wind, view and slope – are issues that continue to inform our architecture.

Topography, climate and urban or rural structure offer points of departure for a design language that seeks to respond to location, context, and function.

The Singapore Library is a block figure, layered with a second shade skin of punctured metal to protect the interior from high humidity, intense periodic rain and moist heat. Upper-level voids cut into the mass induce additional currents of air to circulate and assist the cooling. The design seeks to define a rational form or aesthetic, to differentiate a building in the tropics from more temperate climates.

The idea is to logically and rationally use climate to develop expressive form and regional identity, as well as create an environmentally responsible result.

Similarly, the hillside sites of Batu Maung in Penang present particular opportunity. The island hills drop down to the water, creating terraced or stepped cliff faces for housing and hotel rooms. Two hotels project over the water, creating a microclimate on the piers below the upper mass. The colonnaded building forms offer shade, while induced air currents cool the covered markets and outdoor dining.

An Irish stadium project integrates a large-scale series of stepped, flat field designs and new stadia into the gently rolling landform. Surrounded by recycled water from the catchment, the landform provides a critical anchorage for the design, as well as new parkland recreation for the city.

Another example is found in the glasshouse roof form of the Commonwealth Scientific and Industrial Research Organisation (CSIRO) building in Canberra. Seen as a research centre for the public, the development of science and its application to new technology is on view. The folded glass roof form, naturally breathing as the stepped structural form allows air movement to cool the space, has a formal connection to the greenhouses the scientists customarily inhabit and which occur elsewhere within this scientific environment.

Identity may also result in a search for the expressive power of natural forms, or in technologies beyond architecture, or to offer symbolic reference, as seen in an ark-shaped image for an assembly hall in a junior school project for Xavier College. This figurative shape can be interpreted in multiple ways, even its representational form is ambiguous.

Association depends upon the information or legibility created by individual observers: small children may be more inventive given a prompt. Hence the Xavier Preparatory School is a built reference, a cue to a young child's understanding of his or her environment.

Obviously, the art-laden references assume some prior knowledge of an ancient biblical story; they do, however, additionally prompt a proactive stance or new awareness from the observer through the powerful arguments of abstraction and expressionism.

This state of thinking readily embraces and describes the form of the modern city, the way in which we experience it, and choose to identify with it.

The use of the word 'association' means that the architectural forms seek referential connection; it is not necessarily mimetic, or a figure of replication, but rather a juxtaposition that offers some form of association or communication beyond the object.

The only true constant of the exploratory, inventive model is to have both memory and imagination fuel the creative state of mind, feed the intuitive talent, and generate the objects.

The foregoing discussion is offered as a prompt or explanation. Architecture is architecture; it is not art and it is not science. It is a unique form of physical expression that engages all the senses: the touch and feel of materials and spaces, the visual perception and representation of ideas that stimulate and excite; and, through their emotional substance, offer themselves for useful interpretation as buildings that people will embrace emotionally, and will find useful and sustaining.

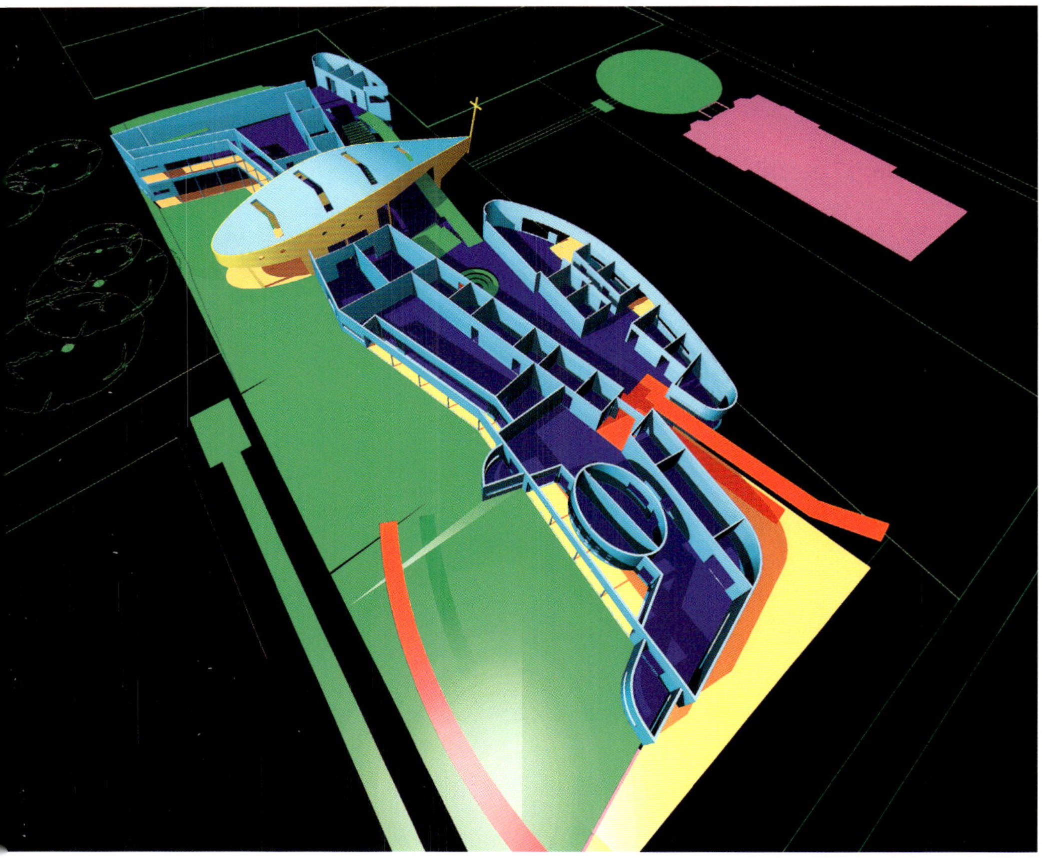

6. BEYOND THE MILLENNIUM: WHERE TO FROM HERE?

'Globalisation' in this new millennium means we are prepared for both large- and small-scale concerns to be addressed. The debates about particularity and universality, global and regional, technological and artistic, autocracy and democracy, continue.

The process of urbanisation now occurring places huge demands on the infrastructure. Cities of five to seven million newly emerging middle-class workers, all requiring better standards of health, education, clean food and water, demand new urban districts growing at great speed. Frequently missing from the public transport system are the broadband communication networks that link things together, minimising dangerous exhausts from an unlimited growth in private automobile ownership. Expanding networks of freeways are currently being installed to make it all work.

Also missing is the middle ground of urban design. Informed layouts that may incorporate adequate public space and private facilities of high amenity appear engulfed by the resultant traffic problems.

In city design there remains a need to create the public realm – promenades, gathering places, market or civic squares – to increase the opportunities for community life to exist and to ensure identity. The relevance of inherent cultures is at the scale of the urban village.

For the architect called in to produce a 'masterplan' there is a limited basis for understanding the real demand, including the political framework. Reconciling the relationship between public entities and the private sector developer is a concern for everyone.

It should come as no surprise to people working on documentation in London to see the fruits of their labour being emailed to Sydney; or for a late night call to Berlin to result in an architect in Melbourne preparing sketches for a housing project in Brandenburg.

This cut into just one section of the millennium rainbow indicates that a full spectrum of colours may be attained; less certain are the global circumstances that veil the point where the sky meets the horizon.

But don't be mistaken, this introduction is not about such dilemmas; rather it endeavours to press all the buttons in order to profess, to see that the instinctive will-to-form of architecture as a discourse is able to question and consolidate; to challenge and confirm the inherent creativity required.

This is an explanatory note about the process and progression of an ongoing, or third field of modern architecture. This architecture pursues a transmission of ideas beyond either of the previous Modern discourses (original or post) to recognise the substantive and the circumstantial; the conditional, flawed, irrational, even impossible decision-making capabilities, particularly in the impoverished yet rapidly expanding cities of Africa, China or Southeast Asia. In the geo-political and socio-economic planning sense, key urban issues of design lie beyond architecture; those of environment, water, food, transportation and adequate shelter for a vast majority of essentially rural populations remain to be addressed in ways yet to be determined.

It needs to be remembered that modern architecture was founded upon a central rational idea related to problem solving as both theory and practice, with the reality of imagining and individual interpretive skill a key ingredient for the human condition. One task ahead is to cast the net for idea making in a bigger exploratory arc to include the reasonability of first world and third world abilities and standards of living remaining in touch and intact: promoting coexistent yet demanding independent human cultures of even greater richness and diversity is part of the encounter.

In such a problematic environment, management demands of time and cost can only be combated by intelligent form making and a capacity to offer artistically and scientifically advanced, fertile and enriched visionary circumstances.

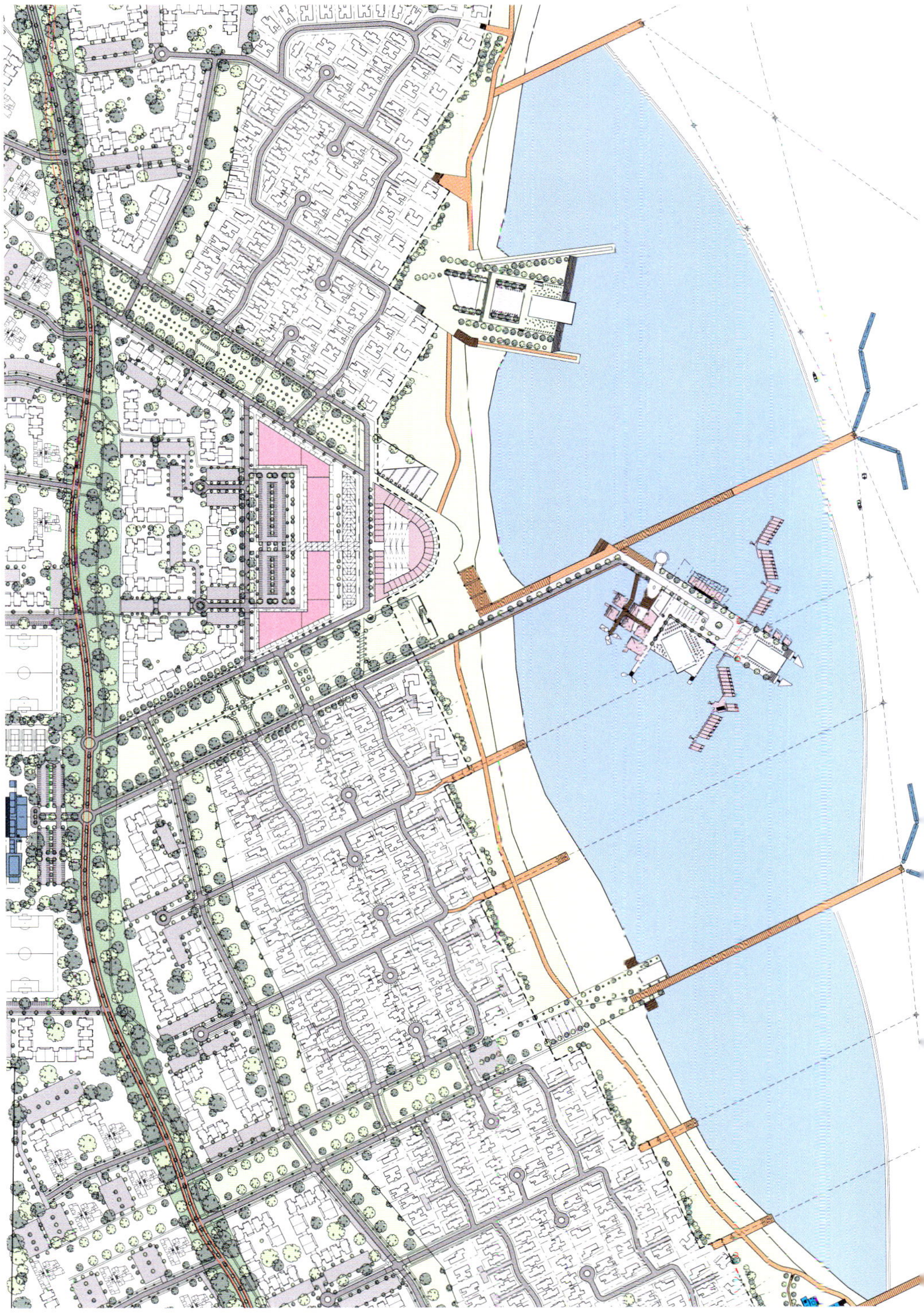

Daryl Jackson Architecture has won significant awards and competitions, in many locations within Australia. Since the inception in 1980 of the Sir Zelman Cowen Awards for best Australian building of the year, the firm has received three such awards, evidence of the assembled talent and commitment to architecture.

Jackson is an RAIA Gold Medallist, and a Professor of Architecture at the University of Melbourne and Deakin University. He has received an Order of Australia for his services to the profession and the community and is an Honorary Doctor of the University of Ballarat.

2006

Mildura Riverfront Masterplan, Mildura, VIC
Planning Institute of Australia, National, Award of Merit
Victoria Local Government Award
Victorian State President's Award

2005

Brindabella Business Park, Canberra Airport, ACT
Green Building Council of Australia 5 Green Star Building Award

Nerang Library, QLD
Gold Coast Urban Design Awards,
The People's Choice Award
Sue Robbins Award for Excellence in Urban Design

2004

Nerang Library, QLD
Royal Australian Institute of Architects,
Gold Coast & Northern Rivers Regions
Building of the Year
People's Choice Award

Australian Greenhouse Office, Federal Department of Environment and Heritage, Canberra, ACT
Royal Australian Institute of Architects (ACT Chapter)
Sustainable Development Award
Indesign Environmental Sustainability Award
Master Builders Association Environmental Award

St Kevins College, Toorak, VIC
City of Stonnington Urban Design Awards,
Best Non-residential Development Award

2003

Victorian County Court, Melbourne, VIC
(In collaboration with Sinclair Knight Mertz and Lyons Architects)
Royal Australian Institute of Architects,
(Victorian Chapter) Interior Architecture Award

AWARD WINNING PROJECTS

Varsity College – Preparatory and Junior School, QLD
Gold Coast Urban Design Award

Gold Coast Arts Centre, QLD
Gold Coast Urban Design Award

Perisher Village (Detailed Village Design Plan), NSW
Planning Institute of Australia Award, NSW

2002

Conservatorium of Music, Sydney, NSW
Royal Australian Institute of Architects, (NSW Chapter) Public Building Award
UNESCO Asia Pacific Heritage Conservation Award
World Architecture Awards – Public/Cultural Buildings – Oceania Regional Finalist

Western Australia Police Academy, Joondalup, WA
(With Peter Hunt Architects)
Royal Australian Institute of Architects (WA Chapter) George Temple Poole Award/Public Institutional Building Award

Channel V TV Studio, Sydney, NSW
BASF Interior Design Award

2001

Subiaco Oval Redevelopment, WA
(With Peter Hunt Architects)
Royal Australian Institute of Architects (WA Chapter) Design Award

2000

CSIRO Discovery Centre, Canberra, ACT
Royal Australian Institute of Architects (ACT Chapter) Canberra Medallion

Council House Refurbishment, Perth, WA
(With Peter Hunt Architects)
Royal Australian Institute of Architects (WA Chapter) Design Award

Couran Cove Resort, Stradbroke Island, QLD
Australian Institute of Steel Construction, Queensland Structural Engineering Steel Design Award

Colonial Stadium, Docklands, VIC (In collaboration with Bligh Lobb Sports Architects Pty Ltd and HOK Sport)
Australian Institute of Steel Construction, Victorian Steel Construction Award

1999

Capital Airport Group – Capital Air Jet Facility, Canberra, ACT
Royal Australian Institute of Architects (ACT Chapter) Canberra Medallion

Couran Cove Resort, Stradbroke Island, QLD
Royal Australian Institute of Architects (QLD Chapter)
Beatrice Hutton Award
Building of the Year Award
Regional Commendation
Commercial Award Commendation

Immigration Museum and Hellenic Archaeological Museum, Melbourne, VIC
Royal Australian Institute of Architects
Presidents Award for Recycled Buildings
The Melbourne Prize – Commendation
John George Knight Award – Conservation
Access Citation Award

Administrative Building Refurbishment and DOFA Fitout
Royal Australian Institute of Architects (NSW Chapter) Award

Port Arthur Historic Site Visitor Centre, TAS
(In collaboration with Philip Lighton Architects)
Royal Australian Institute of Architects (Tasmanian Chapter)
New Buildings – Public Buildings Award

All Hallows' School Library/Science Building, QLD
Royal Australian Institute of Architects (Brisbane) Regional Commendation

1998

Georges Retail Redevelopment, Melbourne, VIC
(In collaboration with Conran Design Partnership)
Royal Australian Institute of Architects,
City of Melbourne Prize
Interior Architecture Medal

Cleveland Library and Administration Centre, QLD
Royal Australian Institute of Architects (Brisbane)
Regional Commendation
Civic Design Award

Sunshine Coast University College, Science Faculty Building, QLD
Royal Australian Institute of Architects
(Queensland Chapter)
Environment Award
Regional Commendation
Maroochy Excellence in Building and Planning
Awards, Institutional Building/Energy Efficiency Award

Australian Institute of Sport, Alpine Training Centre, Thredbo, NSW
BHP Metal Buildings Association National Awards,
Merit Award

Crown Entertainment Complex Riverside Promenade, Melbourne, VIC (In collaboration with Bates Smart and Perrott Lyon Mathieson)
Royal Australian Institute of Architects (Victorian
Chapter) Award of Merit – Urban Design

1997

Australian Institute of Sport Ansett Sports Visitor Centre, Canberra, ACT
Royal Australian Institute of Architects
(ACT Chapter) Canberra Medallion

Capalaba Town Centre Urban Works, Capalaba, QLD
Royal Australian Institute of Architects
Civic Design Award
Regional Commendation

The Northern Grandstand, Brisbane Cricket Ground 'The Gabba', Brisbane, QLD
Royal Australian Institute of Architects (Queensland
Chapter) The F.D.G Stanley Award Commendation

1996

Southern Stand of Subiaco Oval, WA
(With Peter Hunt Architects)
Subiaco Council Design Award

1994

Department of Land Administration Offices, Redlands, WA (With Peter Hunt Architects)
Royal Australian Institute of Architects
(WA Chapter) Merit Award

Penguin Parade, Phillip Island, VIC
Australian Tourism Award
Membrane Structures Association of Australia
Merit Award (1990)
Victorian Tourism Award (1989)

1993

120 Collins Street, Melbourne, VIC
(In collaboration with Hassell Architects)
BOMA Award, National Building Owners & Managers
Association
Royal Australian Institute of Architects
(Victorian Chapter) Award Winner (1992)

1992

Melbourne Cricket Ground, Great Southern Stand, Melbourne, VIC (With Tompkin Shaw & Evans Pty Ltd)
Royal Australian Institute of Architects
Sir Zelman Cowen Award, National award for
the most outstanding architectural work
Victorian Chapter Architecture Medal

University of Canberra,
Boiler House Lecture Theatre, ACT
Royal Australian Institute of Architects
(ACT Chapter) Canberra Medallion

The Hyatt Hotel, Canberra, ACT
Australian Tourism Award

South Brisbane College of TAFE,
Food Technology Building, QLD
Royal Australian Institute of Architects (Queensland Chapter) F.D.G Stanley Award, Finalist

1991

Australian Chancery Complex, Riyadh, Saudi Arabia
Royal Australian Institute of Architects International Award

Australian Institute of Sport Grandstand,
Canberra, ACT
Royal Australian Institute of Architects
(ACT Chapter) Canberra Medallion

1990

The Hyatt Hotel, Canberra, ACT
Australian Council of National Trusts
Australian Heritage Award
National Building Owners and Managers Association Award

1989

The Hyatt Hotel, Canberra, ACT
Royal Australian Institute of Architects
National President's Award
National Interior Design Award
ACT Tourism International Accommodation Award
Heritage Award

Australian Film, Television and Radio School,
North Ryde, NSW
Royal Australian Institute of Architects
(NSW Chapter) Merit Award

Sarina's Restaurant, Taronga Zoo, Sydney, NSW
National ACROD Award

1988

Australian Bicentennial Exhibition
Australian Consulting Engineers Association
National Award, Commendation
Membrane Structures Association of Australia
National Award, Commendation

Lake Ginninderra College, ACT
Royal Australian Institute of Architects
(ACT Chapter) Merit Award

Northcote Library, Northcote, VIC
Royal Australian Institute of Architects and the Australian Library Promotion Council, Citation, Library Design Awards

1987

Australian Defence Force Academy Indoor Sports complex, Campbell, ACT
(In association with Department of Administrative Services Construction Group – ACT Region)
Royal Australian Institute of Architects
(ACT Chapter) Canberra Medallion

Challenge Stadium (formerly Superdrome),
Graylands, WA (With Peter Hunt Architects)
Royal Australian Institute of Architects
(WA Chapter) Design Award

1985

Australian Institute of Sport Training Halls, Canberra, ACT
Third World Biennale of Architecture, Interarch 85, Sofia, Bulgaria Honorary Diploma and Bronze Medal

Singapore High Commission and Chancery, Yarralumla, ACT
Royal Australian Institute of Architects (ACT Chapter) Canberra Medallion

Esprit de Corp Offices and Warehouse, Abbotsford, VIC
Royal Australian Institute of Architects President's Award Citation

1984

Australian Institute of Sport Indoor Training Pool, Canberra, ACT
Royal Australian Institute of Architects
Sir Zelman Cowen Award, National award for the most outstanding architectural work

Australian Institute of Sport, National Sports Centre Swimming Halls, Canberra, ACT
Royal Australian Institute of Architects (ACT Chapter) Canberra Medallion

1983

Hampden Court Apartments, North Sydney, NSW
Royal Australian Institute of Architects (NSW Chapter) Merit Award

1982

McLachlan Offices, Barton, ACT
Royal Australian Institute of Architects (ACT Chapter) Merit Award

Abrahams House, Brighton, VIC
Royal Australian Institute of Architects (Victorian Chapter) Robert Haddon Award

Jackson House, Shoreham, VIC
Timber Promotion Council of Australia. Timber in Architecture Award

Ashburton Branch Library, Ashburton, VIC
Royal Australian Institute of Architects and Australian Library Promotion Council, Library Design Awards, Citation

1981

Canberra School of Art, Acton, ACT
Royal Australian Institute of Architects
Sir Zelman Cowen Award, National award for the most outstanding architectural work
Canberra Medallion

1979

Canberra School of Art, Acton, ACT
Royal Australian Institute of Architects (ACT Chapter)

Balwyn Branch Library, Balwyn, VIC
Royal Australian Institute of Architects and the Australian Library Promotion Council, Library Design Awards, Citation

Royal Melbourne Hospital Staff Housing, North Melbourne, VIC
Royal Australian Institute of Architects (Victorian Chapter) Citation

1978

Canberra School of Music, ACT
Royal Australian Institute of Architects (ACT Chapter) Canberra Medallion

State Bank College, Baxter, VIC
Royal Australian Institute of Architects
(Victorian Chapter) Bronze Medal

Collingwood Swimming Pool, Collingwood, VIC
Royal Australian Institute of Architects
(Victorian Chapter) Citation

1977

Canberra School of Music, ACT
Royal Australian Institute of Architects
(ACT Chapter) Merit Award

1976

City Edge Housing, South Melbourne, VIC
Royal Australian Institute of Architects
(Victorian Chapter) Bronze Medal

Boyle House, Mornington, VIC
Royal Australian Institute of Architects
(Victorian Chapter) Citation

St Paul's School, Woodleigh, VIC
Royal Australian Institute of Architects
(Victorian Chapter) Citation

Yooralla Special Day School, Glenroy, VIC
Royal Australian Institute of Architects
(Victorian Chapter) Citation

South Drummond Street Conservation Study, Carlton, VIC
Royal Australian Institute of Architects
(Victorian Chapter) Citation

1974

Library Resource Centre, Methodist Ladies' College, Kew, VIC
Royal Australian Institute of Architects
(Victorian Chapter) Citation

1973

Princes Hill High School, North Carlton, VIC
Royal Australian Institute of Architects
(Victorian Chapter) Bronze Medal

1970

Lauriston Girls' School, Armadale, VIC
Royal Australian Institute of Architects
(Victorian Chapter) Bronze Medal

1969

Harold Holt Memorial Swimming Pool, Malvern, VIC
(In association with Kevin Borland)
Royal Australian Institute of Architects
(Victorian Chapter) Citation

SELECTED PROJECTS

The apartments were a competition exercise, a submission that illustrated how two very tall object-like residential towers could be juxtaposed to accept and allow a city viewline to pass through their compositional form.

The base structure is a waterfront plinth containing retail, restaurant, offices and car parking. This supports a residential roof garden, a raised arbor from which the much thinner towers emerge to challenge each other in the sky. On the way to the top a bridge link connects the two, with shared residential facilities: spas, pools, restaurant, club and health club.

The tectonics of sculpted conjunction are elaborated via a series of through-block openings and punctuations, three-level garden apartments, and folded metal exterior sun screens to both east and west exposures.

The central expressive idea is to avoid the repetitive monochromatic structure of the typical high-rise residential tower. This one escaped the attention of the development company, as it focused on the yield.

YARRA EDGE

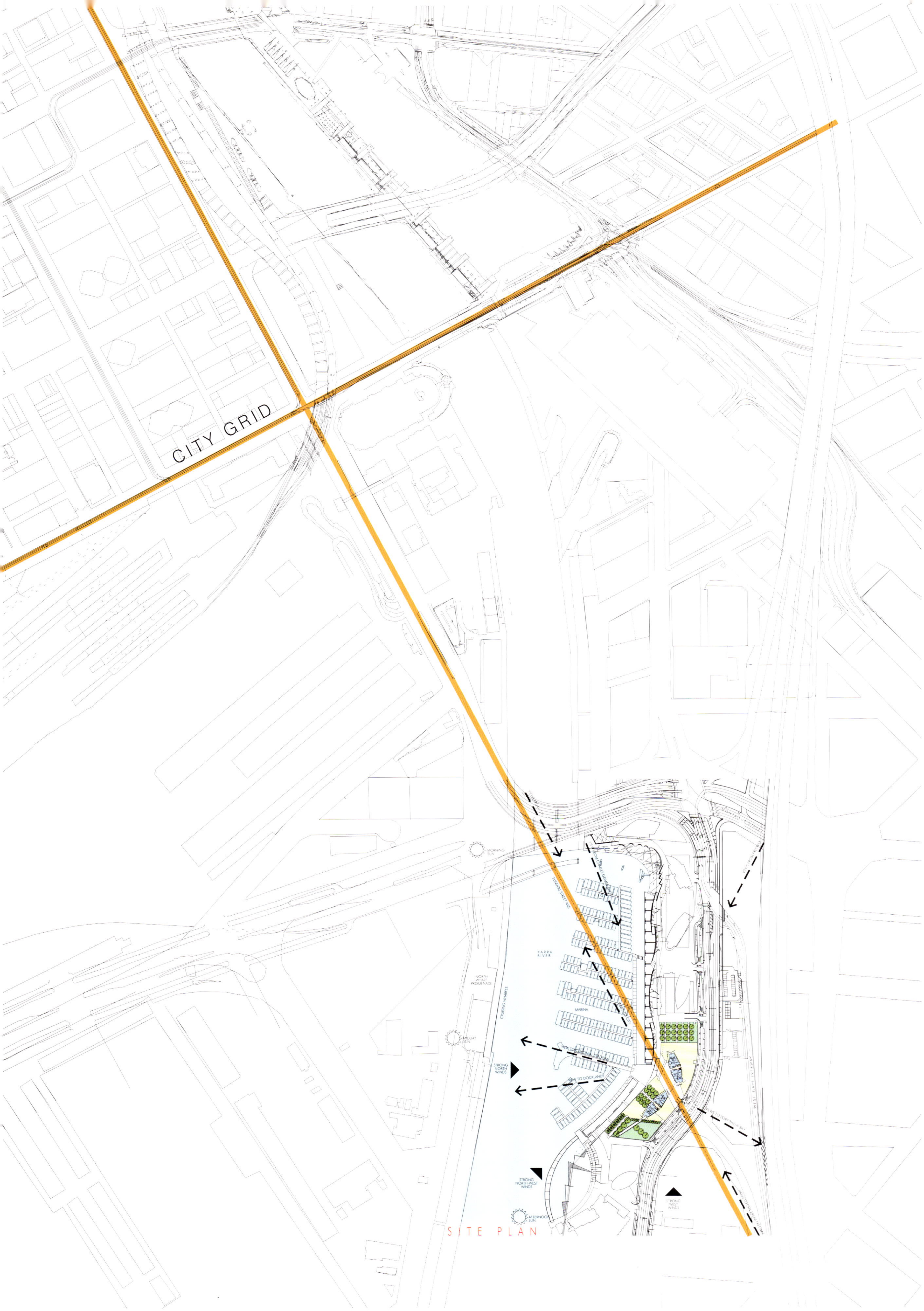
CITY GRID
CHARLES GRIMES BRIDGE
MONTAGUE STREET
MORNING SUN
FLINDERS STREET AXIS
VIEWS FROM FREEWAY
YARRA RIVER
NORTH WHARF PROMENADE
CRUISING WHARFES
MARINA
MIDDAY SUN
STRONG NORTH WINDS
VIEW TO DOCKLANDS
VIEWS TO PORT PHILLIP BAY
WEST GATE FREEWAY
STRONG NORTH-WEST WINDS
STRONG WEST WINDS
AFTERNOON SUN
SITE PLAN

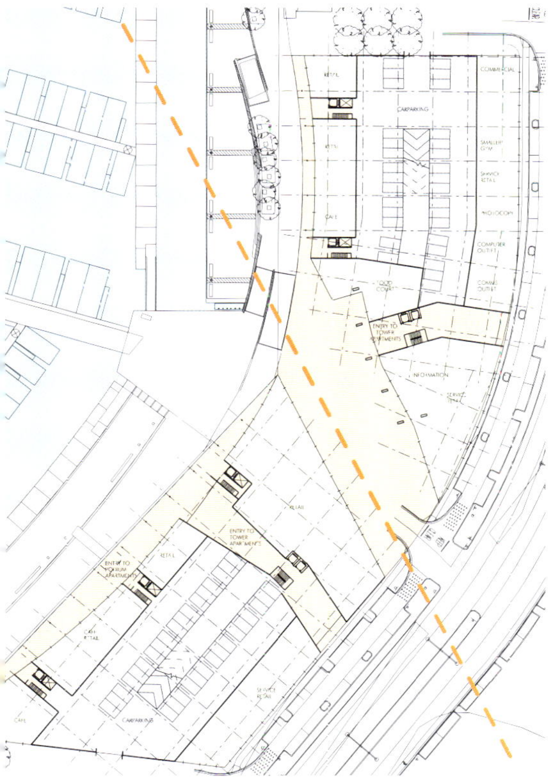

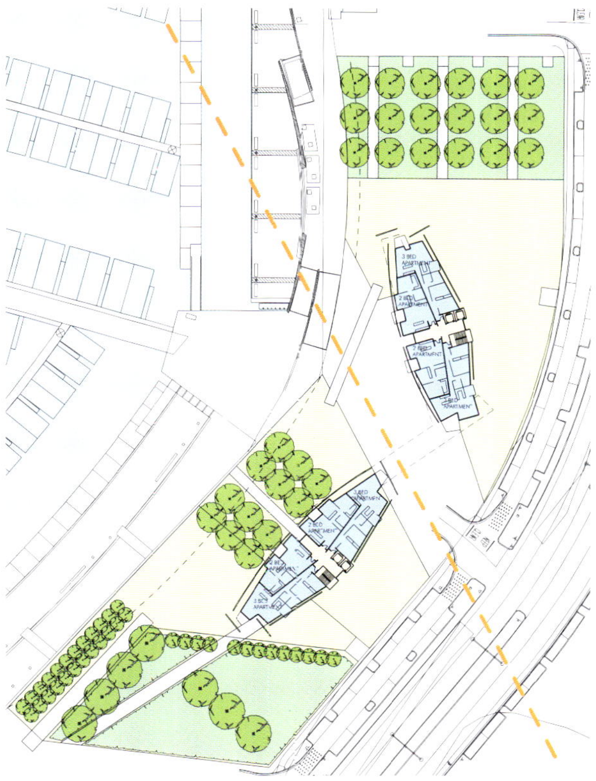

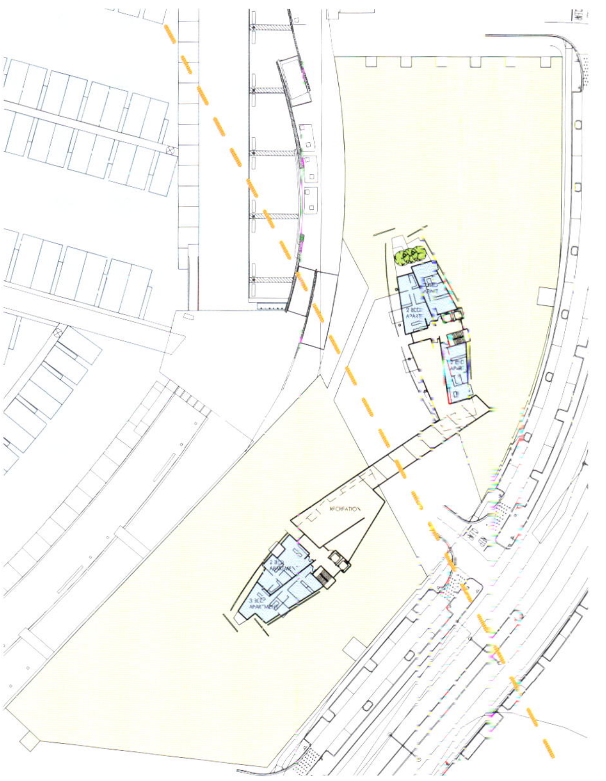

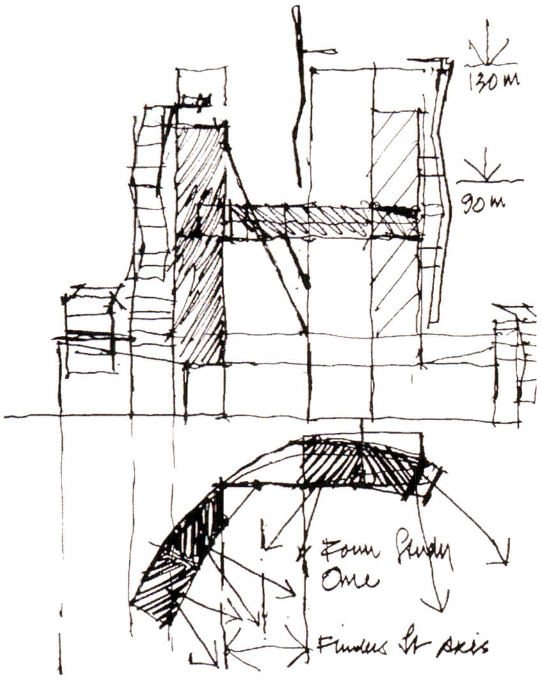
130m
90m
Form Study
One
Flinders St Axis

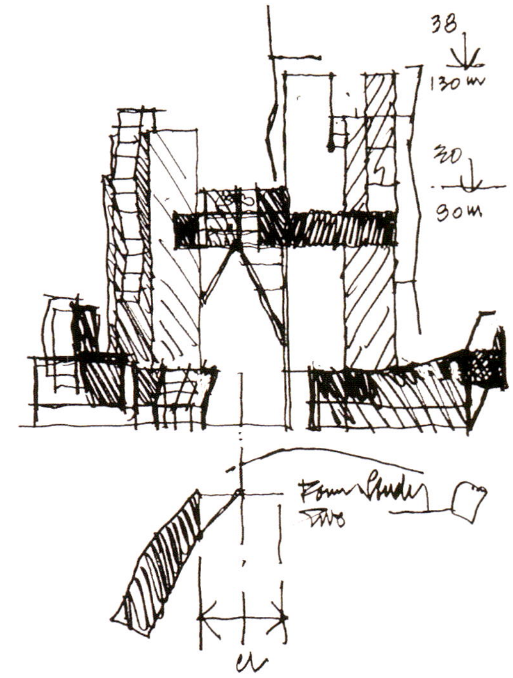
38
130m
30
90m
Form Study
Two

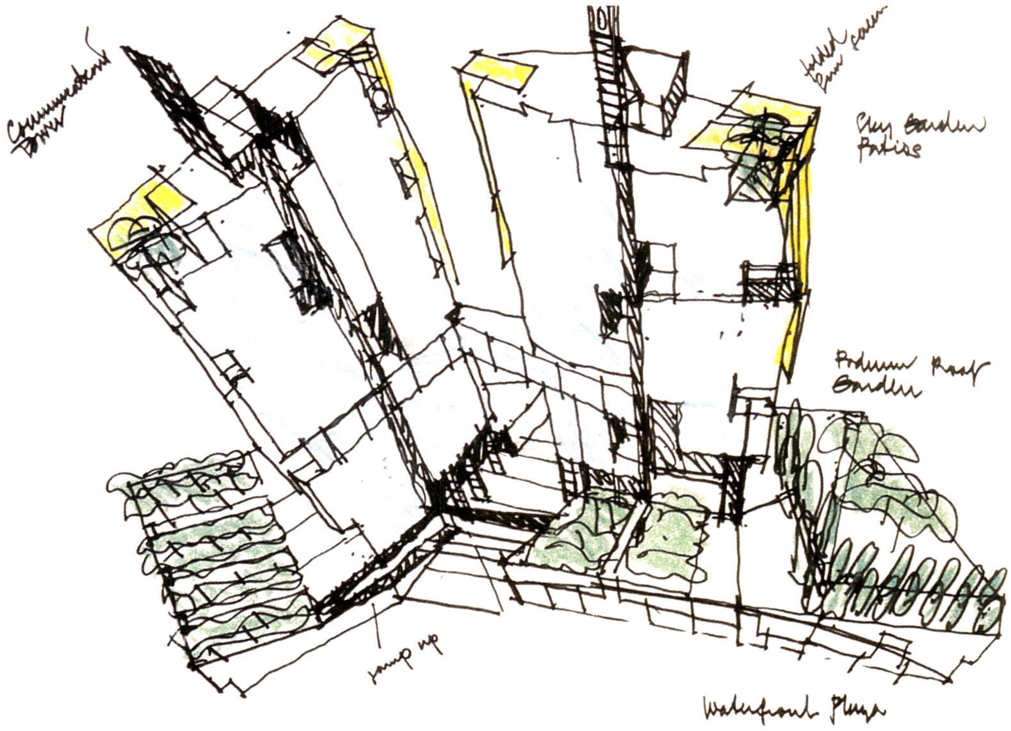
City Garden
Patios
Podium Roof
Garden
ramp up
Waterfront Plaza

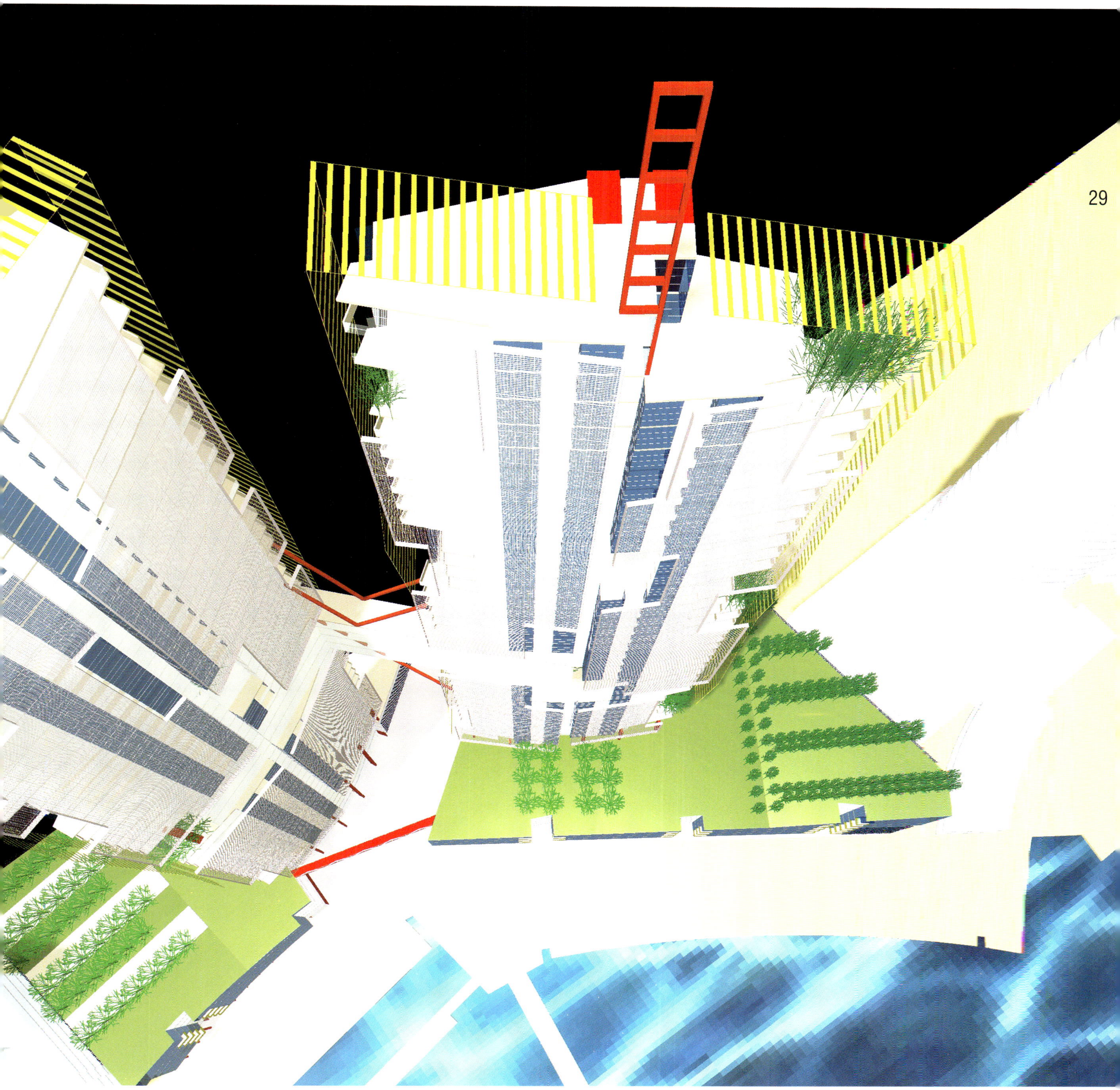

The new Georges provides a unique shopping and restaurant environment that is distinctly global yet inherently Melbourne. While the redevelopment is in the spirit of the original 1880s design, it has produced a spacious, challenging and distinctly modern interior.

Products and services include three exceptional restaurants, and retail spaces that encapsulate the finest in quality and style from local and international designers for men and women and for the home.

The interior atrium was reinstated, and once again plays an important role in establishing a vista of open spaces and modern folded steel staircases, which provide access to four floors of distinguished shopping. The fine plaster detailing, the cast-iron columns and rich spatial layering characteristic of the building's earlier decorative fitout styles are key features of the interior store presentations. So too are finely detailed glass restaurant lanterns and metal screens, the new stone and timber flooring, and the exposed service trunking on the skyline above the top floor.

GEORGES

JACLIN CHOUCHANA

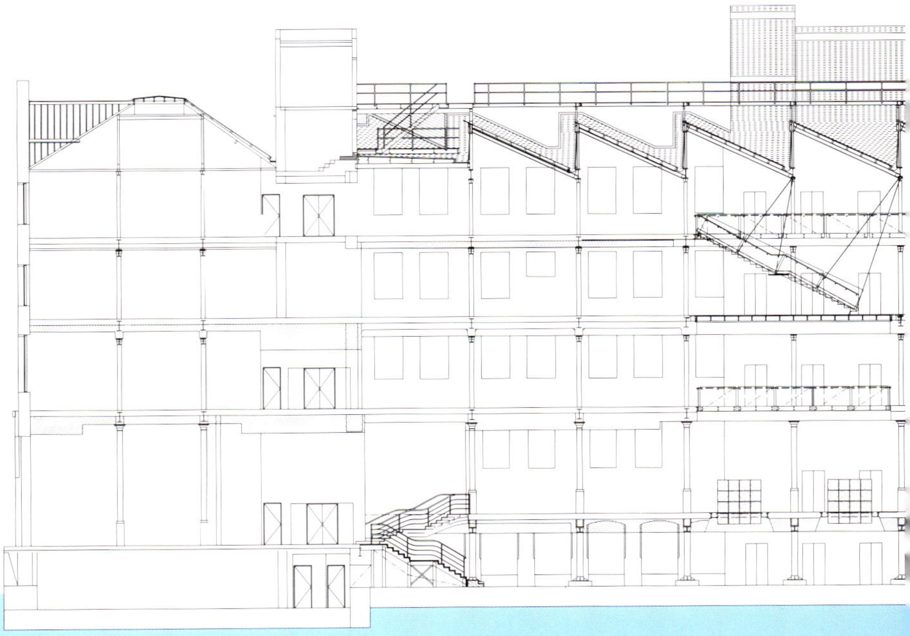
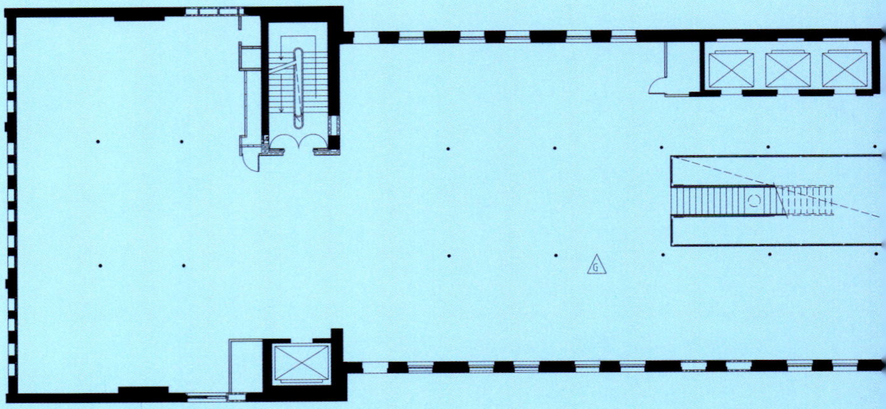
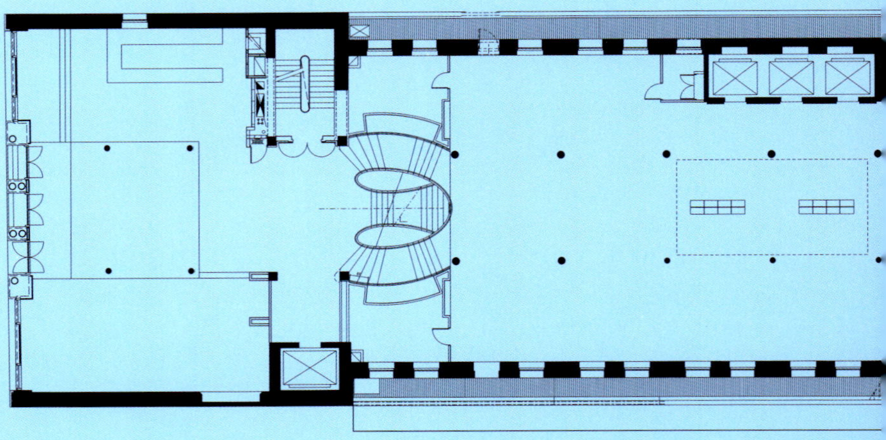
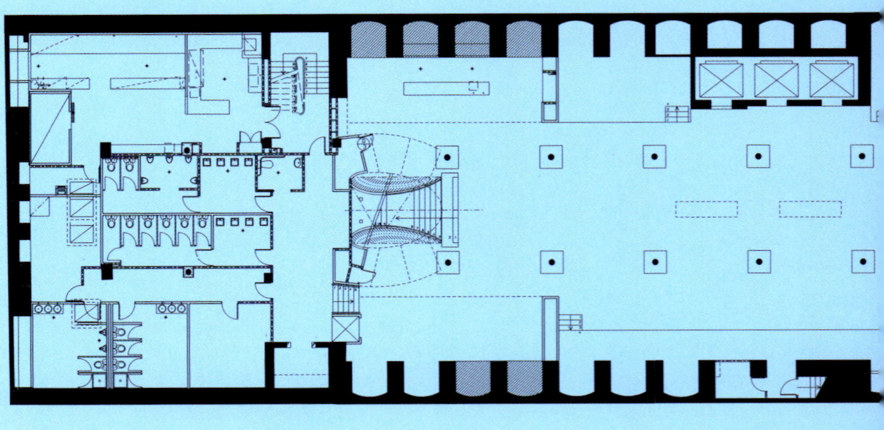

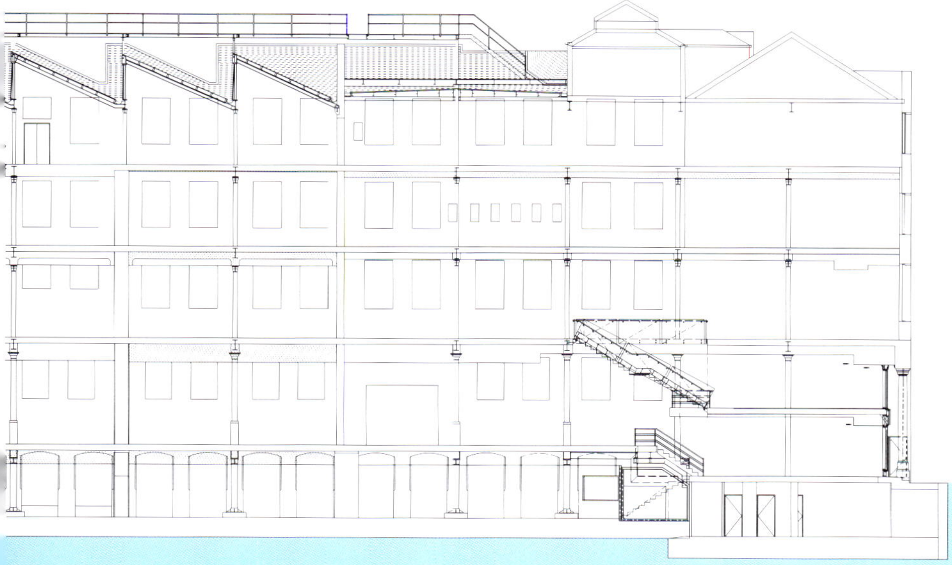

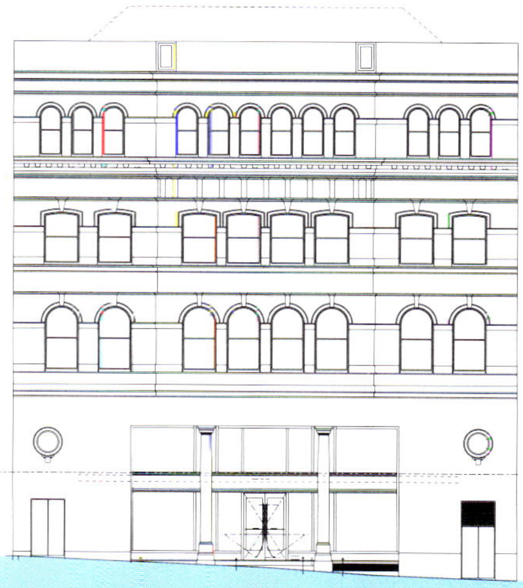

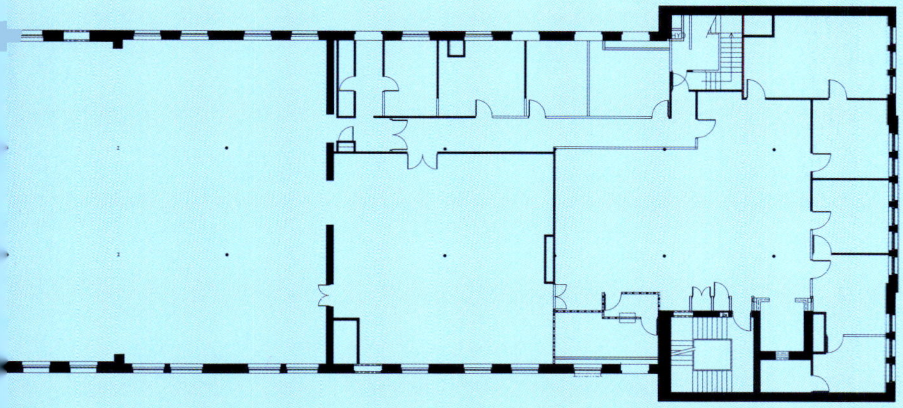

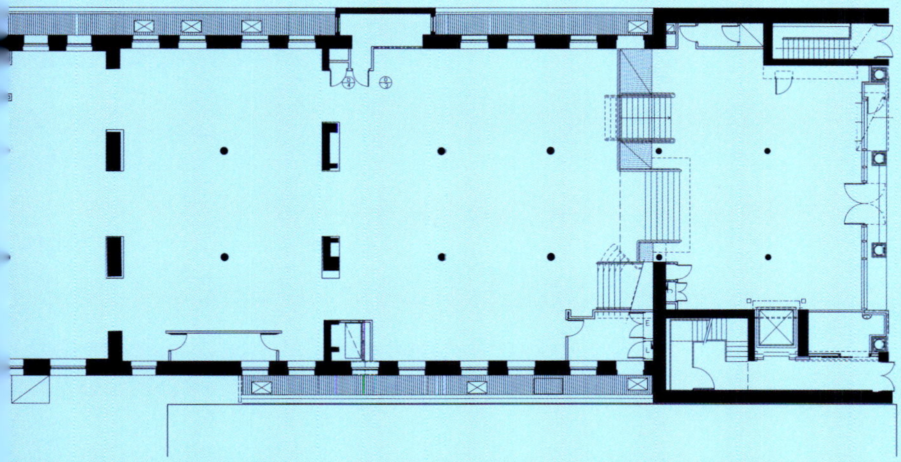

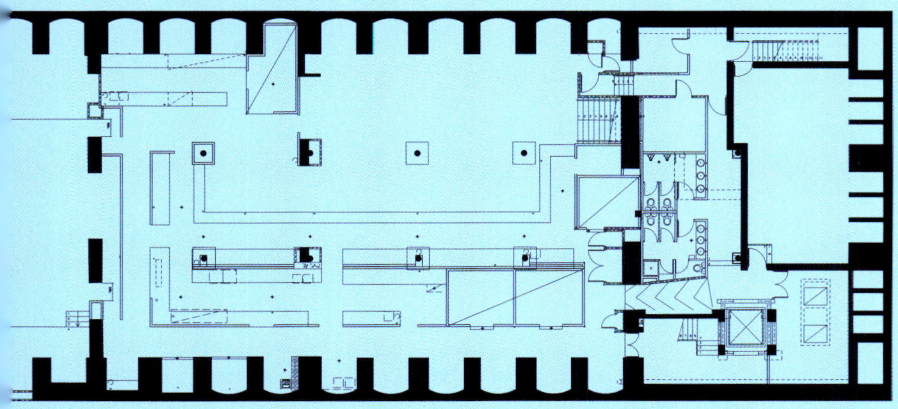

The interior fitout of the restaurant and retail areas has a simplicity that sits comfortably within the original but redefined chalk-white spaces. A simple palette of materials including bluestone, dark timber, glass and stainless steel is used throughout the store to ensure a consistency in style and a high level of future flexibility.

The three restaurants each have a distinct style: the Brasserie has a refinement seen in the ocean liners of the 1930s, while the Loft and Canteen take on a technical vocabulary relevant to the urban consumer, with the hanging steel stair and city skyline brought into the space via the roof glazing.

The flow of the spaces and simplicity of the design of the fixturing allows the clothing on the fashion floor to be the focus, while the new retailing concept for the cosmetics area makes a strong statement on the ground floor with the dark timber joinery, and blue glass display boxes that also filter natural light to the Brasserie below.

Translucent elements, white on white, natural timber and interior daylight are the key elements of a creative collaboration between Daryl Jackson, Sir Terence Conran and Stephen Bennett, the retail principal.

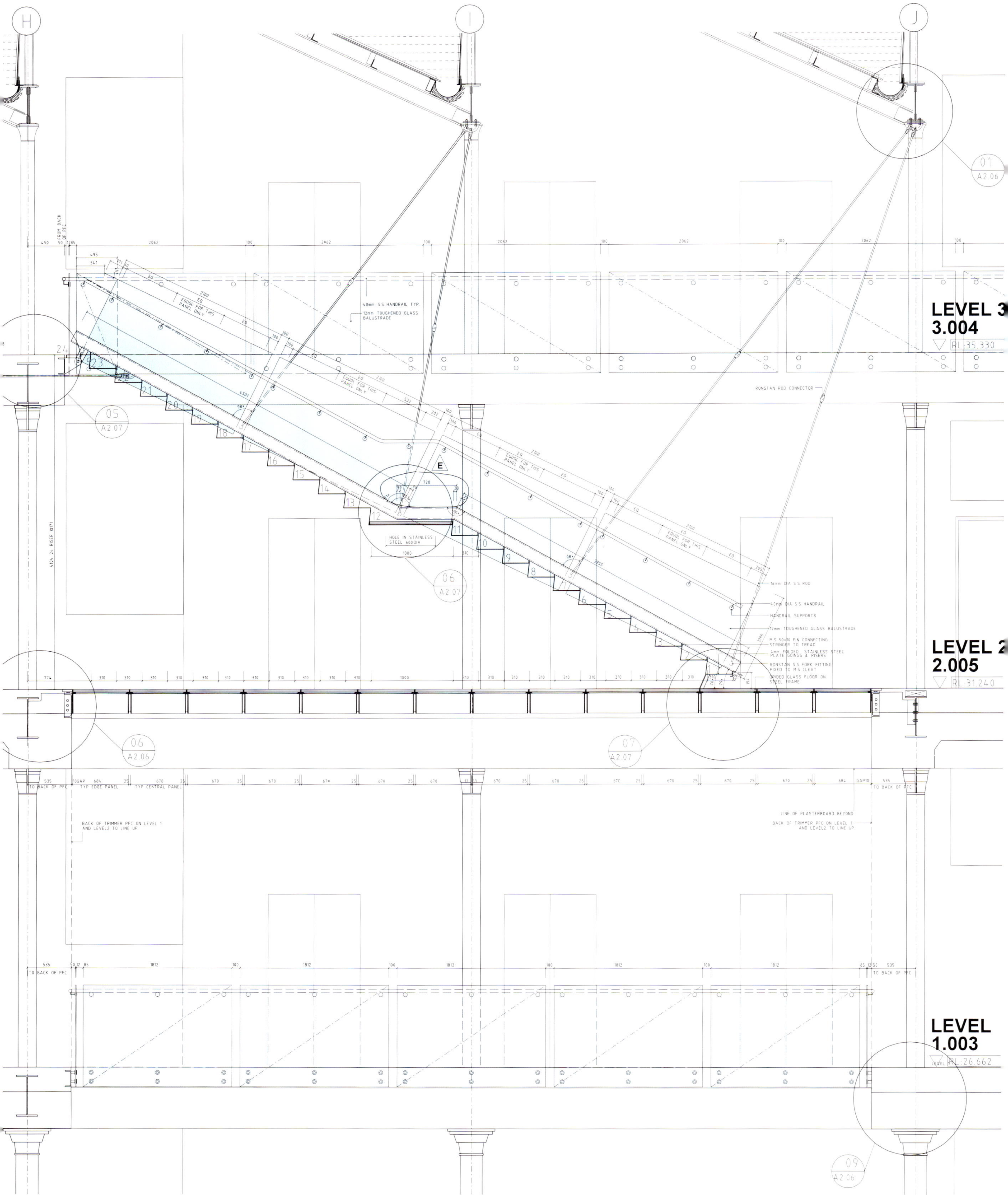
H
I
J
LEVEL 3
3.004
RL 35.330
LEVEL 2
2.005
RL 31.240
LEVEL 1.003
RL 26.662
40mm S.S HANDRAIL TYP
12mm TOUGHENED GLASS BALUSTRADE
EQUAL FOR THIS PANEL ONLY
RONSTAN ROD CONNECTOR
HOLE IN STAINLESS STEEL 600DIA
16mm DIA S.S ROD
40mm DIA S.S HANDRAIL
HANDRAIL SUPPORTS
12mm TOUGHENED GLASS BALUSTRADE
M.S 50x10 FIN CONNECTING STRINGER TO TREAD
4mm FOLDED STAINLESS STEEL PLATE GOINGS & RISERS
RONSTAN S.S FORK FITTING FIXED TO M.S CLEAT
GRIDED GLASS FLOOR ON STEEL FRAME
4104 24 RISER @171
TO BACK OF PFC
TYP EDGE PANEL
TYP CENTRAL PANEL
BACK OF TRIMMER PFC ON LEVEL 1 AND LEVEL2 TO LINE UP
LINE OF PLASTERBOARD BEYOND
FROM BACK OF PFC
01 A2.06
05 A2.07
06 A2.07
06 A2.06
07 A2.07
09 A2.06
E

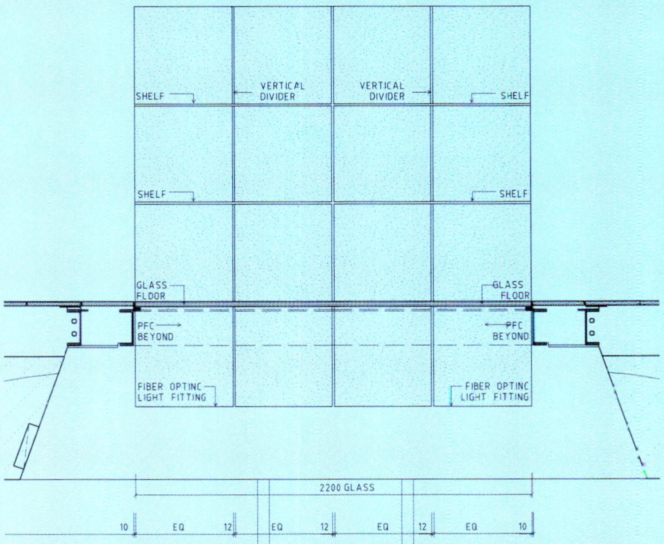

SHELF
VERTICAL DIVIDER
VERTICAL DIVIDER
SHELF
SHELF
SHELF
GLASS FLOOR
GLASS FLOOR
PFC BEYOND
PFC BEYOND
FIBER OPTINC LIGHT FITTING
FIBER OPTINC LIGHT FITTING
2200 GLASS
10 EQ 12 EQ 12 EQ 12 EQ 10

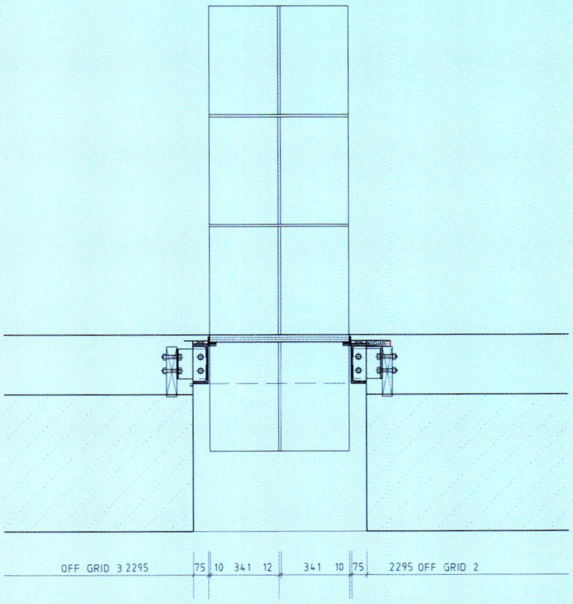

OFF GRID 3 2295
75 10 341 12 341 10 75
2295 OFF GRID 2

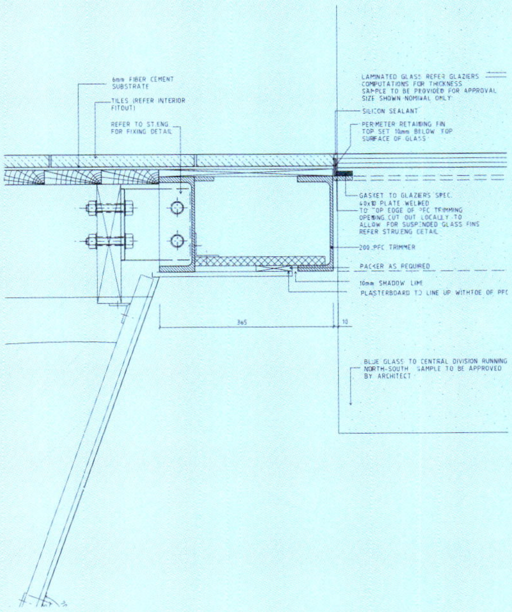

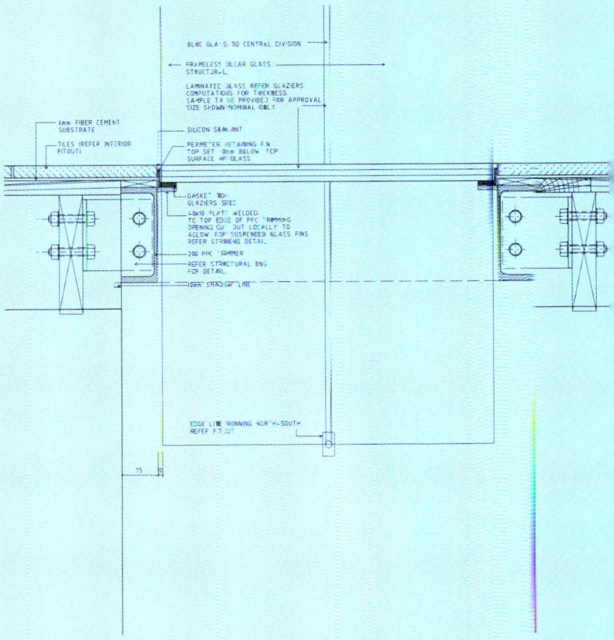

The masterplan is realised as a topographic and urban land sculpture. It brings together the existing Abbotstown House, its villa gardens and park, and overlays a formally set down sports complex suitable for a sports training academy and an all-purpose football and athletics stadium.

This urban arrangement creates a sports complex or village centre by juxtaposing the stadium and the arena on opposite sides of a great public court. This is the focal point of the layout.

The following features became the principal design elements of the masterplan:

The concentration of buildings around a pedestrian plaza offers an urban experience, allowing the perimeter landscape to remain, thus promoting the feeling of being in a park.

Entertainment areas and hotels are located to the south of the town square beyond the shadows formed by the arena and the stadium, ensuring sun penetration to the complex and offering a view to the surrounding hills.

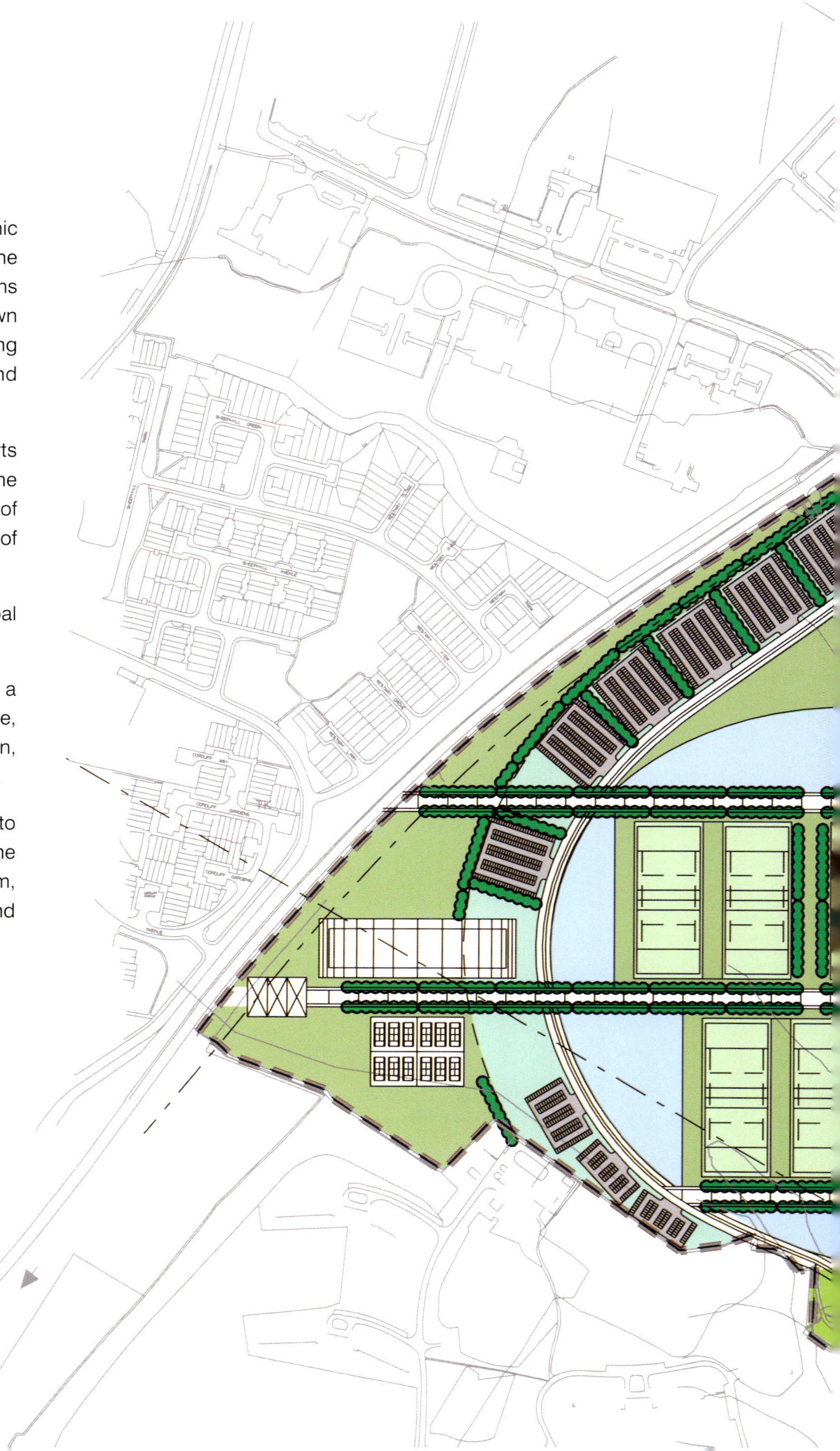

STADIUM IRELAND

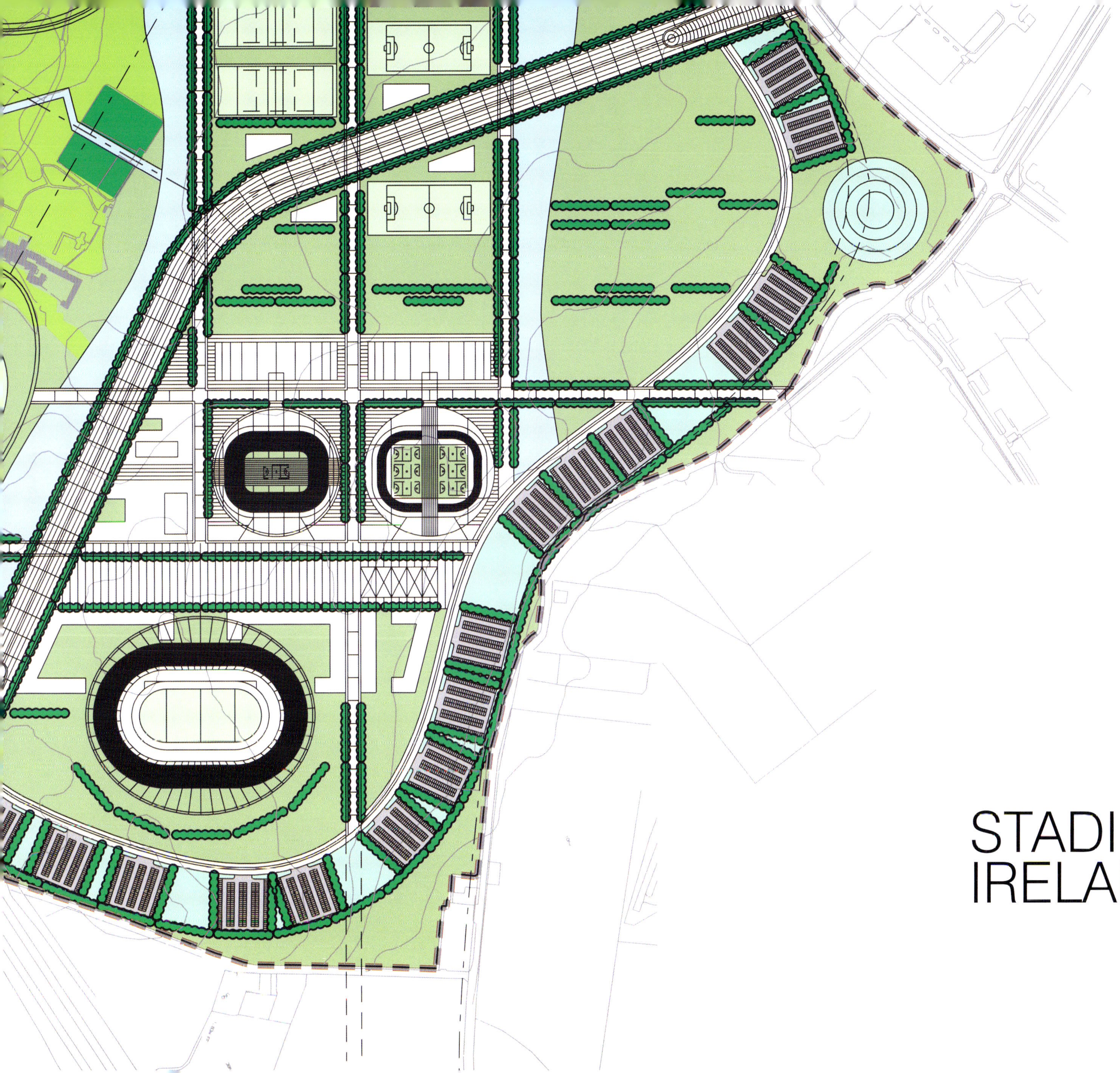

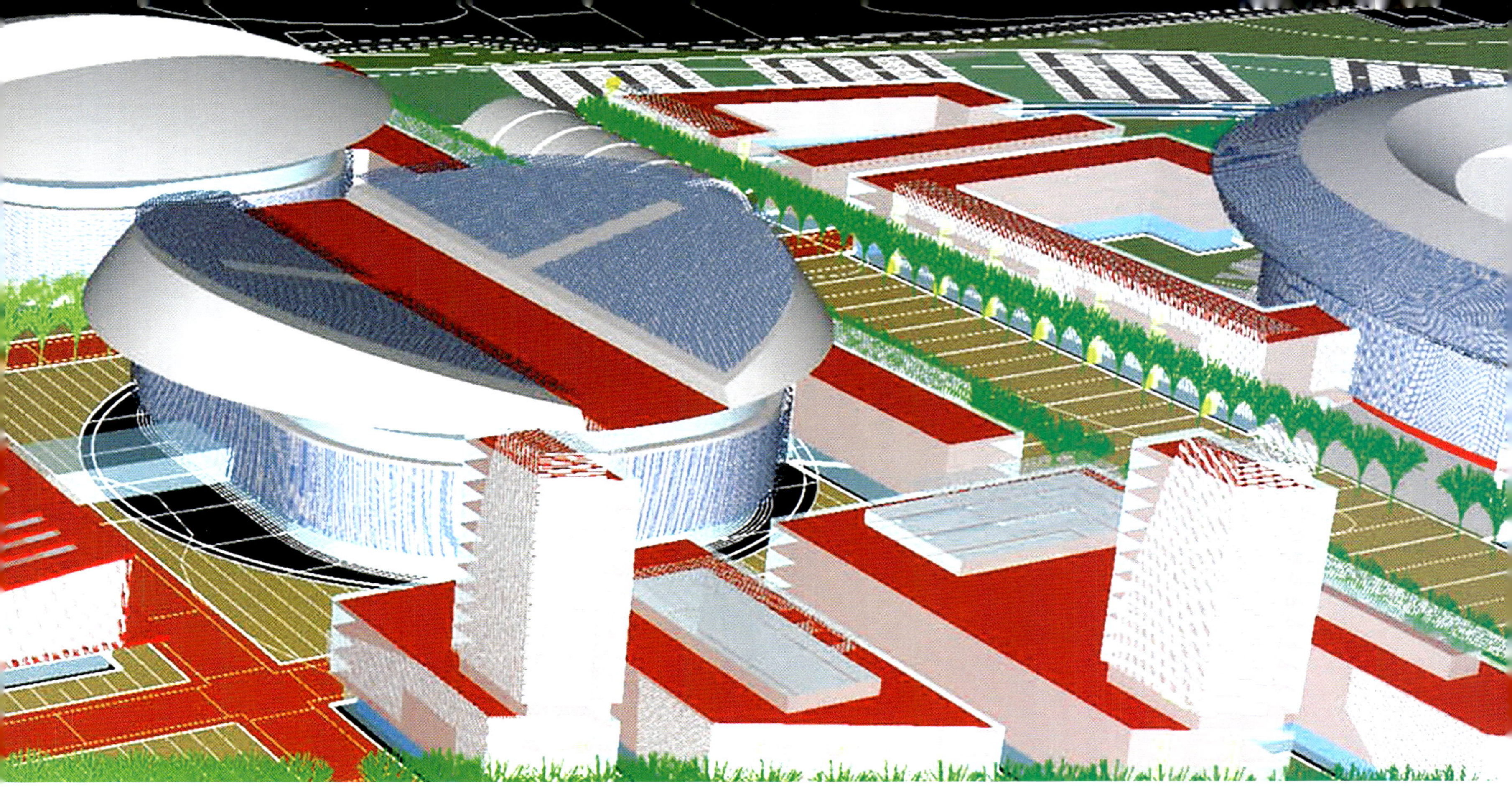

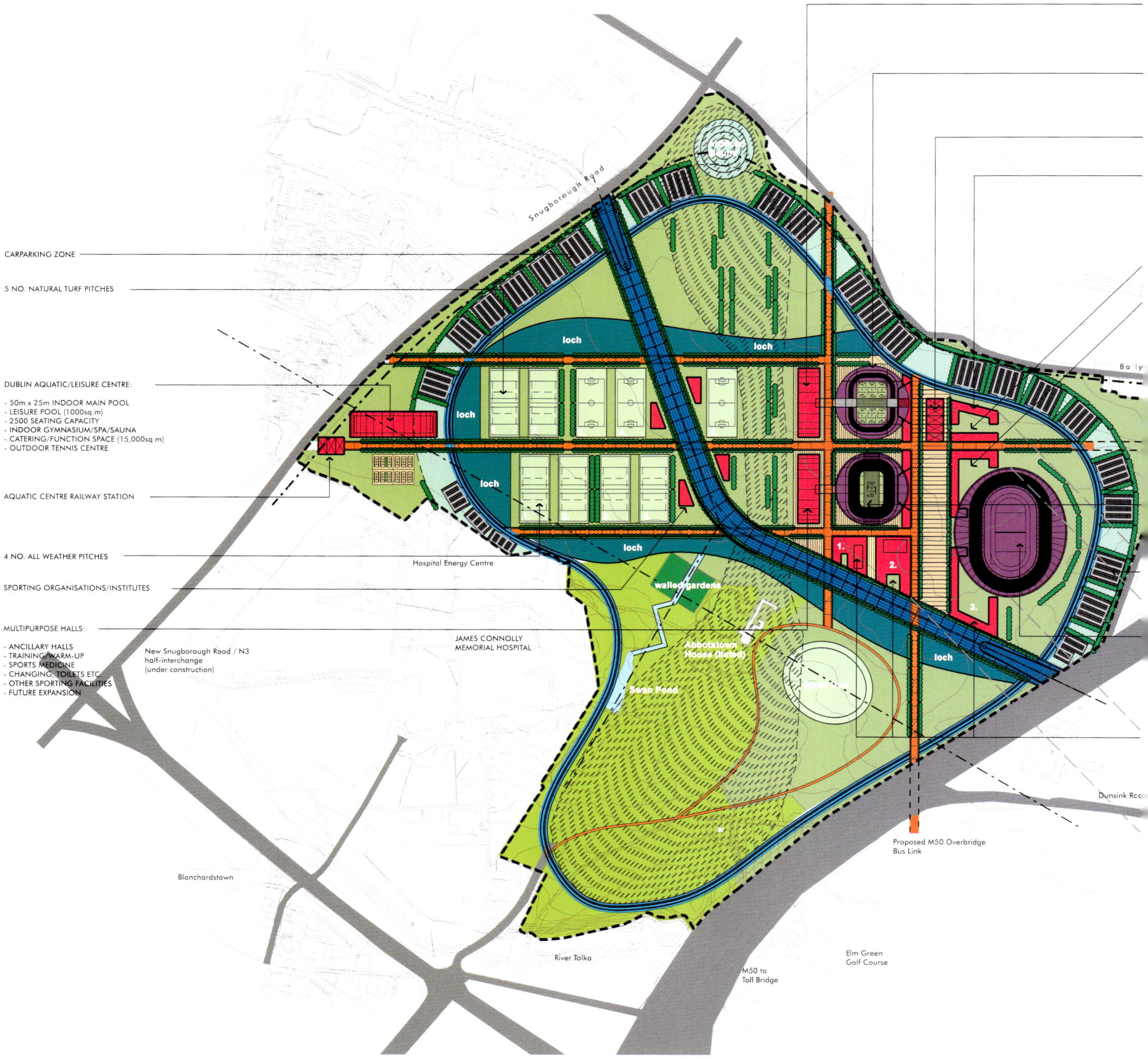

CARPARKING ZONE
5 NO. NATURAL TURF PITCHES
DUBLIN AQUATIC/LEISURE CENTRE:
- 50m x 25m INDOOR MAIN POOL
- LEISURE POOL (1000sq.m)
- 2500 SEATING CAPACITY
- INDOOR GYMNASIUM/SPA/SAUNA
- CATERING/FUNCTION SPACE (15,000sq.m)
- OUTDOOR TENNIS CENTRE
AQUATIC CENTRE RAILWAY STATION
4 NO. ALL WEATHER PITCHES
SPORTING ORGANISATIONS/INSTITUTES
MULTIPURPOSE HALLS:
- ANCILLARY HALLS
- TRAINING/WARM-UP
- SPORTS MEDICINE
- CHANGING, TOILETS ETC.
- OTHER SPORTING FACILITIES
- FUTURE EXPANSION
Snugborough Road
loch
loch
loch
loch
loch
loch
Hospital Energy Centre
walled gardens
JAMES CONNOLLY
MEMORIAL HOSPITAL
Abbotstown
House (listed)
Swan Pond
New Snugborough Road / N3
half-interchange
(under construction)
Blanchardstown
River Tolka
M50 to
Toll Bridge
Elm Green
Golf Course
Proposed M50 Overbridge
Bus Link
Dunsink Rd
1.
2.
3.

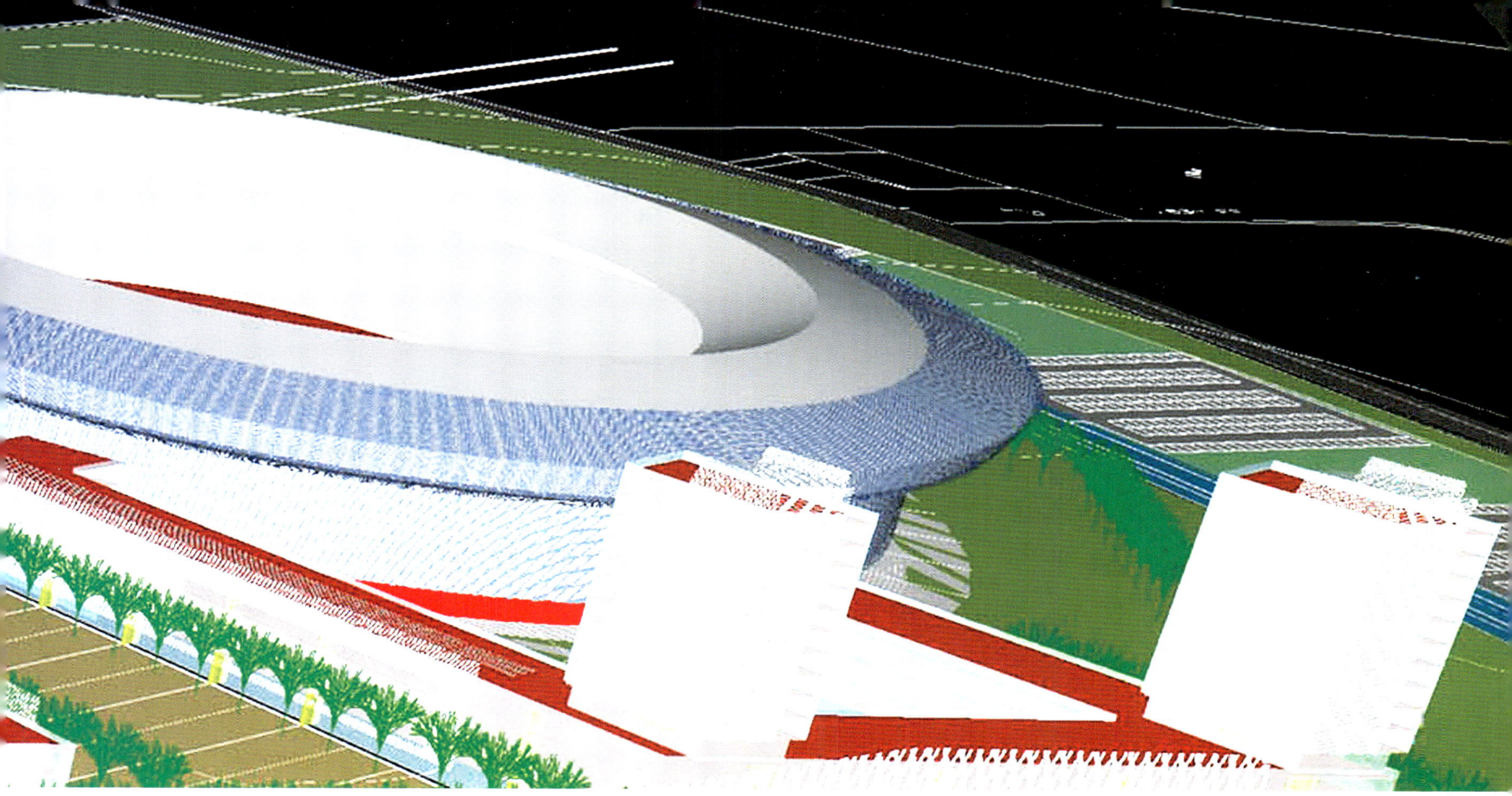

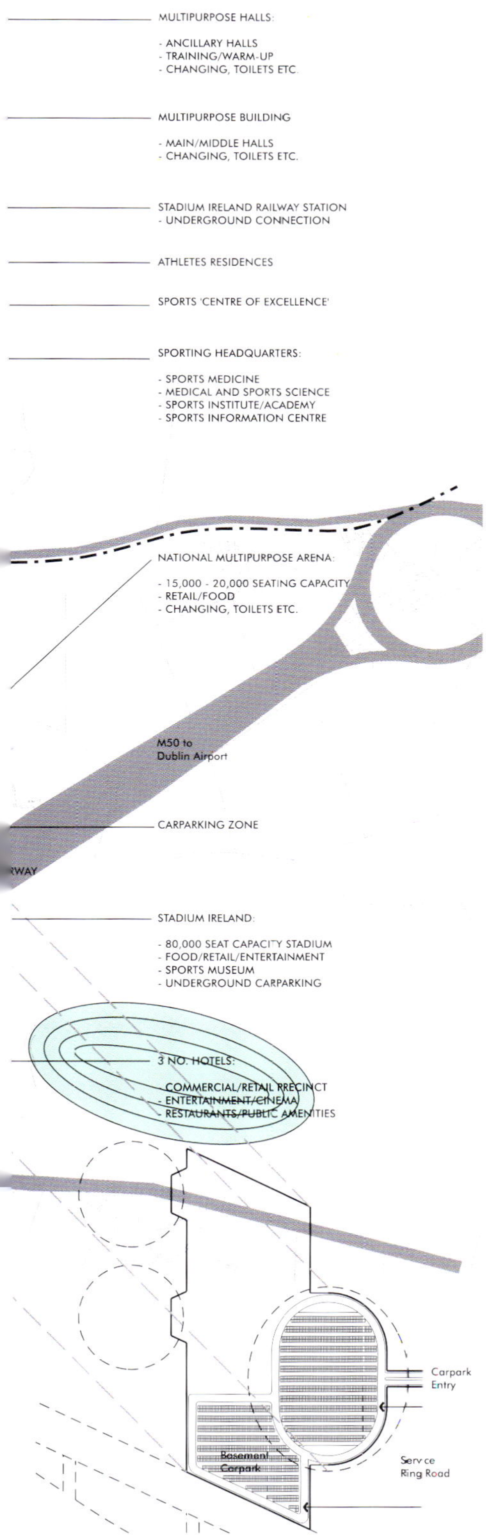
MULTIPURPOSE HALLS:
- ANCILLARY HALLS
- TRAINING/WARM-UP
- CHANGING, TOILETS ETC.
MULTIPURPOSE BUILDING
- MAIN/MIDDLE HALLS
- CHANGING, TOILETS ETC.
STADIUM IRELAND RAILWAY STATION
- UNDERGROUND CONNECTION
ATHLETES RESIDENCES
SPORTS 'CENTRE OF EXCELLENCE'
SPORTING HEADQUARTERS:
- SPORTS MEDICINE
- MEDICAL AND SPORTS SCIENCE
- SPORTS INSTITUTE/ACADEMY
- SPORTS INFORMATION CENTRE
NATIONAL MULTIPURPOSE ARENA:
- 15,000 - 20,000 SEATING CAPACITY
- RETAIL/FOOD
- CHANGING, TOILETS ETC.
M50 to
Dublin Airport
CARPARKING ZONE
STADIUM IRELAND:
- 80,000 SEAT CAPACITY STADIUM
- FOOD/RETAIL/ENTERTAINMENT
- SPORTS MUSEUM
- UNDERGROUND CARPARKING
3 NO. HOTELS:
- COMMERCIAL/RETAIL PRECINCT
- ENTERTAINMENT/CINEMA
- RESTAURANTS/PUBLIC AMENITIES
Carpark
Entry
Basement
Carpark
Service
Ring Road

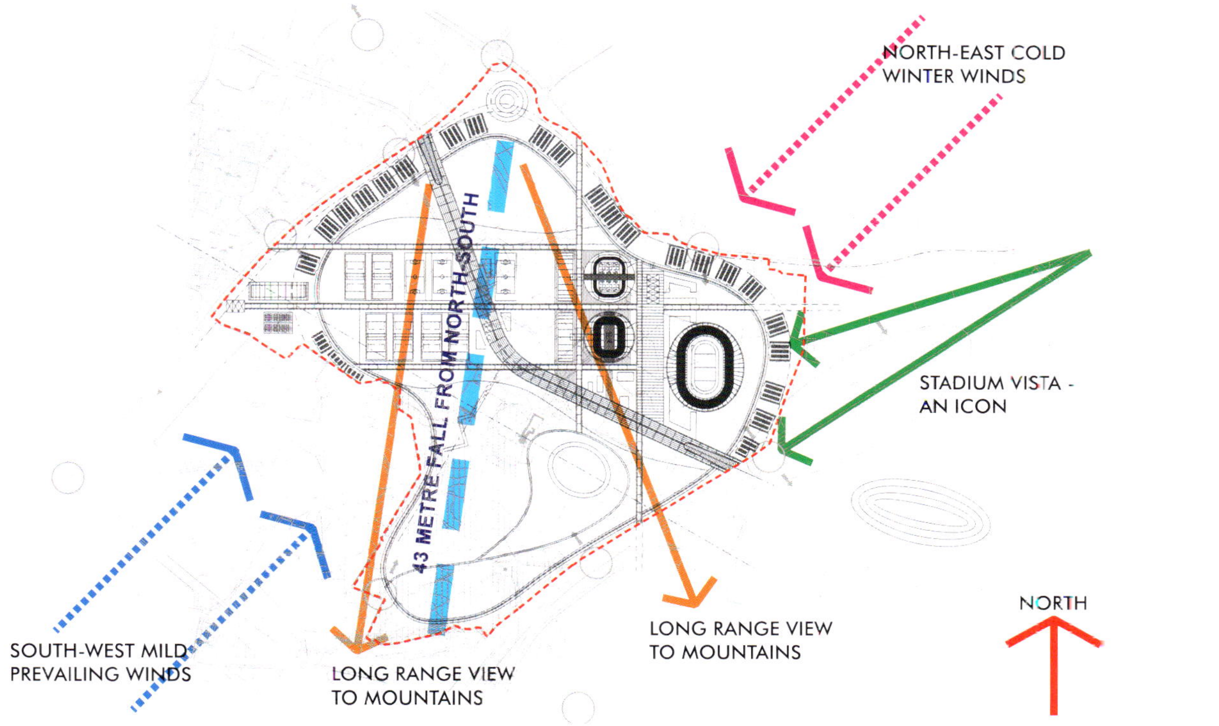
NORTH-EAST COLD
WINTER WINDS
43 METRE FALL FROM NORTH-SOUTH
STADIUM VISTA -
AN ICON
SOUTH-WEST MILD
PREVAILING WINDS
LONG RANGE VIEW
TO MOUNTAINS
LONG RANGE VIEW
TO MOUNTAINS
NORTH

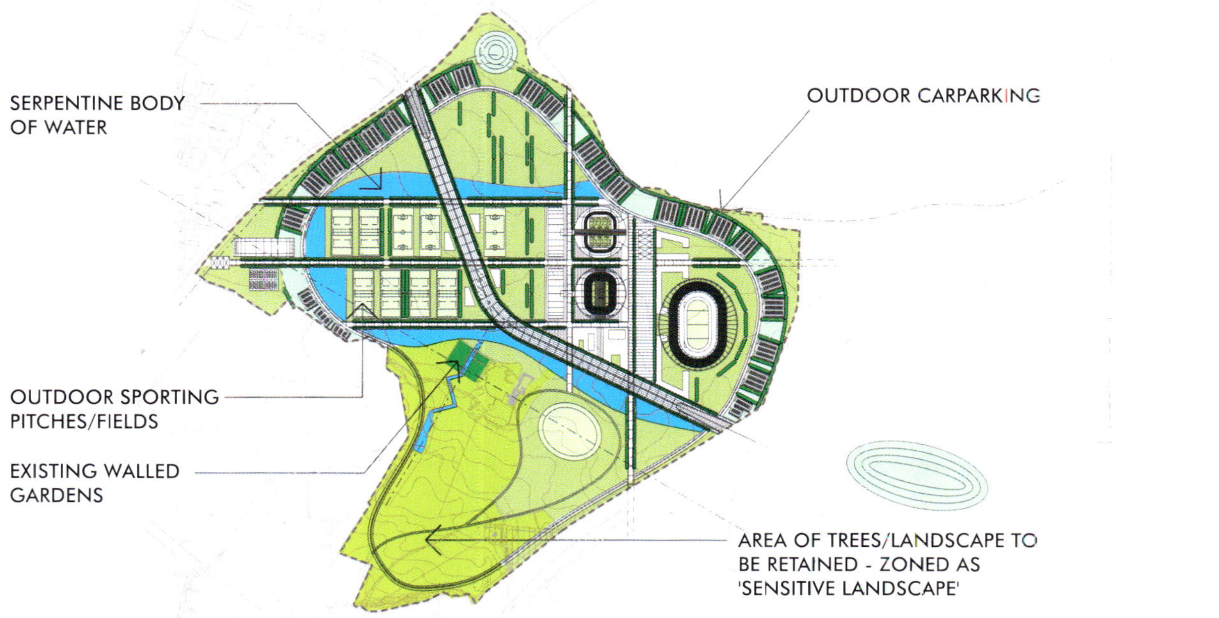
SERPENTINE BODY
OF WATER
OUTDOOR CARPARKING
OUTDOOR SPORTING
PITCHES/FIELDS
EXISTING WALLED
GARDENS
AREA OF TREES/LANDSCAPE TO
BE RETAINED - ZONED AS
'SENSITIVE LANDSCAPE'

The retention and use of water as a serpentine series of linked ponds or lochs is both a pictorial and a practical idea. Solar or wind powered pumps ensure reticulation while excess surface drainage may be collected. Recycled water overflow passes through existing ponds to the river below. It was envisioned that the ponds be stocked with fish.

The planting of perimeter trees will enclose the bounds of the park to offer the campus a distinctive presence while providing greater wind protection to the outdoor training fields.

The use of the tree canopy to reinforce the field grid figure is also important: it mediates the effect of wind on the games, provides protection for spectators and, just as importantly, provides a sense of landscape scale to the outdoor 'rooms' so established.

The use of the grid as 'landscape' also ties the sub-elements together, drawing the aquatic centre into the composition, so that together with the water elements, the least dramatic section of the existing park is given a new sense of purpose.

The organised landscape contrasts with the natural expression of the whole park and allows a 'natural' green corridor to bisect the east–west field grid, to establish the vista and strong form of the Abbotstown House park through the whole campus.

Finally, there is a desire to see the landscape of Ireland as a key metaphor for the campus. It is the green of the grass that counts, and part of the amenity for visitors from the city is the very nature of the park itself.

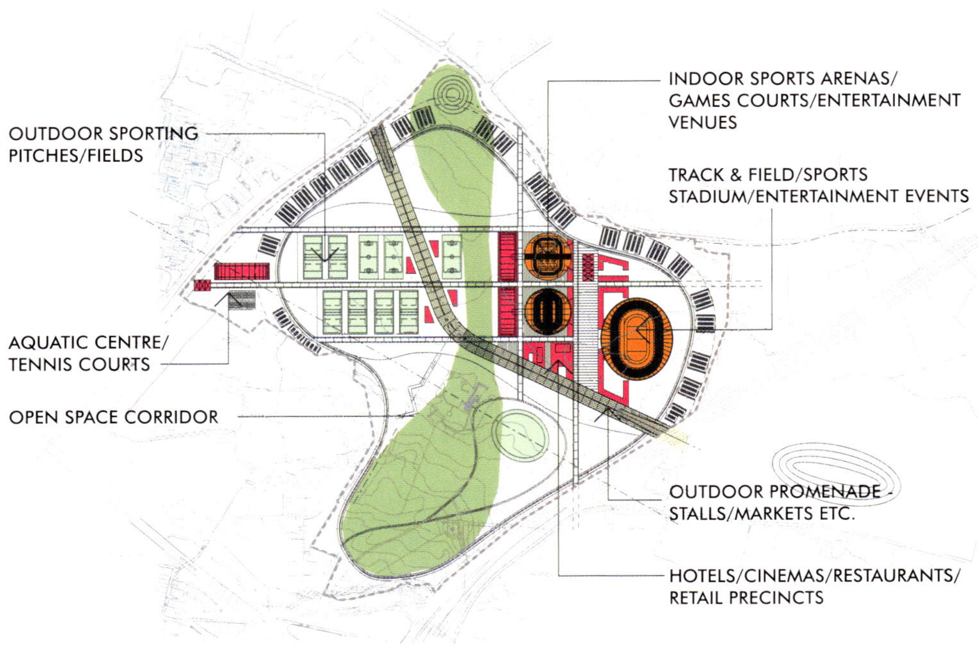

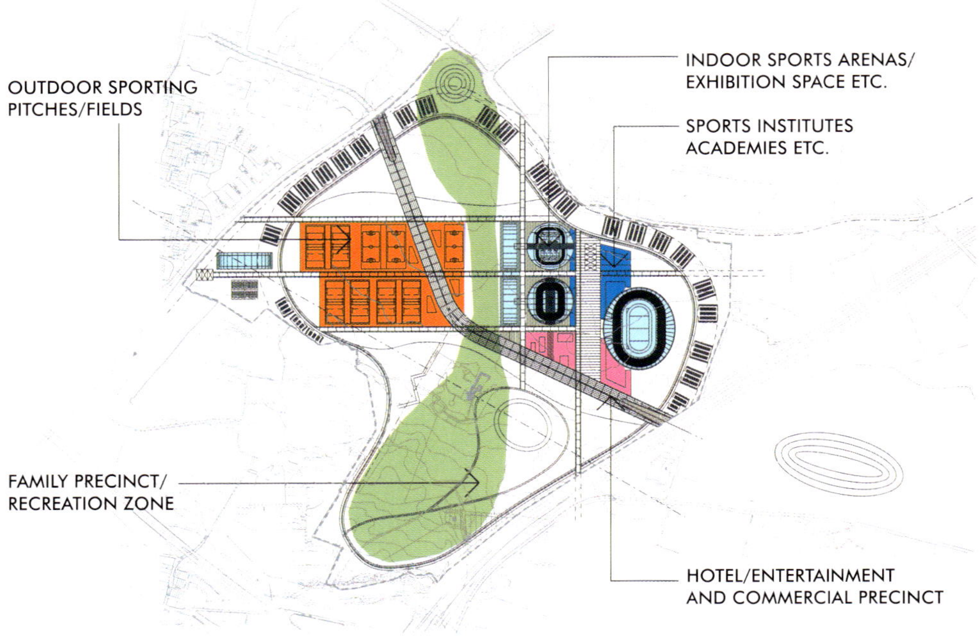

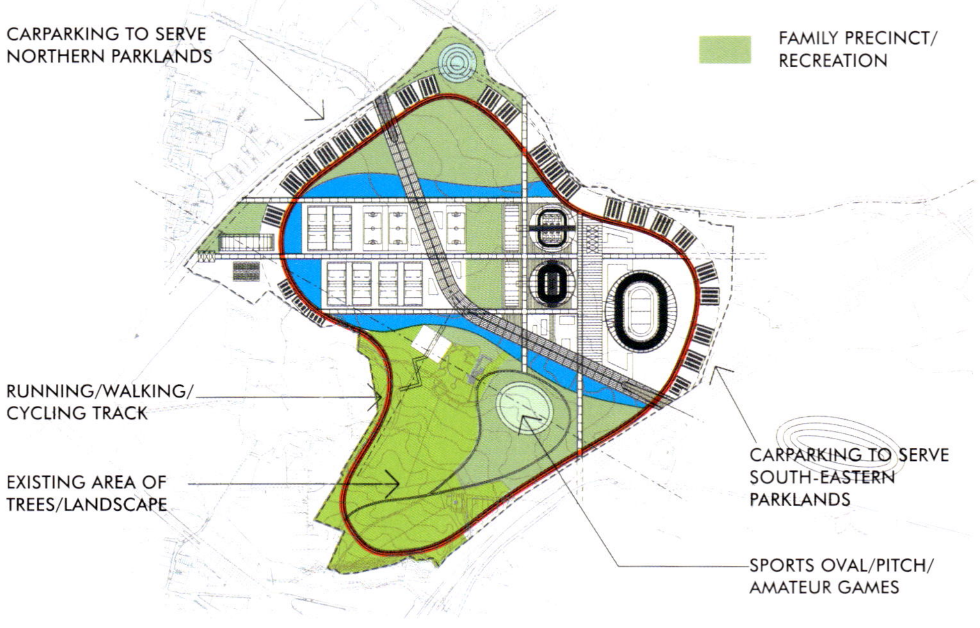

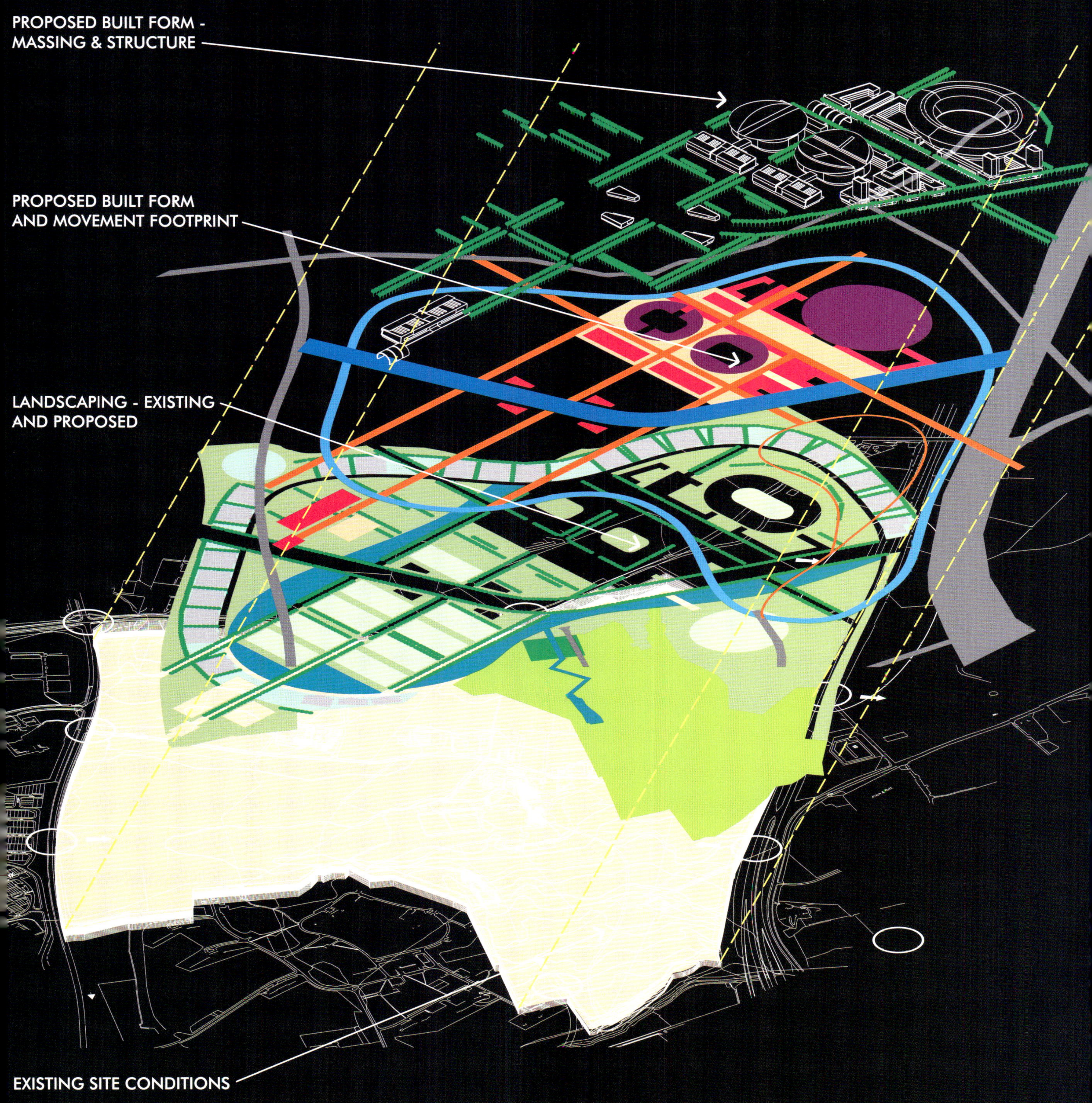
PROPOSED BUILT FORM -
MASSING & STRUCTURE
PROPOSED BUILT FORM
AND MOVEMENT FOOTPRINT
LANDSCAPING - EXISTING
AND PROPOSED
EXISTING SITE CONDITIONS

Cannons Gymnasium is built into the subterranean arches of London's Cannon Street railway station. Its long, bare, brick barrel vaults, once used for storage, now house a series of aerobic, weights, and exercise rooms. This project illustrates the steam room, sauna and spas.

The bathhouse has a Byzantine theme, with deep blue glazed surfaces on a new cross-wall, and blue and yellow glass mosaic tiles highlighting the spa area. Views of the Thames from the rest area emphasise a theatricality and sense of make-believe, with the hot, wet, colourful interior juxtaposed with the often grey and gloomy weather outside.

CANNONS GYMNASIUM

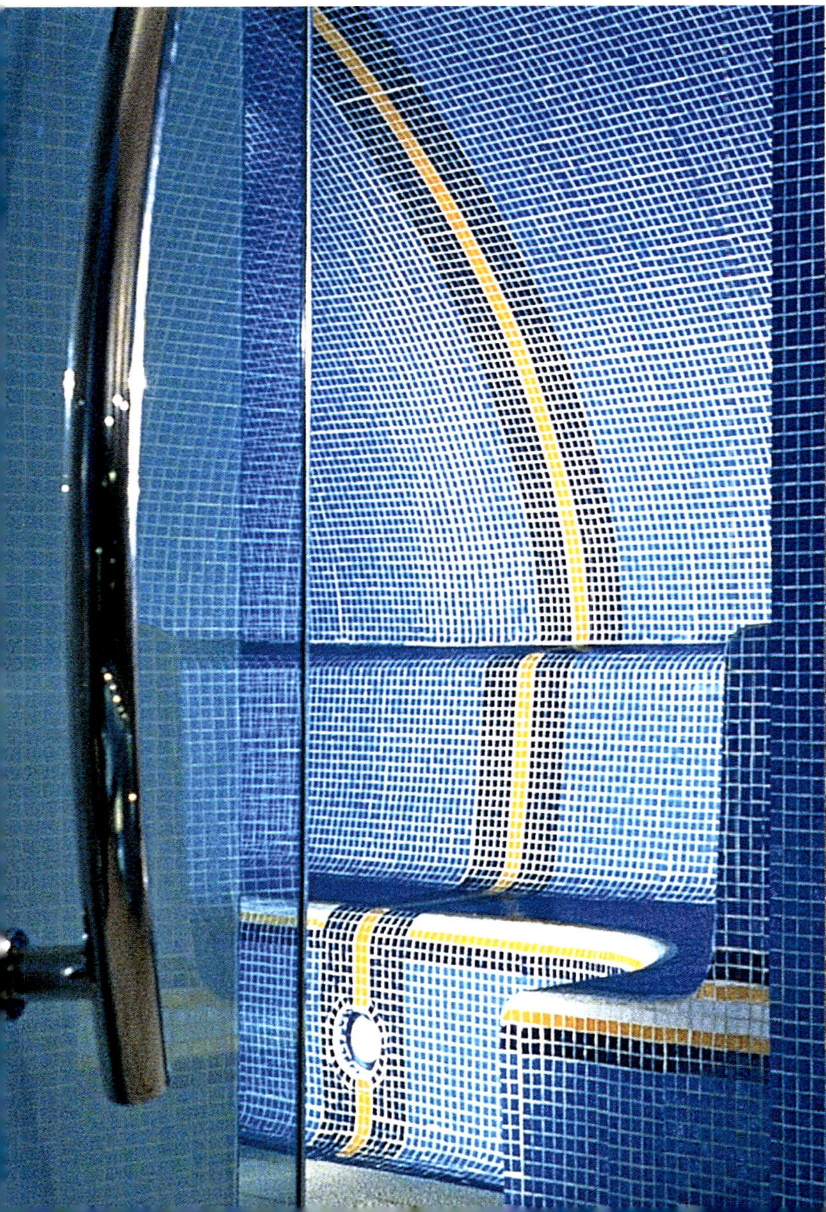

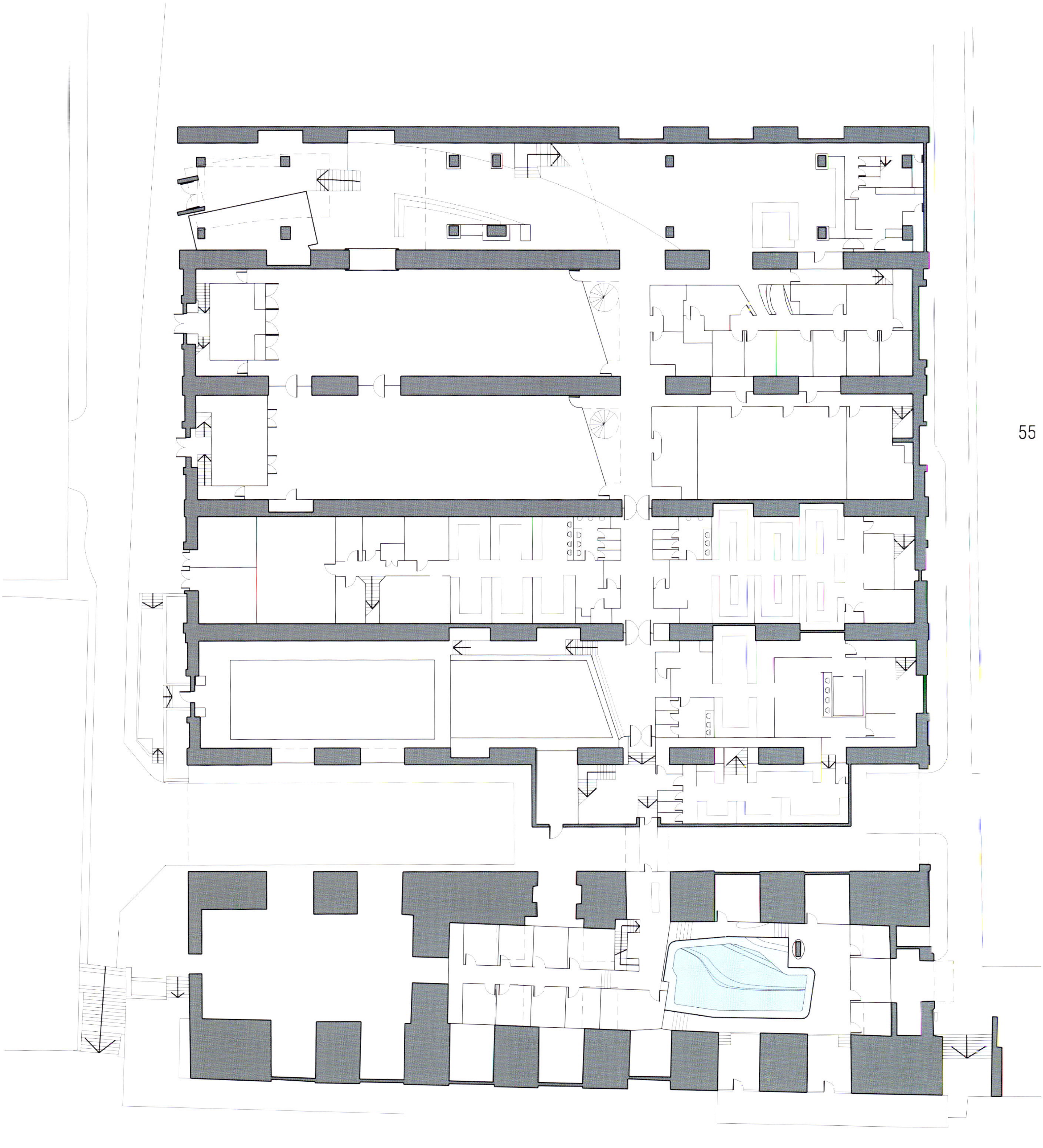

Urban resorts are relatively unusual; although relatively common in Mediterranean regions, they are rarely found in Asia.

Visitors to Penang customarily experience international beach hotels, spaced 500 metres or so apart, each with their own enclave and self-sufficient sub-tropical imagery.

The project was an exercise in planning a micro-city on the edge of the island where an outmoded fish farm, factory and village previously existed.

The design intent is to create a resort township of some substance, providing leisure and residential facilities for national and international visitors as well as work opportunities for the residents. The structure uses the steeply sloping hillside for terraced apartments that overlook the sea, providing accommodation for a critical mass of holiday residents to complement the itinerant hotel guests.

Two hotels are designed to resemble large ocean liners that are berthed, permanently in this case, above the water and projected out from the land mass. Both blocks are raised above piers of retail, open air street dining and restaurants.

The upper reaches of the land enable individual houses to be constructed, with the waterfront – the essence of a marine-based exchange with boats to local beaches and to other island resorts – completing the scheme.

This project remains unbuilt.

PENANG
BATU MAUNG

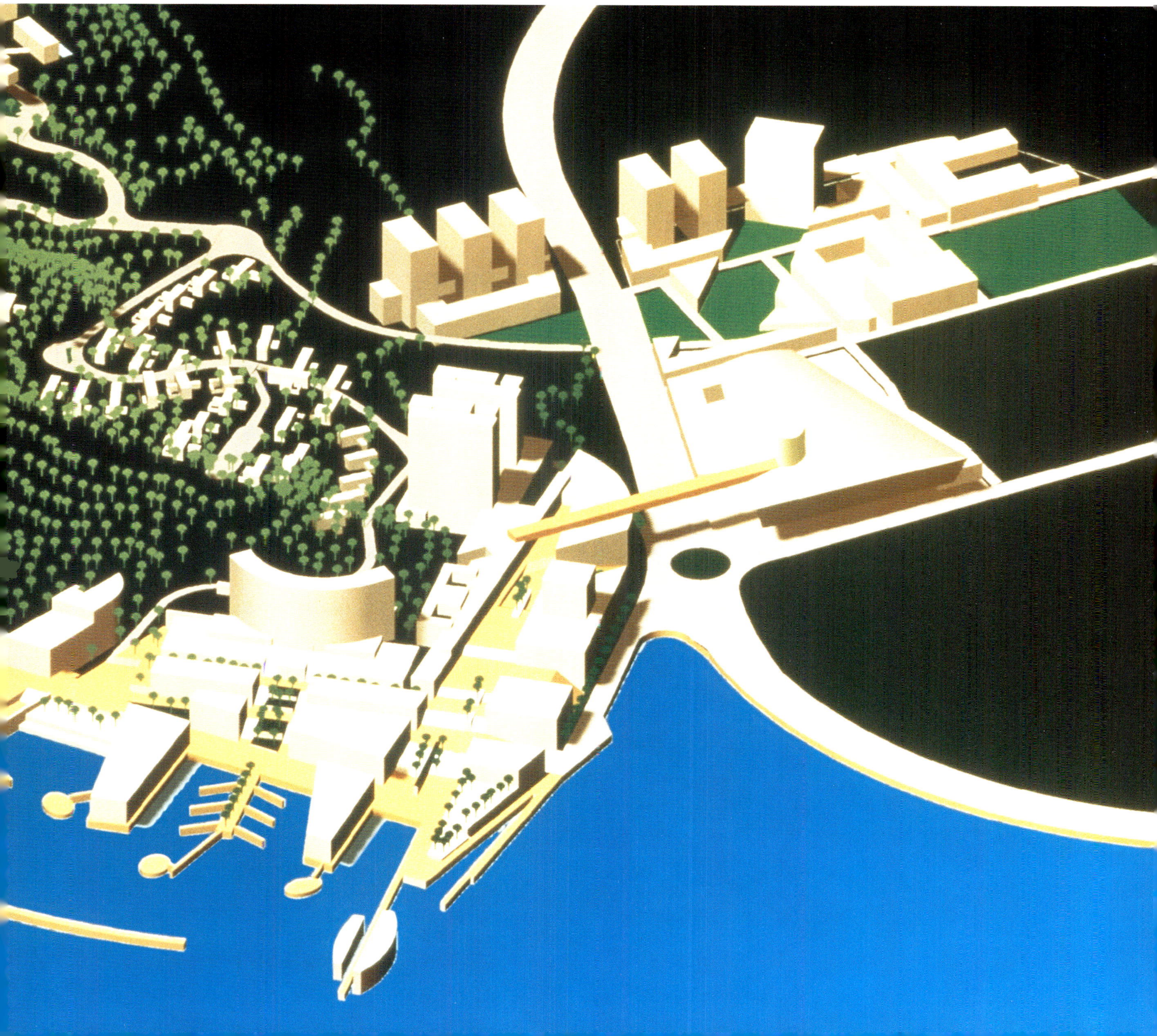

LEGEND
1 3 level shop house
2 16 level affordable housing
3 3 level bus depot, exhibition centre, shops and food court
4 3–5 level apartments
5 5–16 level apartments
6 School
7 Football field
8 Luxury bungalows
9 20 level apartments
10 3–5 level waterfront apartments
4–5 level terraced apartments
4–5 level boulevard apartments
11 3-star hotel
12 Boat slipway
13 Floating seafood restaurant
14 Retail shopping centre
15 Marina
16 Gateway/link
17 Park
18 Forest/orchard
Pools/water
Roads
Pedestrian
Planters
Existing buildings to remain
EXISTING TEMPLE
EXISTING BUILDINGS
OFFICE TOWER
(3)(3600sqm)
MEDICAL CENTRE

LEGEND
1 Pedestrian only areas
2 Primary pedestrian routes

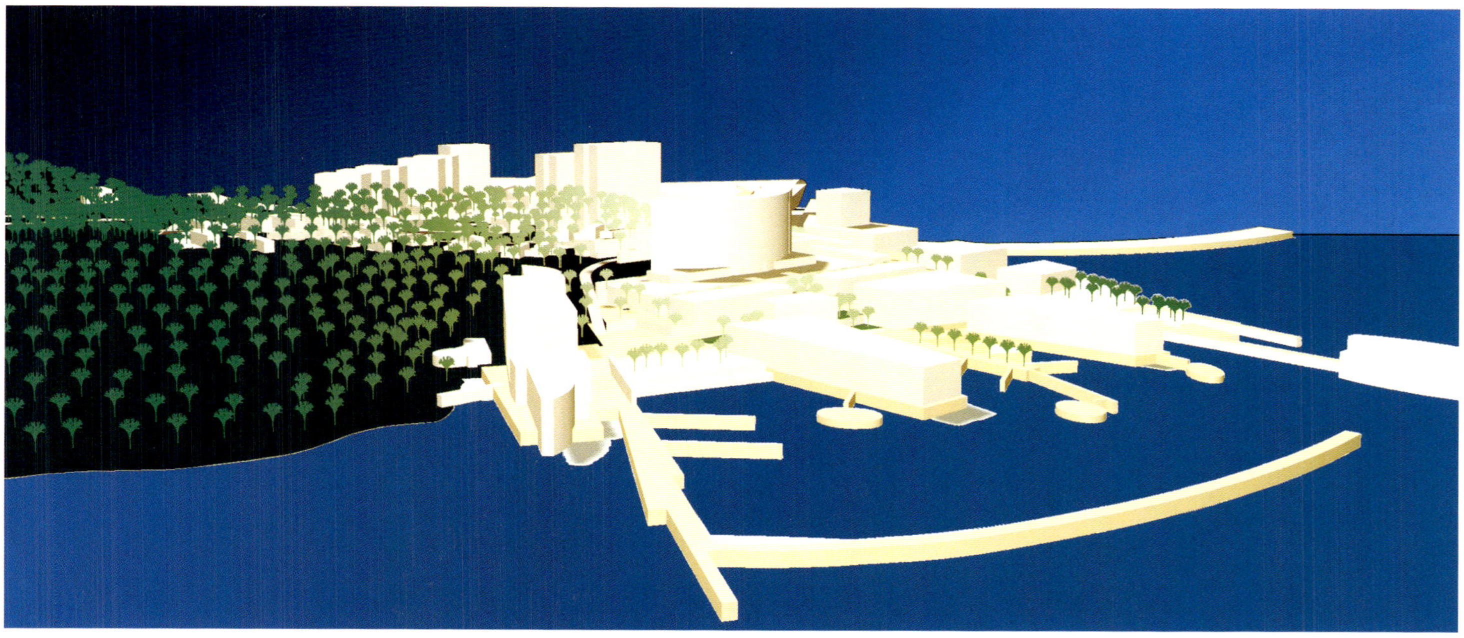

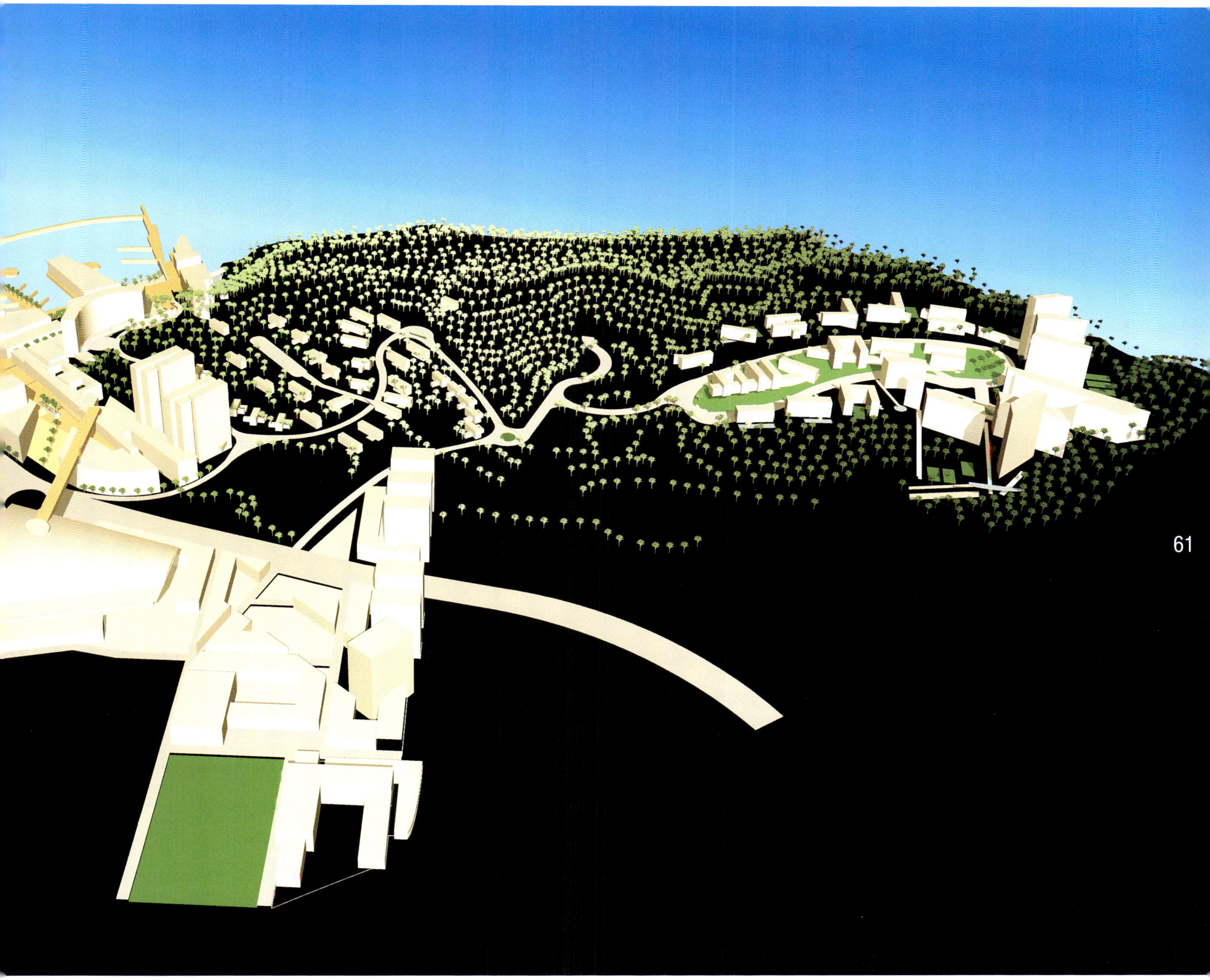

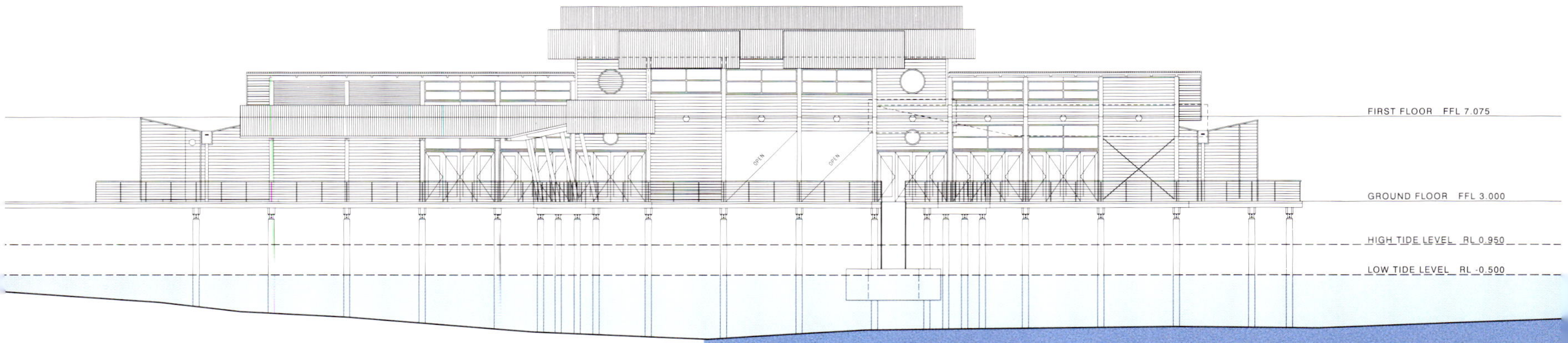

South Stradbroke Island is a remarkable piece of South Queensland coastline. Its detachment from, yet proximity to, the Gold Coast mainland presents both significant values and challenges to the visitor.

Broadwater and the inlet to Couran Cove offer safe sailing and an intimate waterway. The east-side surf beach and uninterrupted dunal foreshore stretch north and south to meet the far horizon: sky, sea and sand meet each other via an easy infinity.

Between these land edges is mature native bushland that incorporates secret pieces of tropical rainforest.

The maritime village hotel is perched within this setting, touching the land lightly as a gull might use its legs to land on the beach.

All the buildings have been designed to convey an attitude towards and for the landscape, to infiltrate the bush, to hover over the water of the new cove outline, and in particular to make connections via the long jetty that forms a promenade between the inner and outer lagoons.

COURAN COVE RESORT

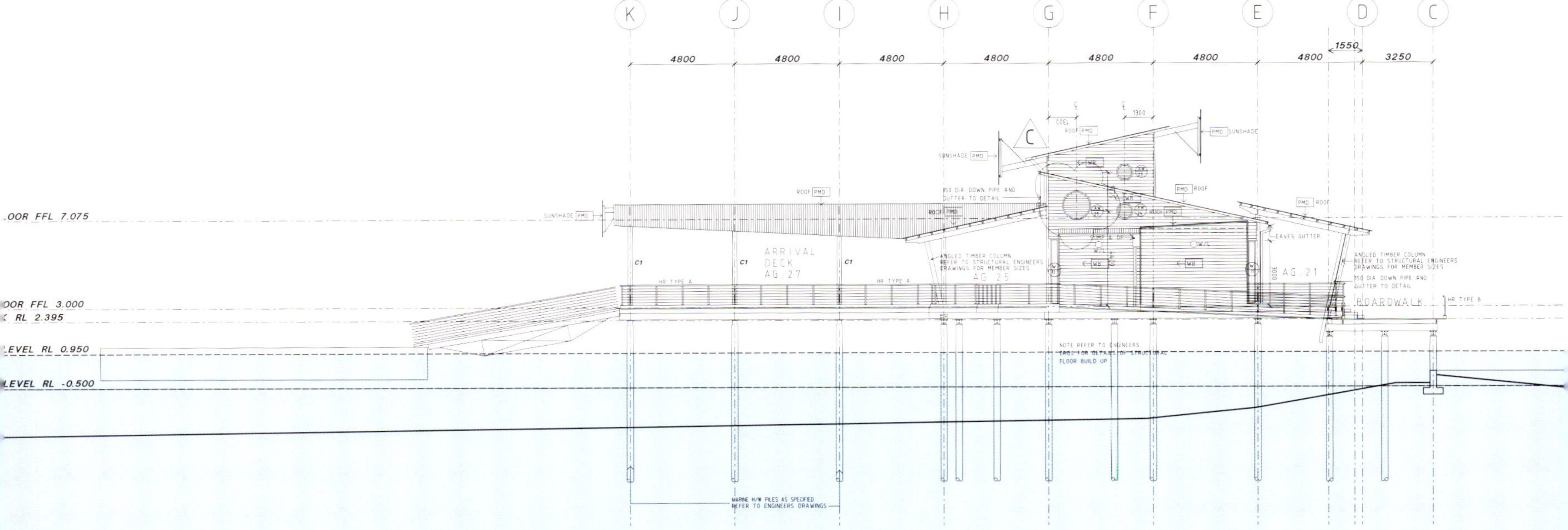
K J I H G F E D C
4800 4800 4800 4800 4800 4800 4800 1550 3250
SUNSHADE
ROOF
OOR FFL 7.075
OOR FFL 3.000
RL 2.395
LEVEL RL 0.950
LEVEL RL -0.500
ARRIVAL DECK AG 27
AG 25
AG 21
BOARDWALK
ANGLED TIMBER COLUMN REFER TO STRUCTURAL ENGINEERS DRAWINGS FOR MEMBER SIZES
150 DIA DOWN PIPE AND GUTTER TO DETAIL
EAVES GUTTER
HR TYPE A
HR TYPE B
MARINE H/W PILES AS SPECIFIED REFER TO ENGINEERS DRAWINGS

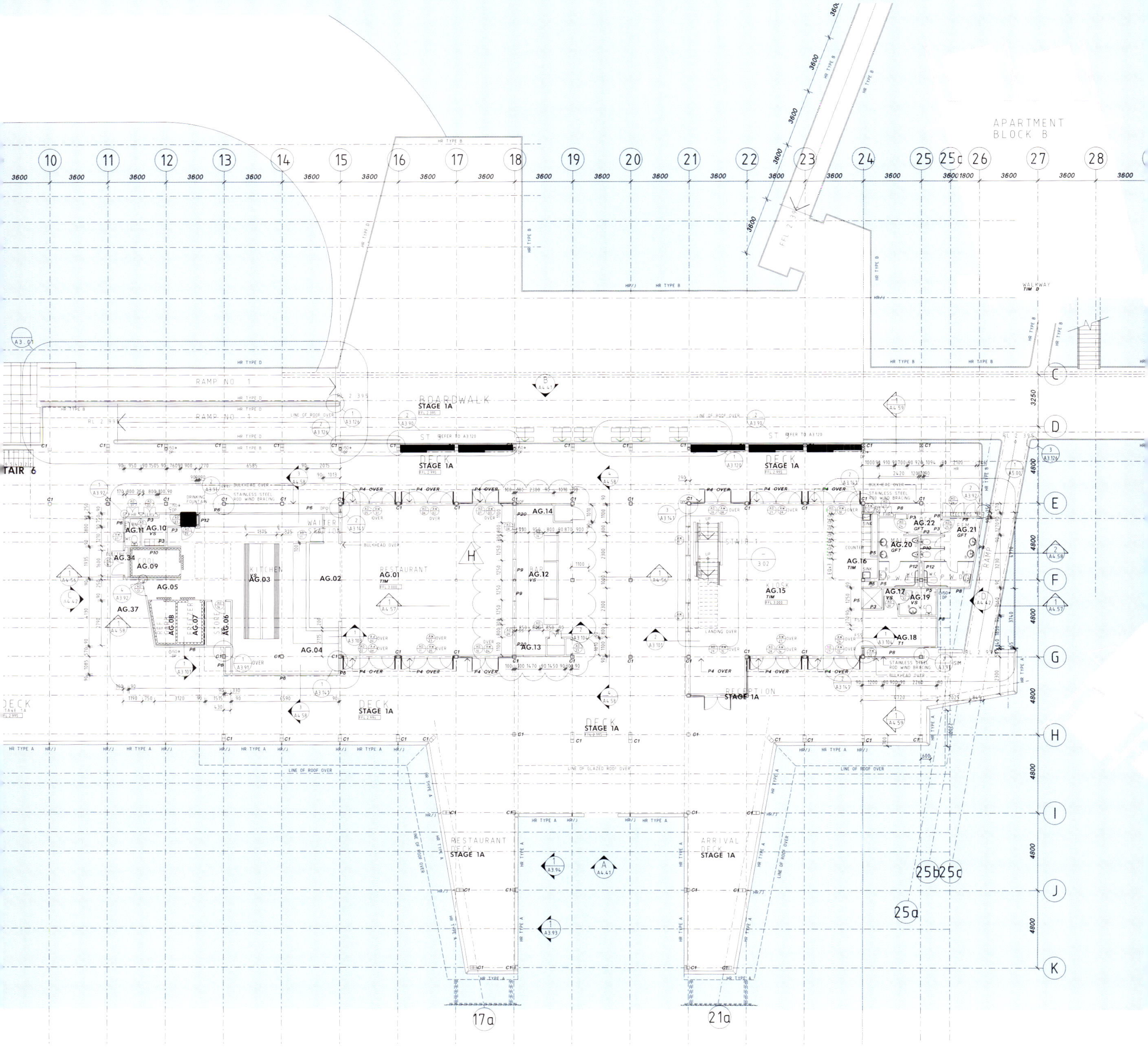
APARTMENT BLOCK B
10 11 12 13 14 15 16 17 18 19 20 21 22 23 24 25 25c 26 27 28
3600
RAMP NO. 1
BOARDWALK STAGE 1A
DECK STAGE 1A
WALKWAY
TAIR 6
AG.01 RESTAURANT
AG.02
AG.03 KITCHEN
AG.04
AG.05
AG.06
AG.07
AG.08
AG.09
AG.10
AG.11
AG.12
AG.13
AG.14
AG.15 KIOSK
AG.16
AG.18
AG.19
AG.20
AG.21
AG.22
AG.34
AG.37
STAIR 1
RECEPTION STAGE 1A
RESTAURANT DECK STAGE 1A
ARRIVAL DECK STAGE 1A
C D E F G H I J K
4800
17a 21a 25a 25b 25c

OARDWALK RL .395
OARDWALK RL .800

The buildings possess a character that recognisably belongs to Queensland, deploying white corrugated iron, saw textured and stained timber, painted weatherboards, louvre panels and batten sunshades in a number of colours and combinations.

This use of the vernacular is regional maritime architecture at its best, exploiting shadows cast by the sub-tropical light and allowing the sky's reflection in the water to lap against the pier structure upon which the two-storey units are built.

There are differences of scale between the deep-verandahed loggias of the dining, recreation and conference pavilions and the smaller verandahs on each of the houses, and between the robust, marina arrivals pier and the personalised jetties attached to each waterfront dwelling.

As with maritime buildings anywhere there is a sensitive adherence to principles of structure and to a limited use of primary materials. These elements combine to form a coherent village atmosphere where, due to the consistency of the approach, each building contributes to the whole and the overall impression is strengthened.

Spa Island is the centrepiece of the inner lagoon, connected to the reception and restaurant area by a footbridge. Children and adults share a series of wading and bathing areas, spas, and a 25-metre competition swimming pool.

Sunbaking accompanied by a massage is an option, while shade-giving umbrellas and a large flowing canopy offer protection.

Set apart from the Gold Coast by the water that separates it from the mainland, Couran Cove is distinguished by its ecosystem, which remains largely intact, and by the attention paid to tree retention, use of materials, and dunal or forest protection. These are relatively new values for tourist projects, yet sustainability is one of the lessons the Australian landscape can offer.

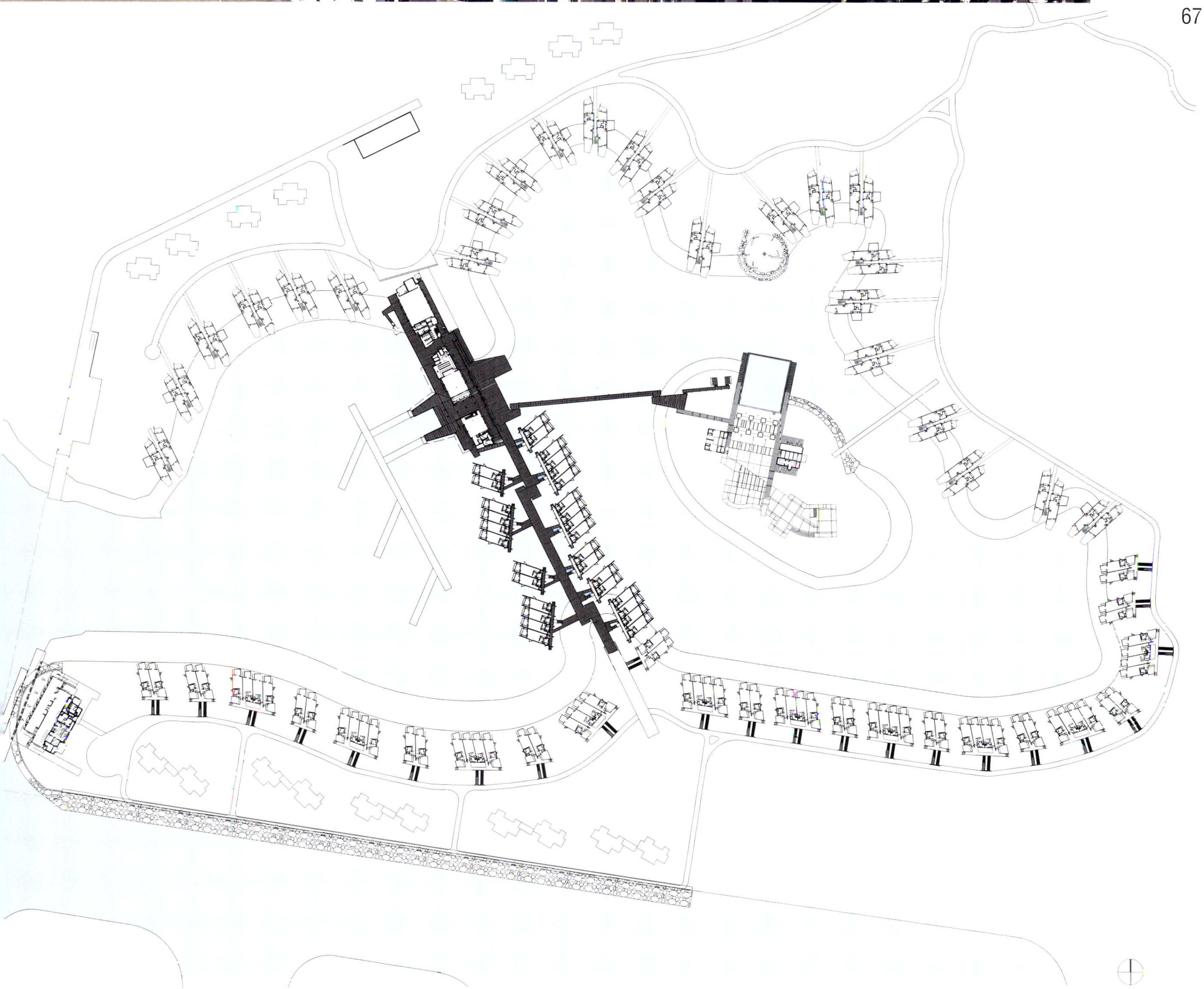

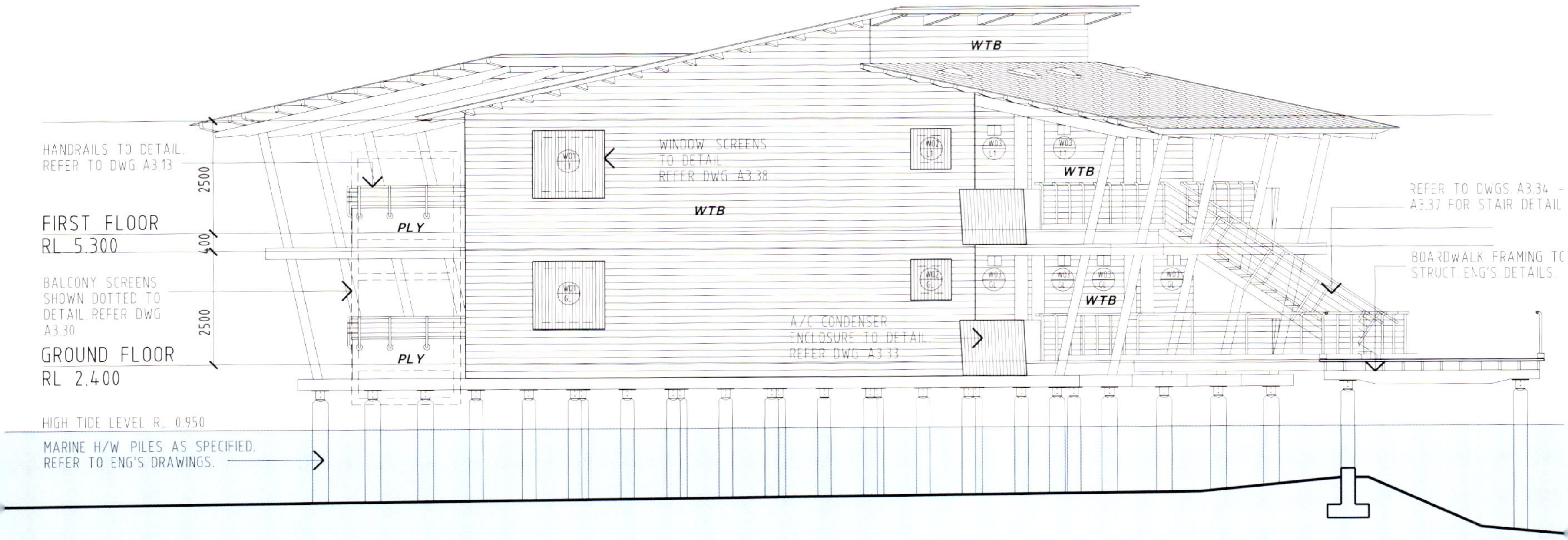

WTB
HANDRAILS TO DETAIL. REFER TO DWG A3.13
WINDOW SCREENS TO DETAIL REFER DWG A3.38
FIRST FLOOR RL 5.300
PLY
BALCONY SCREENS SHOWN DOTTED TO DETAIL REFER DWG A3.30
GROUND FLOOR RL 2.400
A/C CONDENSER ENCLOSURE TO DETAIL REFER DWG A3.33
REFER TO DWGS A3.34 - A3.37 FOR STAIR DETAIL
BOARDWALK FRAMING TO STRUCT. ENG'S. DETAILS.
HIGH TIDE LEVEL RL 0.950
MARINE H/W PILES AS SPECIFIED. REFER TO ENG'S. DRAWINGS.

D1
D1.1
D2
D3
D4
D4.1
D5
DA
DB
DB.1
DC
DD
DE
DF
DF.1
DG
DH
BALCONY RM.2
APP.1 LIVING AREA RM.1
APP.2 LIVING AREA RM.1
APP.3 LIVING AREA RM.1
APP.4 LIVING AREA RM.1
KITCHEN RM.3
DRESS RM.4
BATH RM.5
WALKWAY
SCREEN TO DETAIL REFER DWG A3.30
WINDOW SCREEN TO DETAIL REFER DWG A3.38
SLIDING FLY SCREEN TIMBER LOUVRES TO DETAIL
A/C CONDENSING UNIT ENCLOSURE
FOR BOARDWALK CONNECTION REFER DWGS A1.12 & A1.13
A2.03

Business Centre

This two-tier stand with a capacity for 45,000 spectators has a central area for dining and club entertainment. It can be viewed as a cross-section with one side of the stand facing the action, primarily football and cricket matches. View lines, proximity to the play and comfortable seating are the key requirements.

The steel structure becomes an element for the tectonics of cantilever, guyed masts and backstays. The fibreglass canopy protects spectators from sub-tropical rain and sun. Its umbrella form, spiky and stick-like, is a deliberate contrast to the concrete plinth of the base and the solid form of the steel elevation.

The 'Gabba' is a significant feature of inner-suburban Brisbane.

BRISBANE CRICKET GROUND

4
GATE

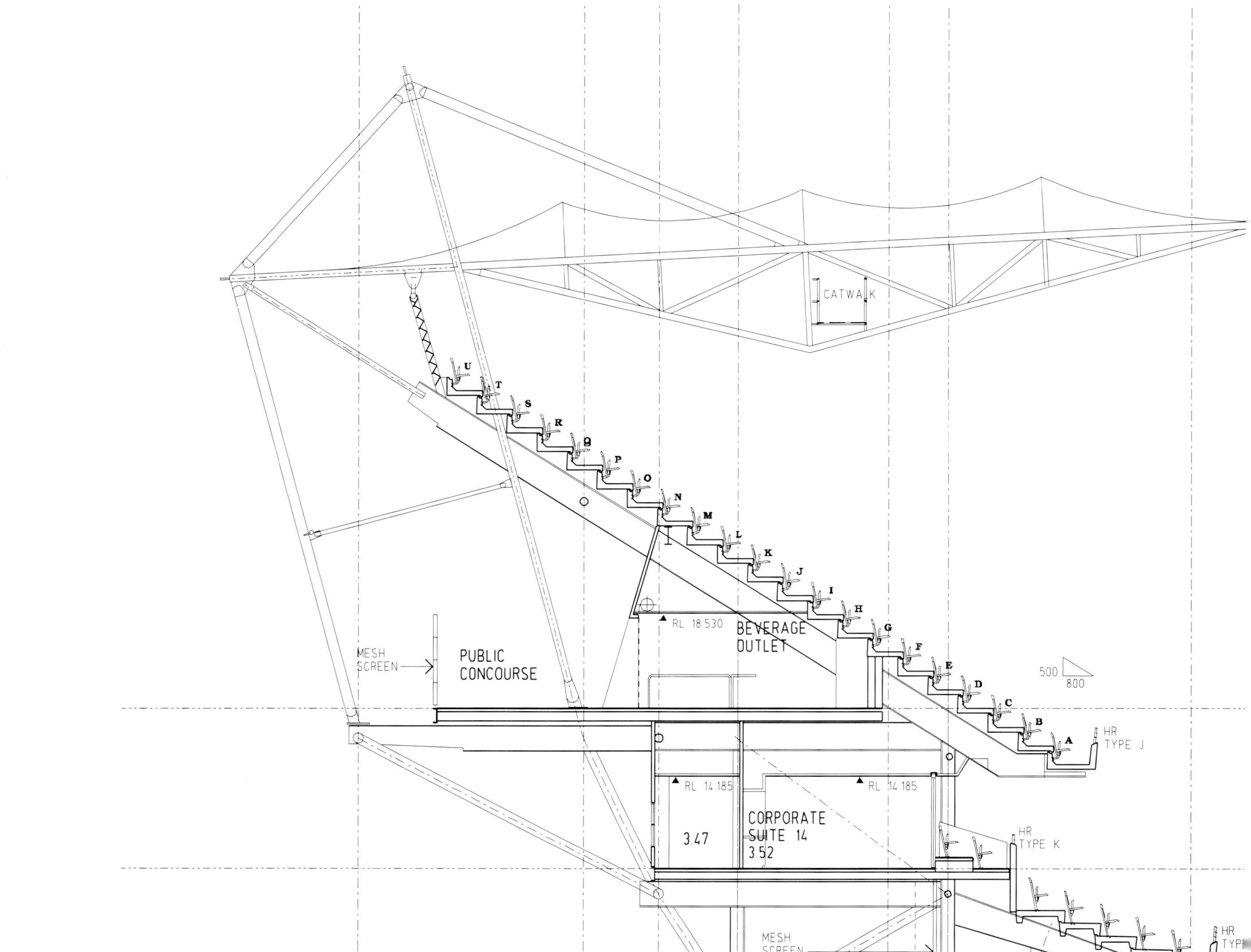
CATWALK
U T S R Q P O N M L K J I H G F E D C B A
RL 18 530
BEVERAGE OUTLET
MESH SCREEN
PUBLIC CONCOURSE
500
800
HR TYPE J
RL 14 185
RL 14 185
CORPORATE SUITE 14
3.52
3.47
HR TYPE K
HR TYPE
MESH SCREEN
PUBLIC CONCOURSE 2.37
N M L K
STANLEY STREET
CONC PLINTH
PLANT ROOM 1.78
SERVIC TUNNEL 1.72
COMPACTED FILL
TANKING MEMBRANE TO RETAINING WALL REAR FACE TO GROUND
MOISTU BARRIE

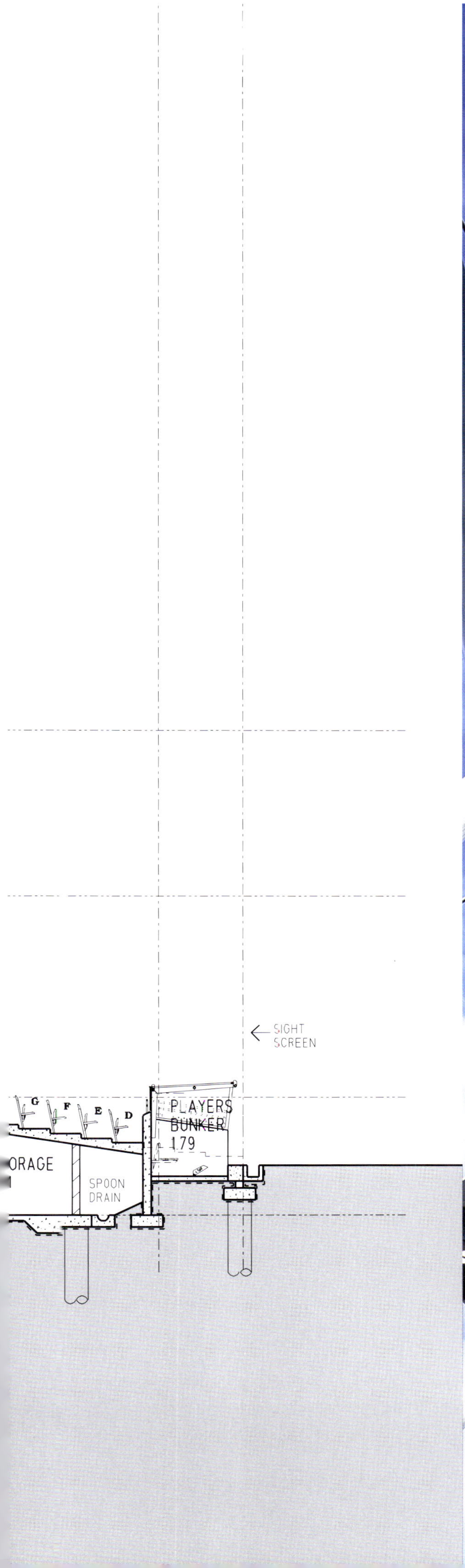
SIGHT
SCREEN
PLAYERS
BUNKER
179
G
F
E
D
ORAGE
SPOON
DRAIN

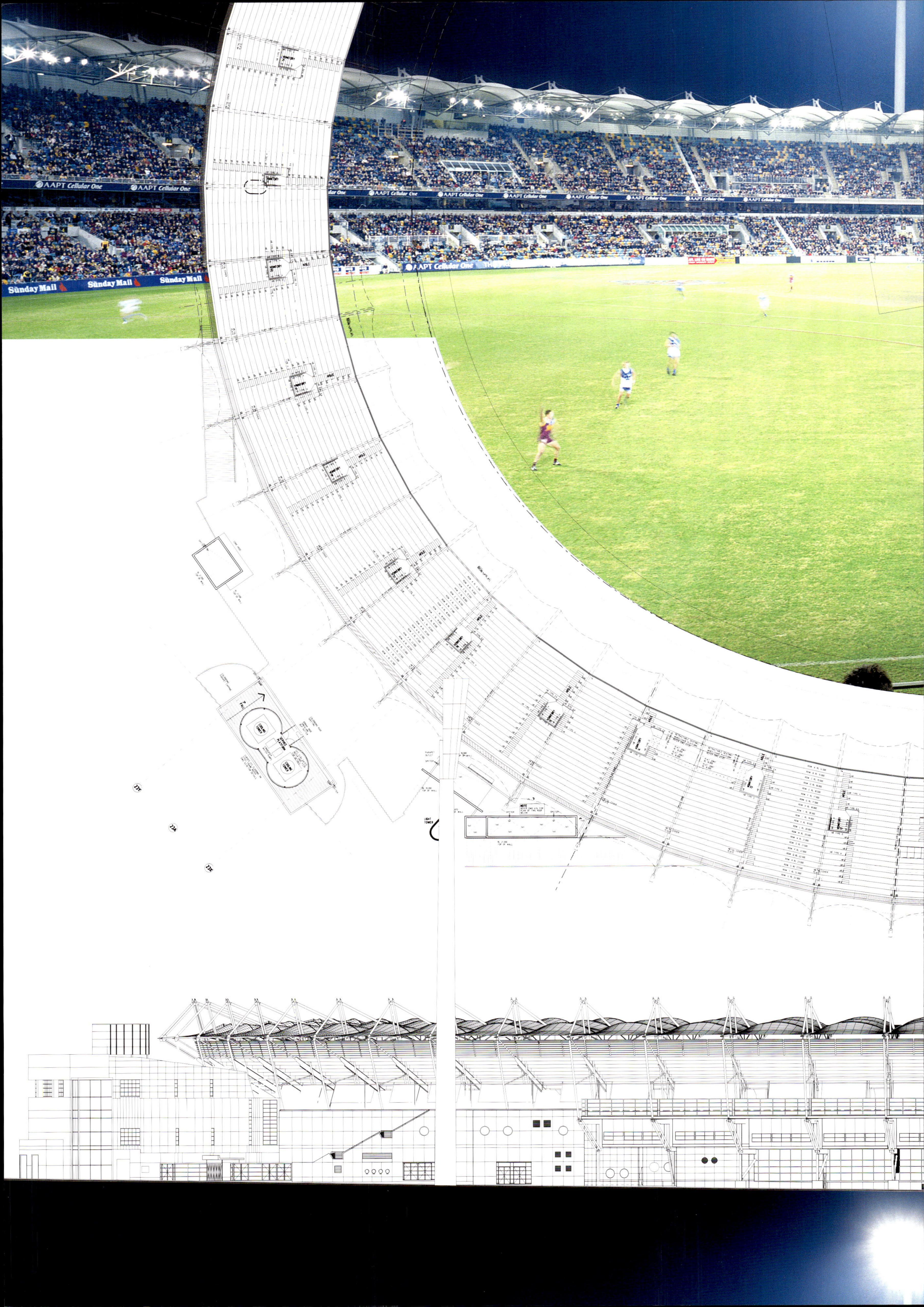
AAPT Cellular One
Sunday Mail
LIGHT TOWER

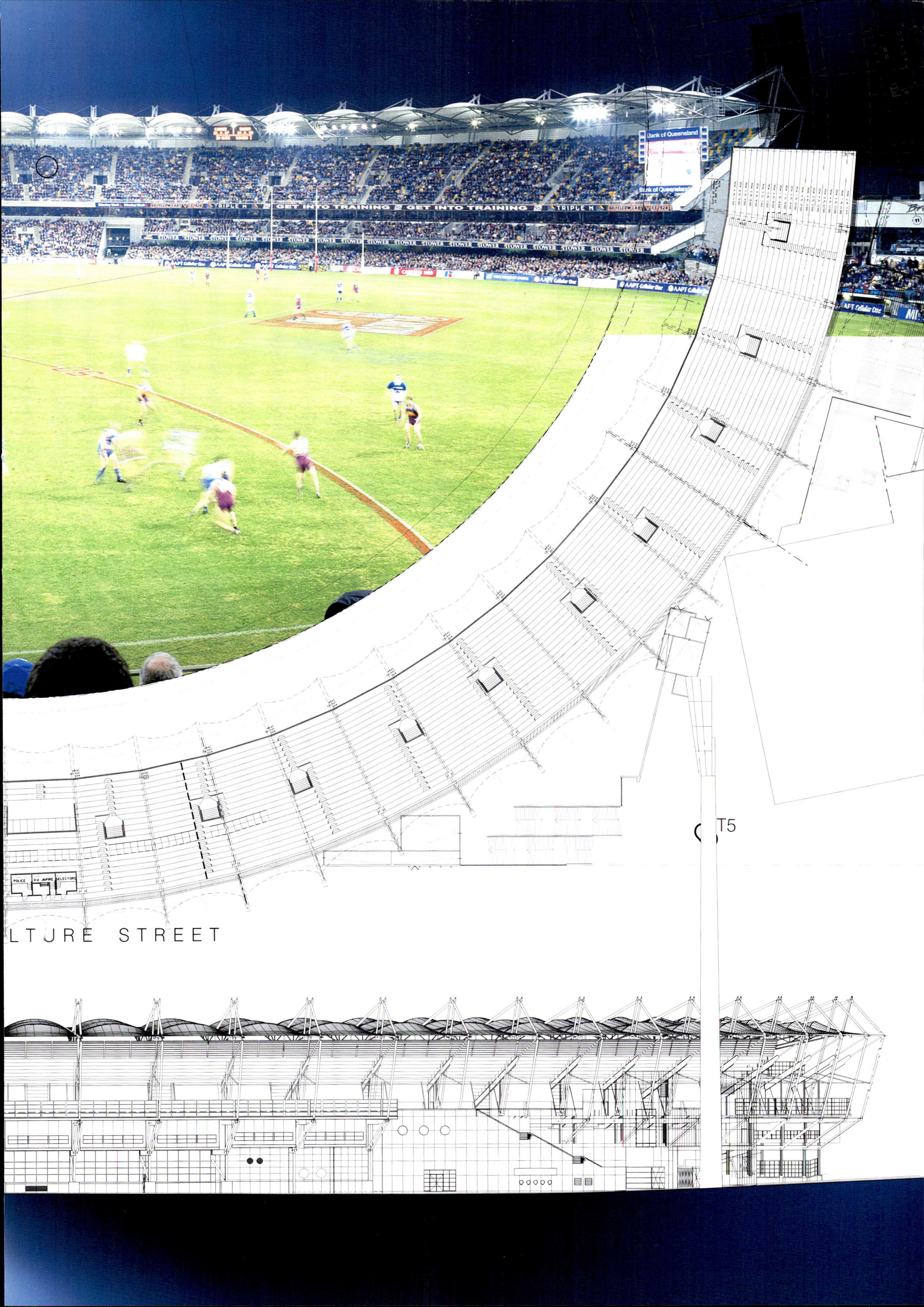
Bank of Queensland
GET INTO TRAINING
TRIPLE M
TOWER
POLICE
SELECTORS
T5
LTURE STREET

This project represents a downtown university-led renewal and involves appropriating the former post office and courthouse and connecting with the city art gallery. These actions create a new public space and are critical urban actions that redefine this part of the city and further distinguish the precinct.

These two new public spaces help redefine the area: one is an open grass bank and urban plaza, the other an inner-city block court with a new performance theatre entered from the arch beneath the post office tower. They link two historic streets in the centre of the city.

Pedestrian pathways between the old and new elements bind the complex together. Curved walls and intricate passages cut between open spaces and building blocks bring new life, in the same way that students of design, art and theatre create a vibrant and diverse urban drama.

The architecture is carefully laminated into an existing 'back wall' context, the new curving inclined walls leaving the free-standing historic buildings alone. On the skyline the key Victorian towers remain dominant, with zinc-faced student housing keyed into the neighbourhood of corrugated iron roofs. For students there is a strong new spatial identity for their studies. For the citizens of Ballarat, a new public space is formed.

UNIVERSITY OF BALLARAT

87

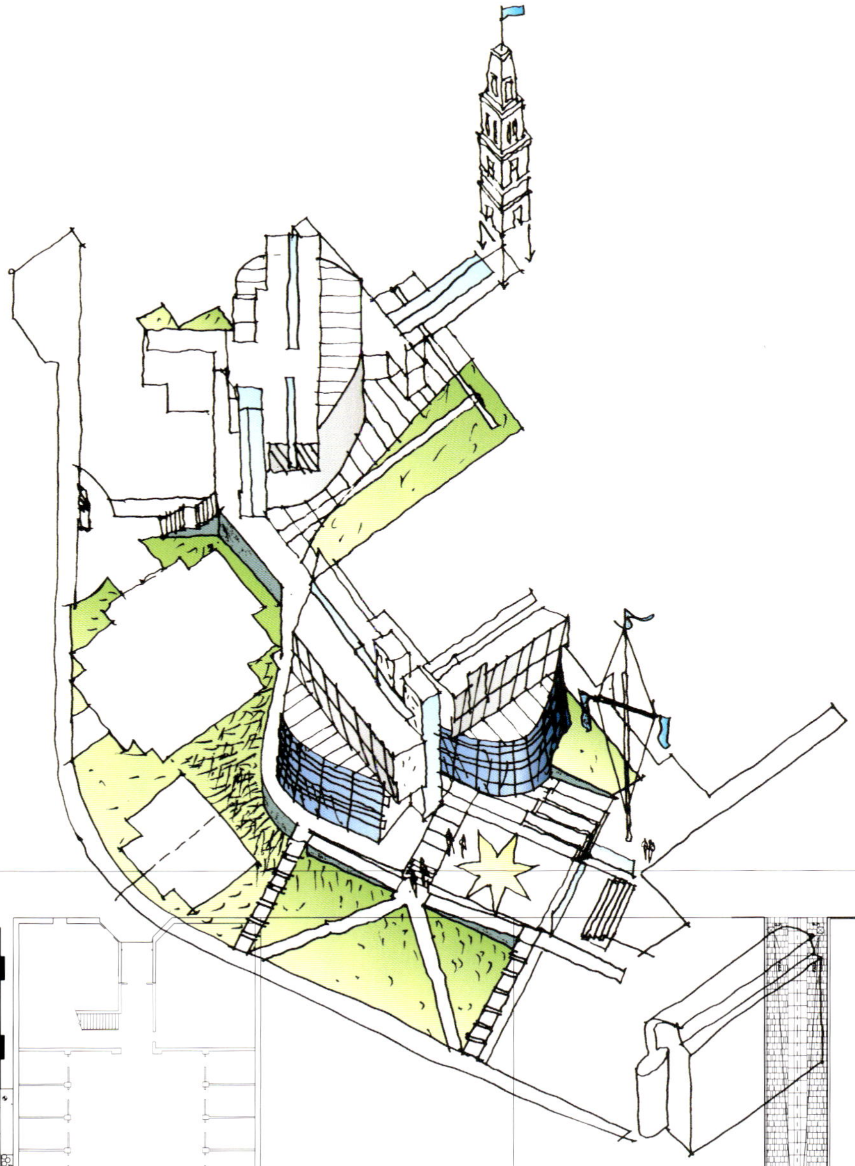

Docklands Stadium is a 52,500-seat indoor arena, a stadium for three codes of football and a theatre for public assembly and entertainment. In addition to church and university convocations, the arena has played host to performers including Barbra Streisand and Bruce Springsteen.

The field surface is specifically sized at 168 metres x 140 metres to enable both Australian Rules football and cricket to be played. Pullout lower-tier seating platforms are designed to host soccer and rugby with spectators close to the 'touch line'. The central moving roof is 35 metres above the natural grass turf. These activities are supported by a full complement of food and beverage services, with quality dining and bars for Medallion Club members and team coteries, and with a nightclub/bar/restaurant precinct catering for general patrons.

A total of 6,500 dining area seats are available, with 60 corporate suites occupying one half of the mid-level upper tier.

A key attribute of the arena is the proximity of spectators to the play. When the roof is closed, this exchange is further heightened, leading to an intimacy that is experienced by both players and patrons.

DOCKLANDS STADIUM

This high-technology stadium has one of the world's largest moving roofs (it opens or closes in seven minutes), with a rectangular sky aperture of 165 metres x 100 metres to mirror the rectangular pitch areas required for soccer and rugby. The design imagery deploys an engineering aesthetic to express four inclined-paired curving bow-shaped trusses appearing above the roof to reflect the interior elliptical form. The curved shape of the bowl is sculpturally expressed (as in a saucer) with an upper ring, bringing roof and wall together. Against the sky, the idea of the moving roof appears to hover like giant wings about to become part of the action. At night, a blue perimeter of light projected into the fascia offers a 'rings of Saturn' surround to the occasion. It accelerates dramatically as the intensity of the match underway increases and the crowd noise intensifies.

The roof is designed to be closed quickly in the event of rain or excessive sunlight, both causing spectator and player discomfort. The field is oriented north–south to accord with international standards for rugby and soccer. (Australian Rules football is played on grounds with a variety of orientations, with north–south as the preferred layout).

Major entries at four corner points are celebrated in giant stair and ramp portals. Painted red and green, these offer a welcoming identity to the place of arrival and herald the excitement of the event.

The experience of the crowd assemblage on the broad perimeter concourse (a form of ritual progression), is an important part of the arrival sequence, and adds to the anticipatory adrenalin that fuels the fans.

The design is driven by the idea that it is the reality of the total experience of the big match or spectacular event that counts; being there is a crucial value. The job of the architect is to see that all the essentials are brought together to ensure this 'atmosphere', the excitement that stimulates the senses and requires emotional, even physical attention.

Colonial

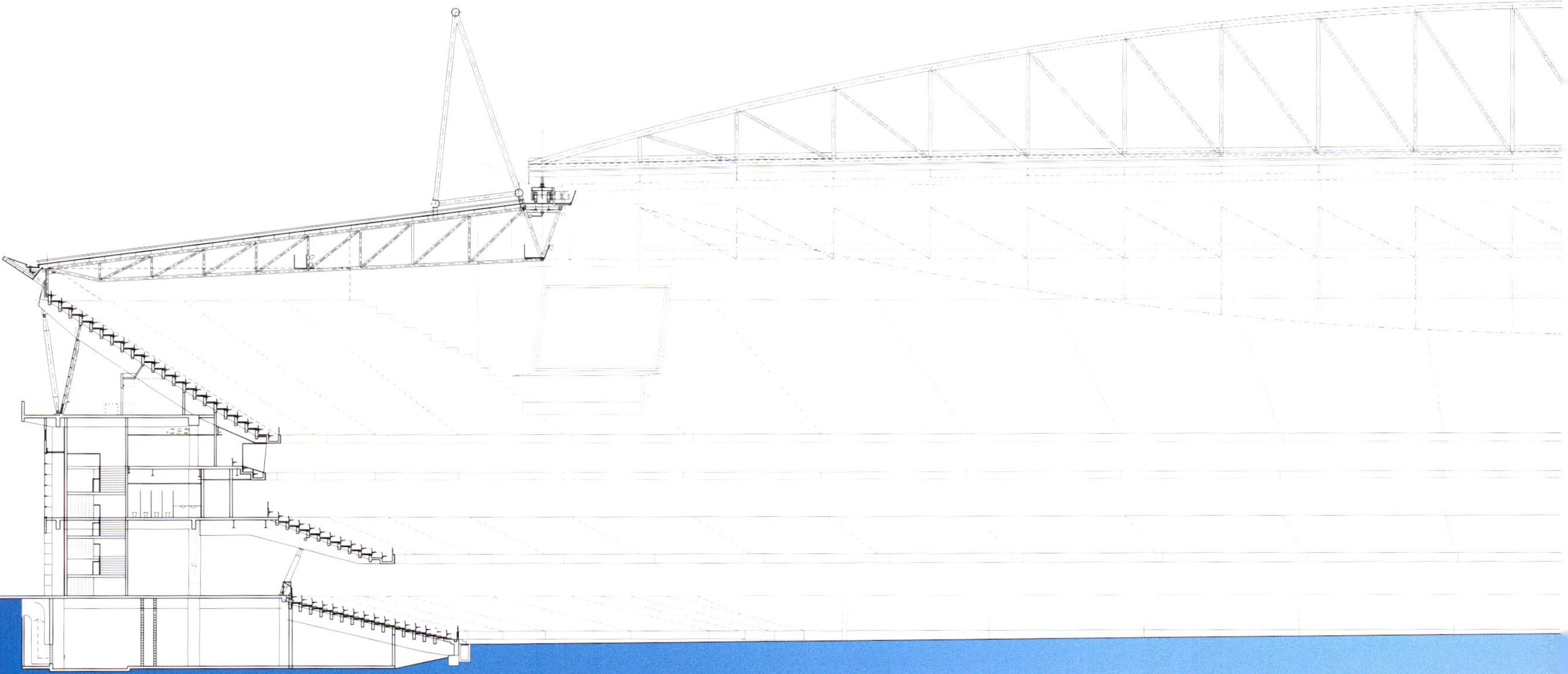

SmokeFree SmokeFree SmokeFree SmokeFree
FOUR'N TWENTY
10/10
Mitre10
tab sportsbet
ANSETT AUSTRALIA
BOYER SPORTS MEDIA
HEINZ
Coca-Cola Coca-Cola
DUNLOP TYRES

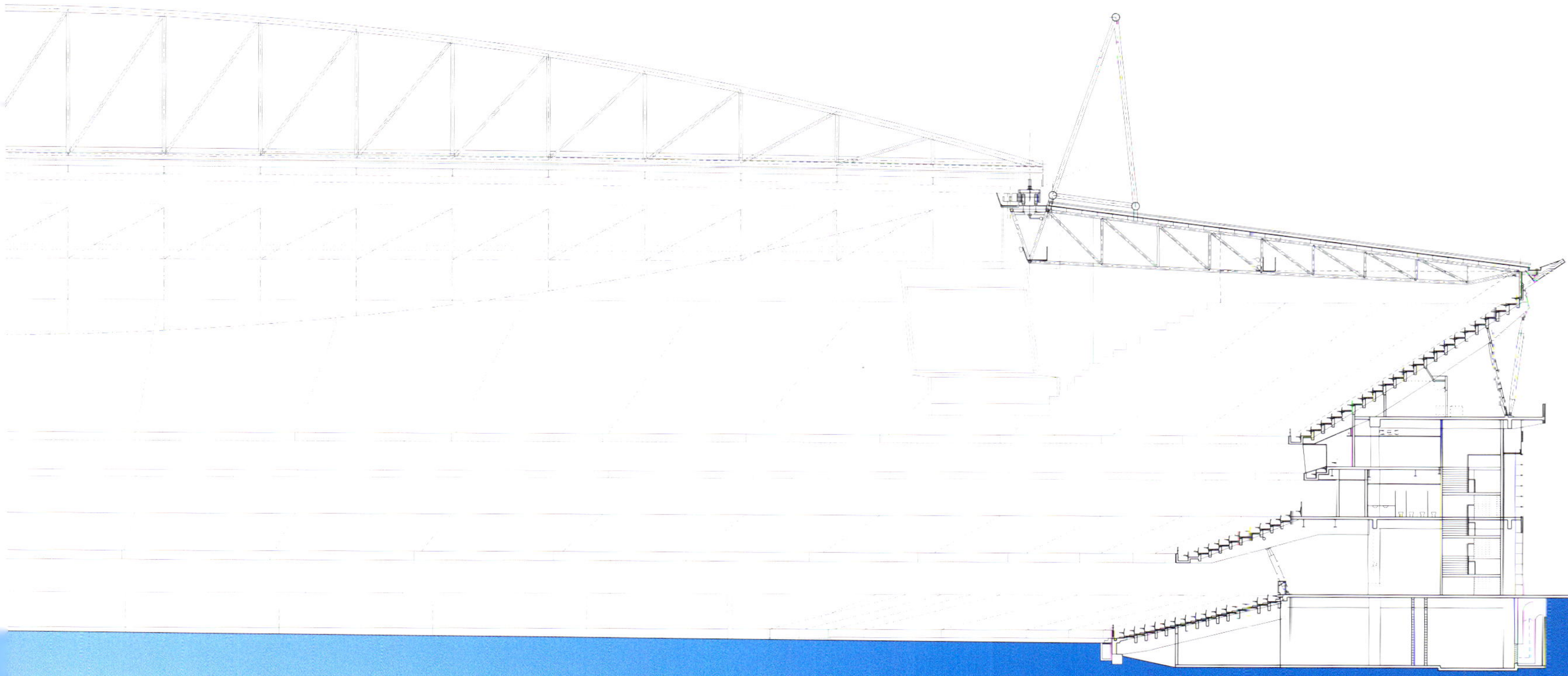

Colonial.
NISSAN
COUGAR BOURBON WHISKEY
SmokeFree
Herald Sun
SmokeFree
EnergyAustralia
seek.com.au
Cracker Barrel

8
Aisle

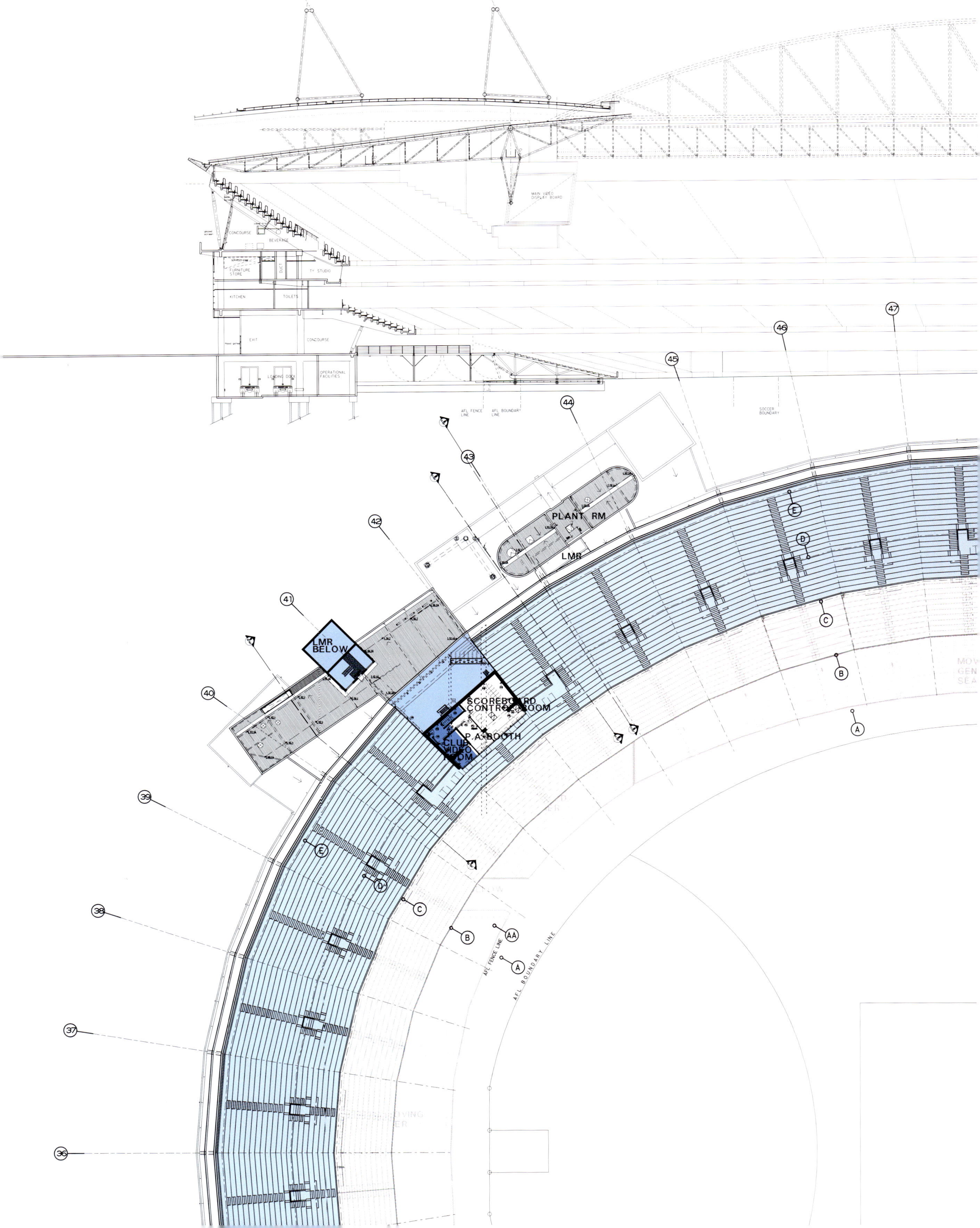
MAIN VIDEO DISPLAY BOARD
CONCOURSE
BEVERAGE
FURNITURE STORE
DUCT
TV STUDIO
KITCHEN
TOILETS
EXIT
CONCOURSE
LOADING DOCK
OPERATIONAL FACILITIES
AFL FENCE LINE
AFL BOUNDARY LINE
SOCCER BOUNDARY
PLANT RM
LMR
LMR BELOW
SCOREBOARD CONTROL ROOM
P.A. BOOTH
CLUB VIDEO ROOM
AFL FENCE LINE
AFL BOUNDARY LINE

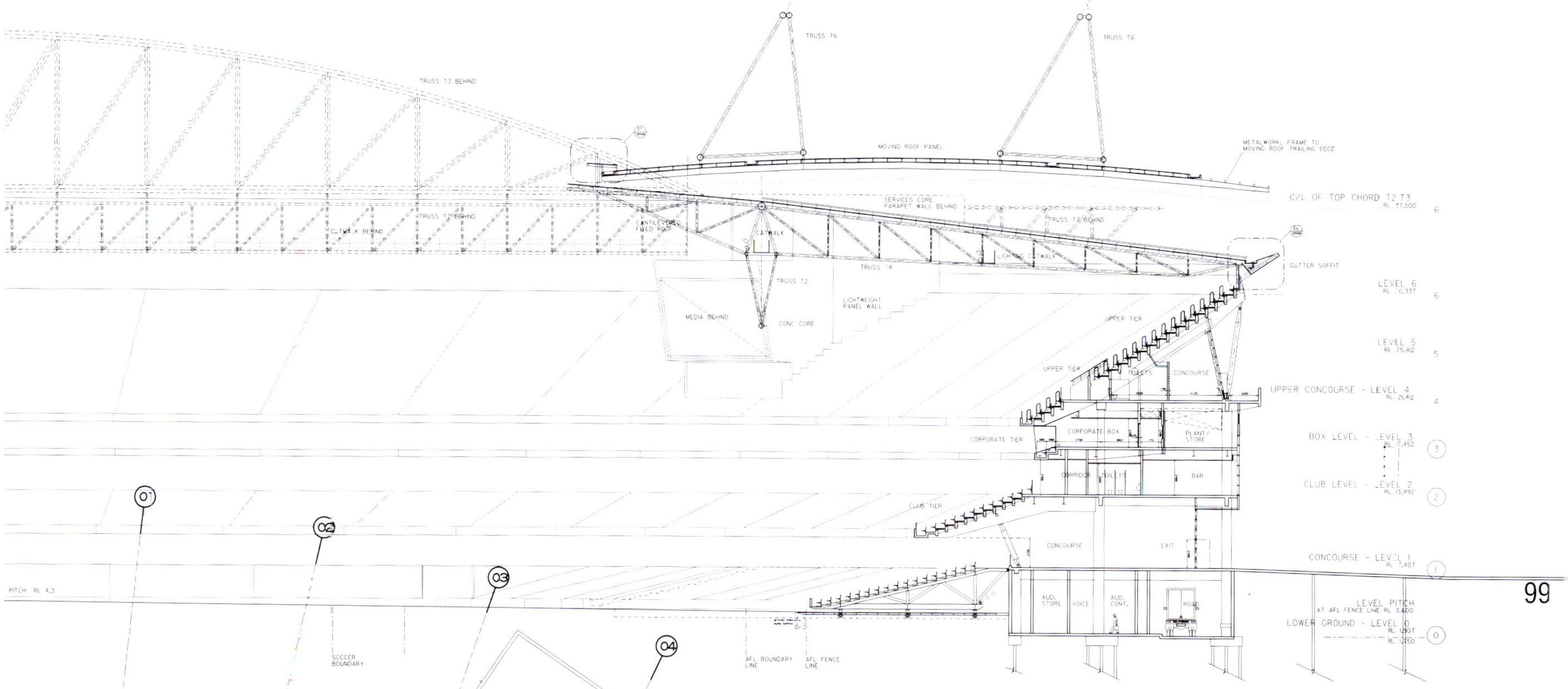
TRUSS T6
TRUSS T6
TRUSS T3 BEHIND
MOVING ROOF PANEL
METALWORK FRAME TO MOVING ROOF TRAILING EDGE
C/L OF TOP CHORD T2 T3
CATWALK
TRUSS T2
MEDIA BEHIND
CONC CORE
GUTTER SOFFIT
LEVEL 6
LEVEL 5
UPPER TIER
UPPER CONCOURSE - LEVEL 4
CORPORATE TIER
CORPORATE BOX
BOX LEVEL - LEVEL 3
BAR
CLUB LEVEL - LEVEL 2
CLUB TIER
CONCOURSE
EXIT
CONCOURSE - LEVEL 1
LEVEL PITCH
LOWER GROUND - LEVEL 0
SOCCER BOUNDARY
AFL BOUNDARY LINE
AFL FENCE LINE

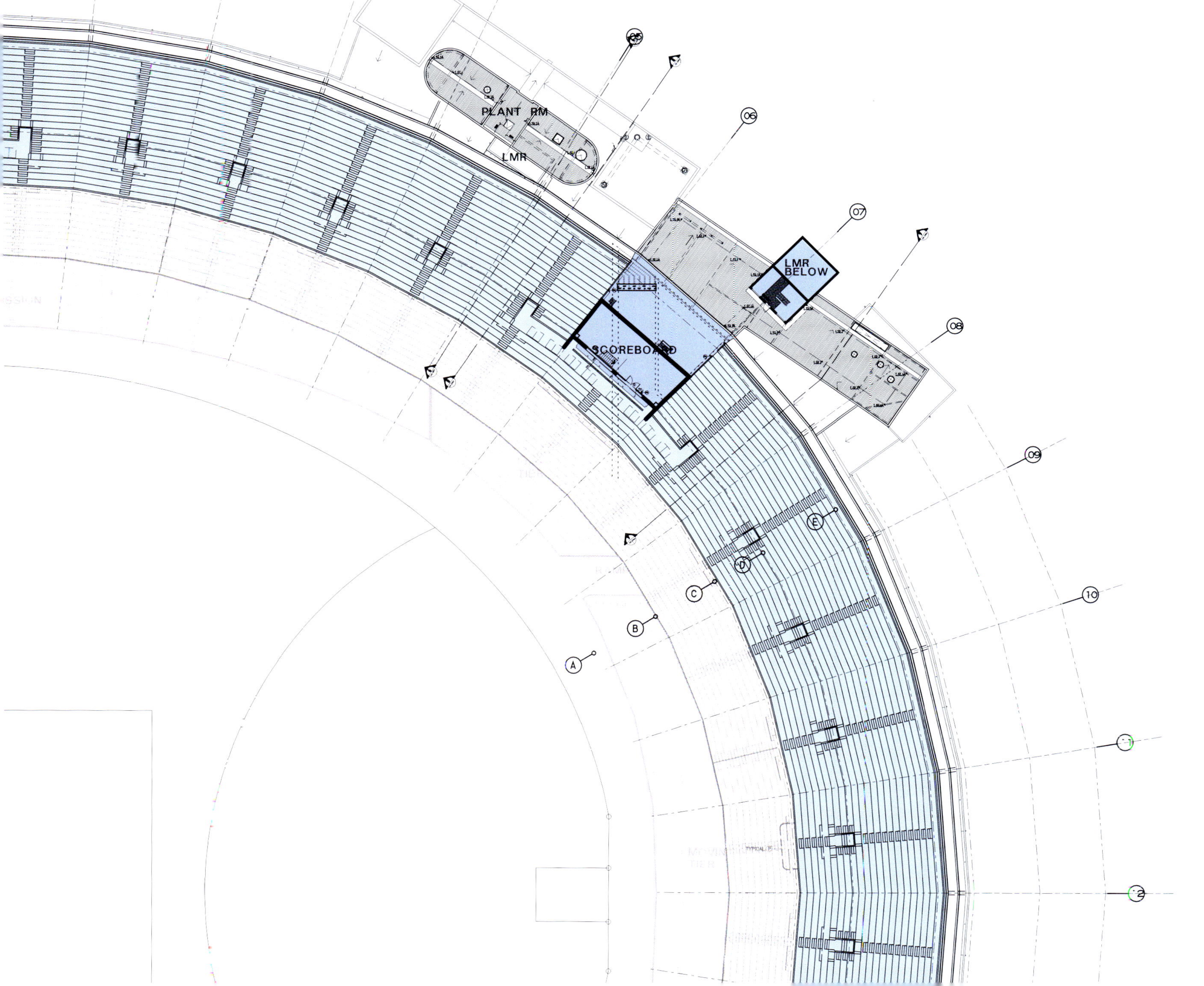
PLANT RM
LMR
LMR BELOW
SCOREBOARD

Dramatically sited on one edge of the central city, the stadium overlooks the waters of the Yarra River upon which Melbourne was founded.

There is unusual transparency: from the interior restaurants and bars, patrons can look across the extensive Victoria Harbour or alternatively, into the very substance of the city. Such facilities may be used for community or corporate functions on non-match days.

It complements one vision of Melbourne, Australia as a sporting/events city in a country that loves playing games and is customarily good at them.

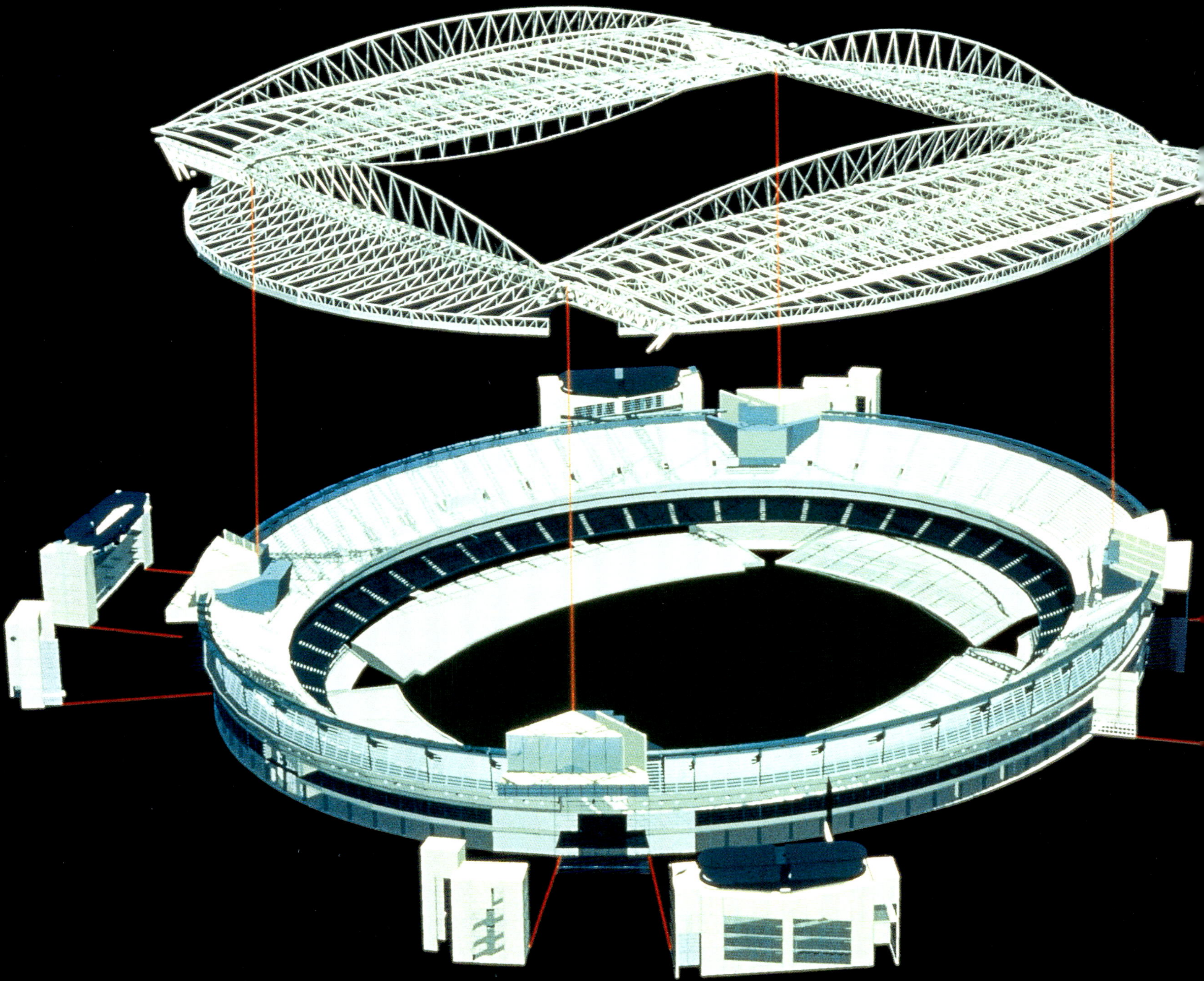

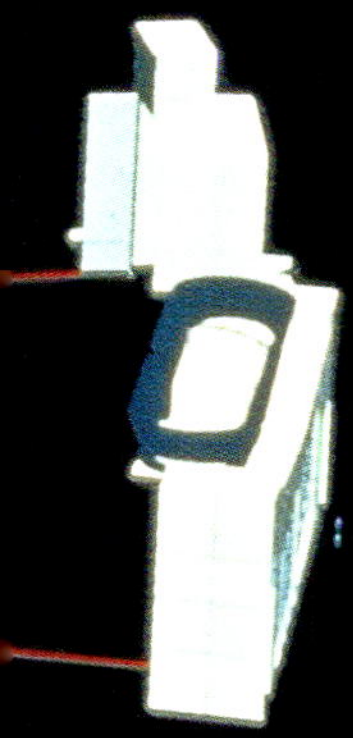

Wesley is a school with a child-centred learning philosophy and an urbane understanding of the intricate relationships between children, parents and schools.

This preparatory school is architecturally focused upon intuitive curiosity, the developing cognition of its pupils and a more structured enquiry. It encourages the development of tool skills through which we form judgments; and the confidence required to innovate and express concepts.

A circular arrival form brings everyone together, as in a living room, and connects home rooms to central resources. A stair with fixed wheels and a house on the landing act as a welcoming joke; so too a wooden bridge with a noisy floor and red viewing slots (that only a child can experience) encountered on the journey through the school.

The ceiling above the circle has an east–west light slot that allows a bar of sunlight to move across the floor, while circular skylights act as planetary metaphors. Elsewhere is a play-ground with face masks and a staircase that leads to a roof terrace from which a slide descends to the sandpit.

WESLEY PREPARATORY SCHOOL

READING
IS
FUN

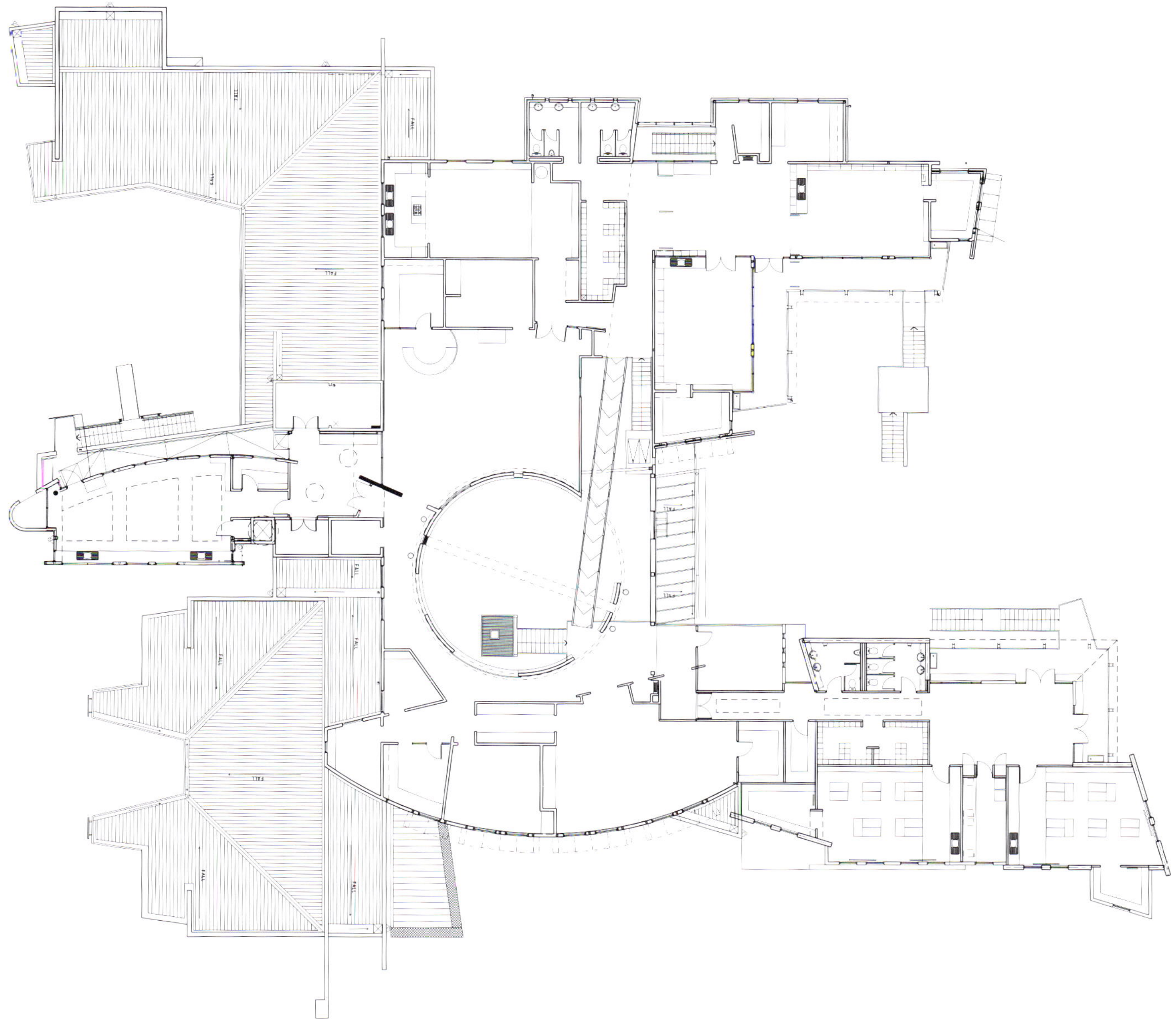

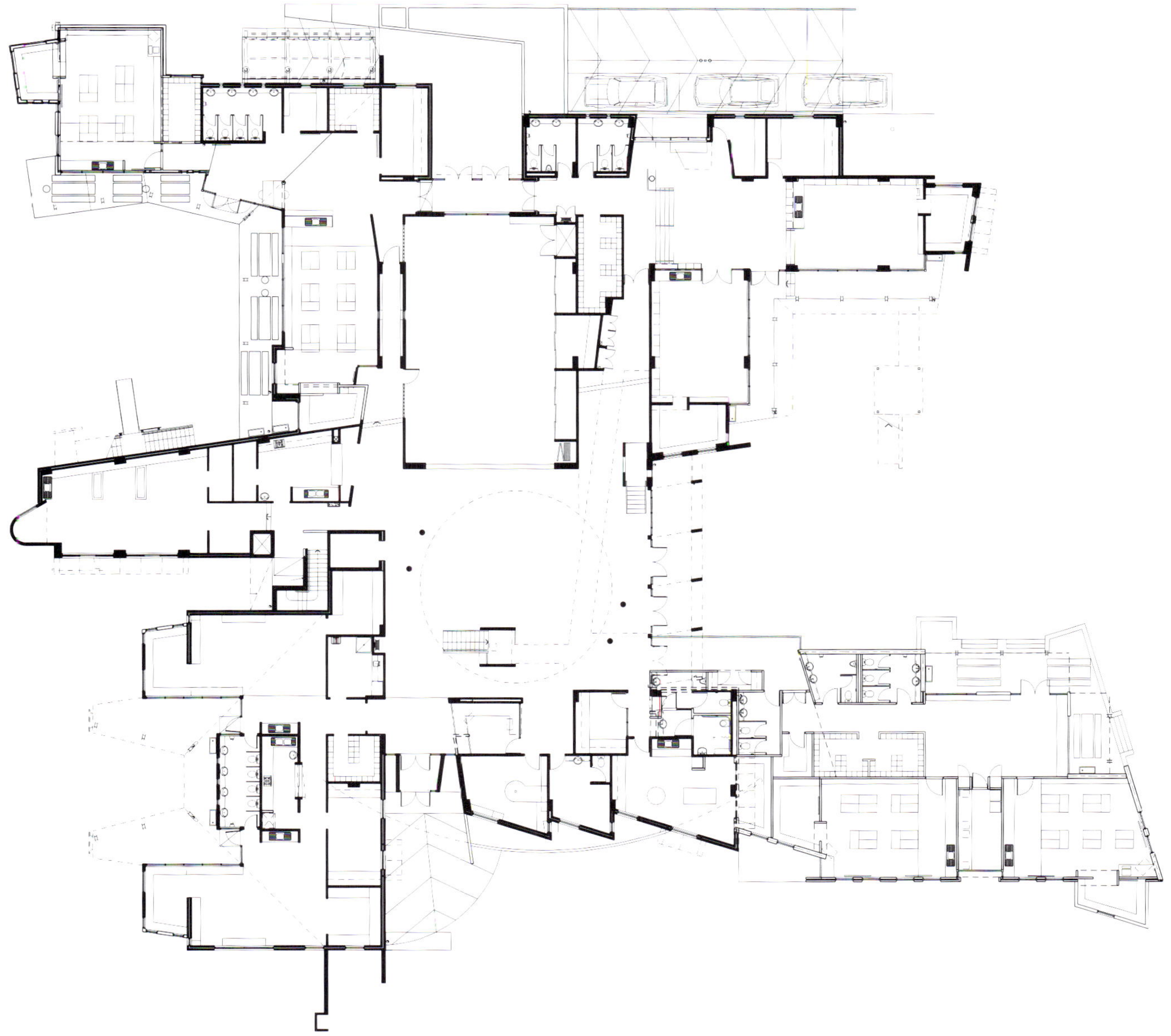

The architecture engages in such ideas in order to create objects that students can literally possess. The forms seek to establish both fantasy and reality as key parts of the one system. Learning for little kids should be serious fun, with love, care and feelings creating the stimulus that ensures continuity.

Verandah edges offer ambiguity for play and imagination; fractured pieces offer differences and identifiable sub-architectures that test eye/mind connections. Optimism is encouraged, and life, form and learning are perceived together.

for

This Commonwealth Scientific and Industrial Research Organisation (CSIRO) Discovery Centre project comprises research laboratories, a conference centre, retail areas, an exhibition hall, bank, cafeteria, and a science education centre called the Green Machine.

A centrally located greenhouse atrium gives the building an introspective winter garden configuration and a focus for public activities.

A tautly gridded, concrete-framed, highly serviced laboratory box of three levels sits to one edge. The public, looking from the atrium, can see the scientists at work from the middle level, which provides a vantage point similar to the bridge on a ship.

The other edge of the block includes the conference centre, the cafeteria and the communications exchange. This enclosure is shaped as a sharply clad element, fragmented, teased out and expanded, with balcony antennae stretched out to meet the landscape. This is the opposite of the controlled but open laboratory grid. The naturally ventilated central greenhouse is visually open to the sky, one face looking towards the city, the other to the bush and the mountains behind Canberra.

CSIRO DISCOVERY CENTRE

DISCOVERY

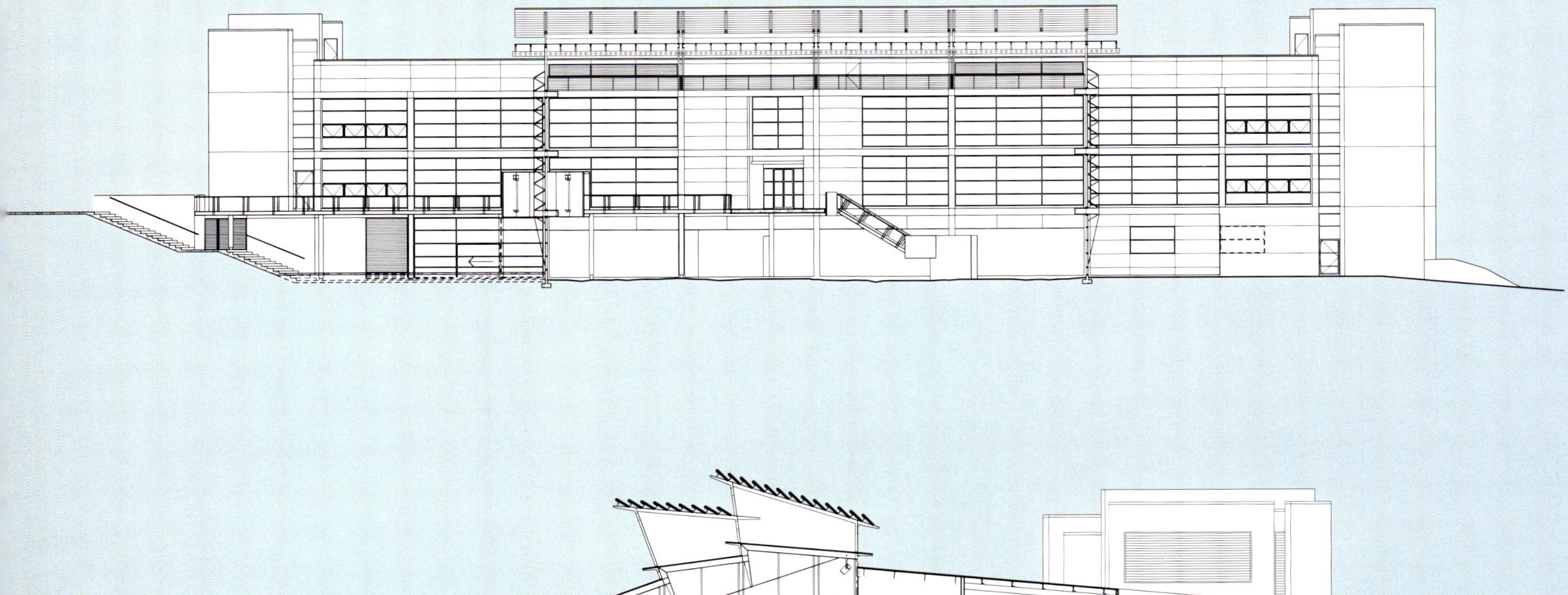

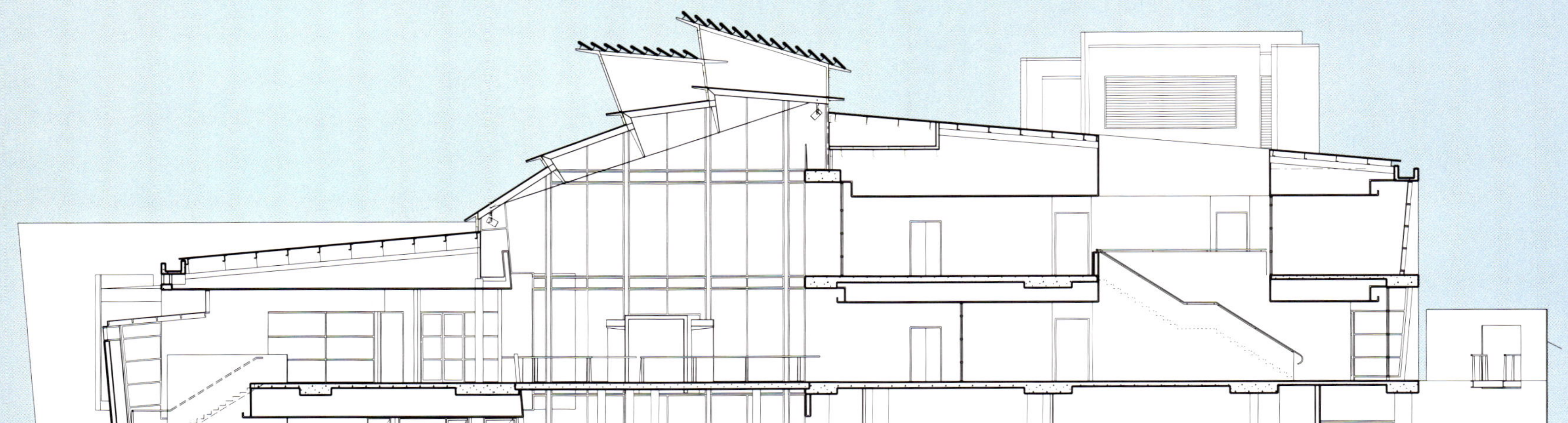

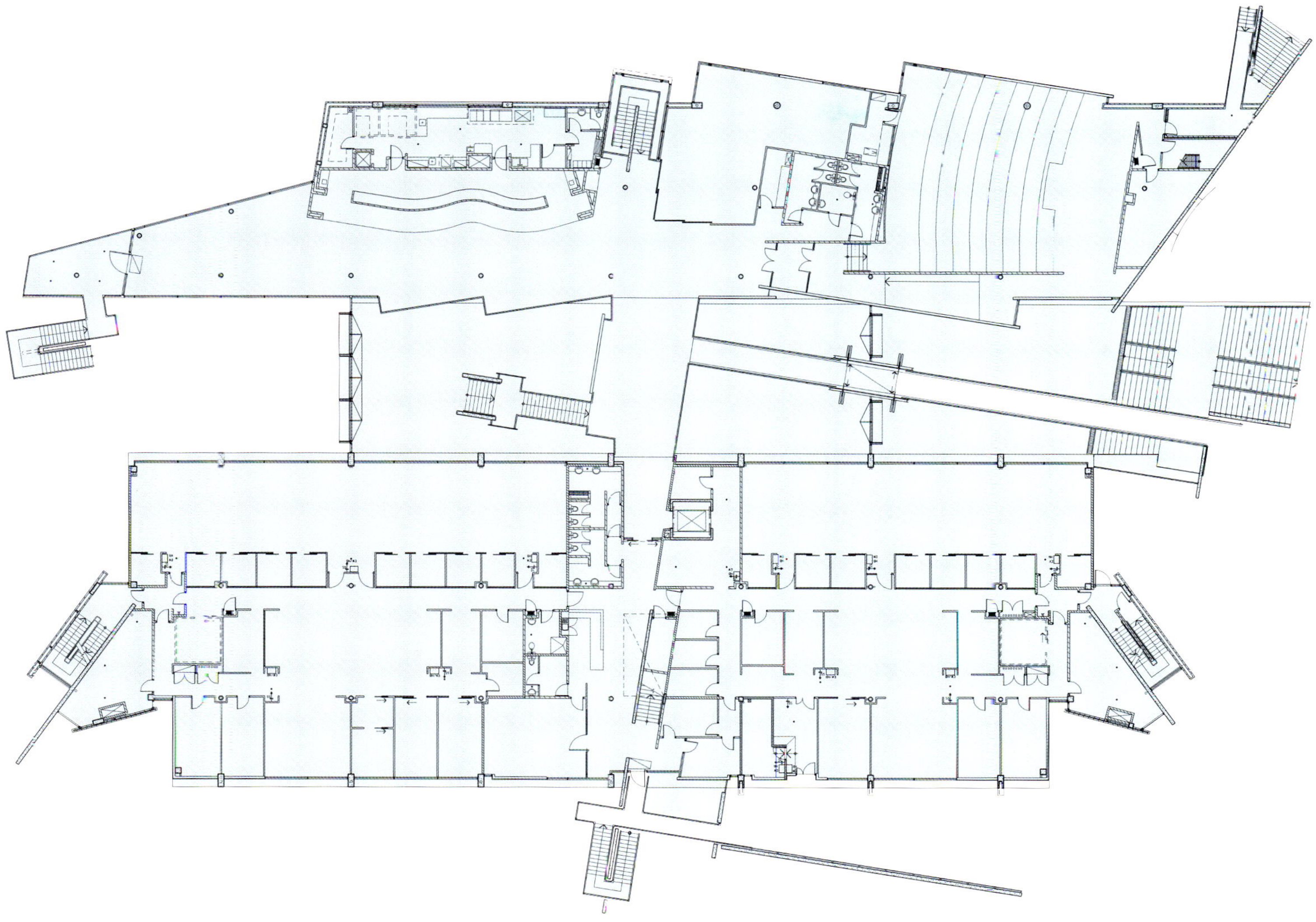

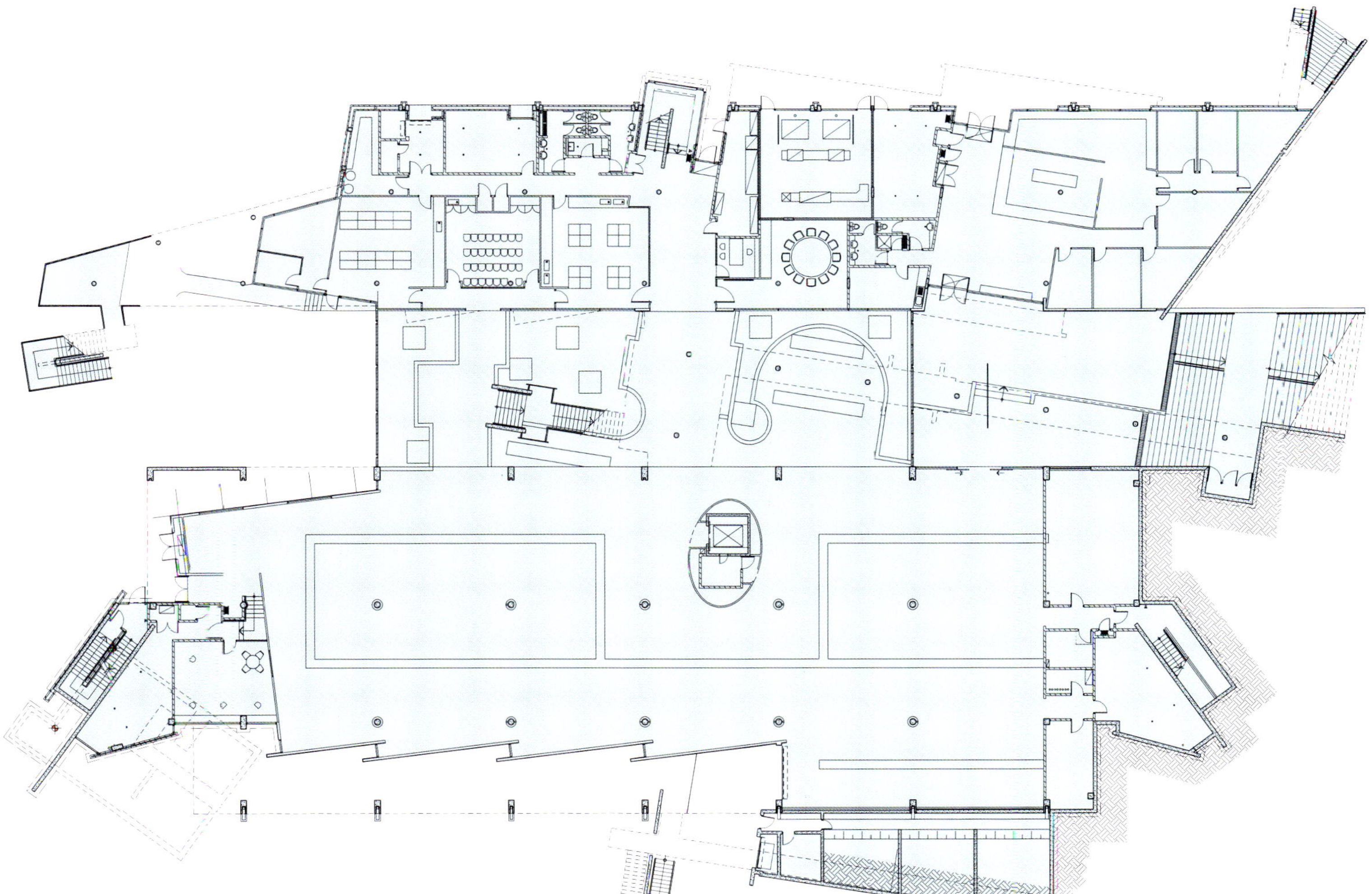

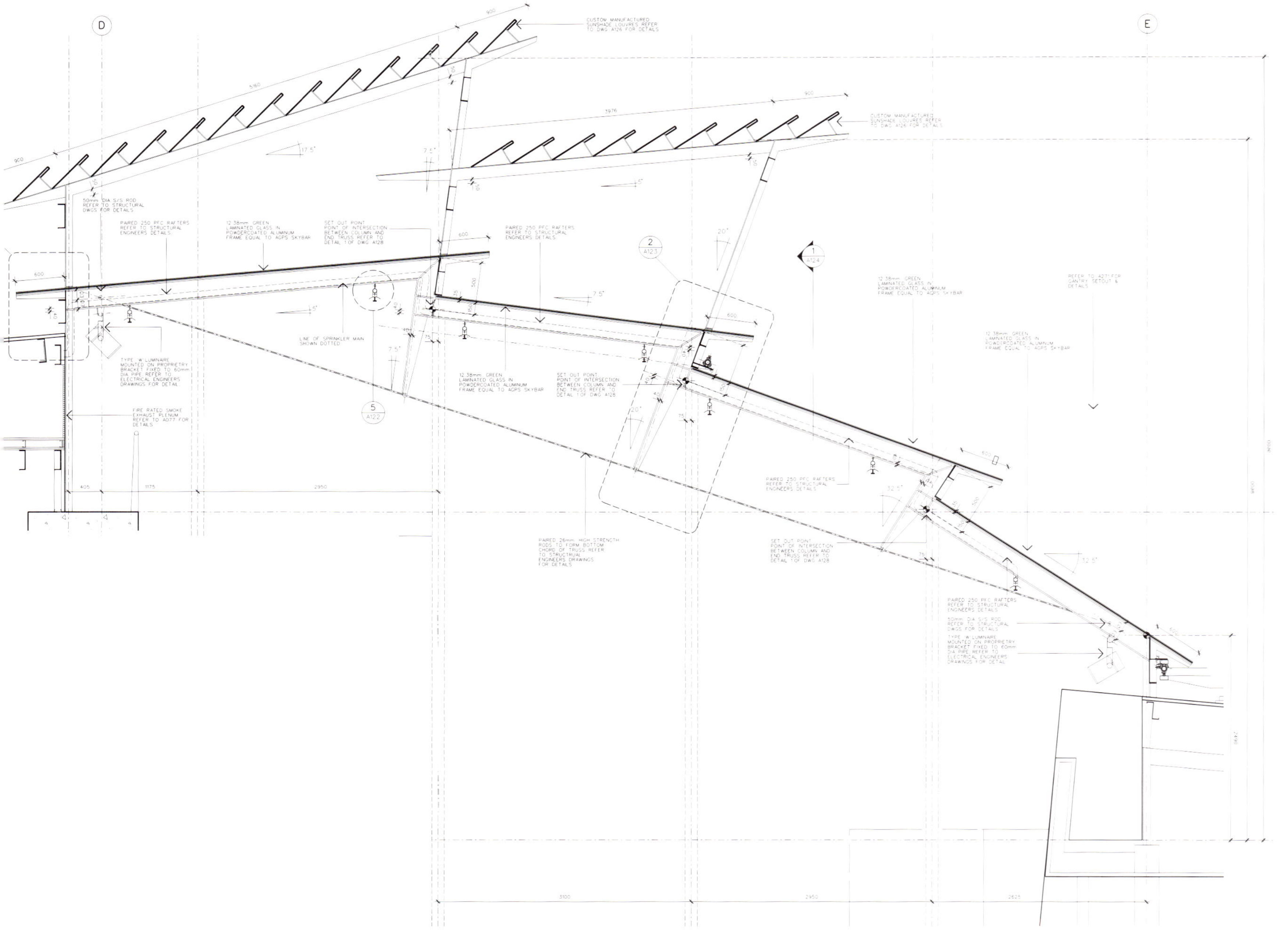

D
E
CUSTOM MANUFACTURED SUNSHADE LOUVRES REFER TO DWG A126 FOR DETAILS
CUSTOM MANUFACTURED SUNSHADE LOUVRES REFER TO DWG A126 FOR DETAILS
50mm DIA S/S ROD REFER TO STRUCTURAL DWGS FOR DETAILS
PAIRED 250 PFC RAFTERS REFER TO STRUCTURAL ENGINEERS DETAILS
12.38mm GREEN LAMINATED GLASS IN POWDERCOATED ALUMINUM FRAME EQUAL TO AGPS SKYBAR
SET OUT POINT POINT OF INTERSECTION BETWEEN COLUMN AND END TRUSS REFER TO DETAIL 1 OF DWG A128
PAIRED 250 PFC RAFTERS REFER TO STRUCTURAL ENGINEERS DETAILS
LINE OF SPRINKLER MAIN SHOWN DOTTED
TYPE 'W' LUMINAIRE MOUNTED ON PROPRIETRY BRACKET FIXED TO 60mm DIA PIPE. REFER TO ELECTRICAL ENGINEERS DRAWINGS FOR DETAIL
FIRE RATED SMOKE EXHAUST PLENUM REFER TO A077 FOR DETAILS
12.38mm GREEN LAMINATED GLASS IN POWDERCOATED ALUMINUM FRAME EQUAL TO AGPS SKYBAR
SET OUT POINT POINT OF INTERSECTION BETWEEN COLUMN AND END TRUSS REFER TO DETAIL 1 OF DWG A128
PAIRED 26mm HIGH STRENGTH RODS TO FORM BOTTOM CHORD OF TRUSS REFER TO STRUCTRUAL ENGINEERS DRAWINGS FOR DETAILS
12.38mm GREEN LAMINATED GLASS IN POWDERCOATED ALUMINUM FRAME EQUAL TO AGPS SKYBAR
12.38mm GREEN LAMINATED GLASS IN POWDERCOATED ALUMINUM FRAME EQUAL TO AGPS SKYBAR
PAIRED 250 PFC RAFTERS REFER TO STRUCTURAL ENGINEERS DETAILS
SET OUT POINT POINT OF INTERSECTION BETWEEN COLUMN AND END TRUSS REFER TO DETAIL 1 OF DWG A128
PAIRED 250 PFC RAFTERS REFER TO STRUCTURAL ENGINEERS DETAILS
50mm DIA S/S ROD REFER TO STRUCTURAL DWGS FOR DETAILS
TYPE 'W' LUMINAIRE MOUNTED ON PROPRIETRY BRACKET FIXED TO 60mm DIA PIPE. REFER TO ELECTRICAL ENGINEERS DRAWINGS FOR DETAIL

EXIT

The new sciences are developing new environments for research. Large, flexibly planned, highly serviced generic laboratories, with open plan office/IT work areas in immediate reach, are key planning elements.

This building houses researchers in two large working wings, located each side of a central administration and meeting block.

Set within the St. Lucia Campus of the University of Queensland, the building presents a powerful identity for world-class research teams.

A double-storey glass foyer receives researchers, staff, students and visitors at a keyed security point. Research teams are brought together from the Commonwealth Scientific and Industrial Research Organisation (CSIRO) and the university Science faculty.

A framework approach to the formulation of space, structure and services acknowledges the inevitability of change and a future that we know will be different. Flexibility in space usage and adaptability of fitout and servicing, equipment design and location, are fundamental design strategies.

Distinct front doors for each laboratory unit (or block) facilitate address from a central interactive communication space on each of the nine floor levels.

UNIVERSITY OF QUEENSLAND BIOSCIENCES

The overall form is integrated with the main campus via a ramped colonnade that leads to the central security point. Sciences and stores entries are located in a lower-level loading dock. Public functions of café, library, conference centre, seminar and IT training areas are placed outside the laboratory environment.

Of great importance is the quality of the working environment: safety, amenity and function are critical, so too are the need for natural light, clustering of elements, and areas for interaction and debate.

In the sub-tropical light and heat of Brisbane, the penetration of excessive sun is unacceptable, hence the double skin of the exterior sunshades. These offer a distinguishing identity to the expression and combine with the rooftop form of the air exhausts and mechanical service to generate a feeling for the new sciences and the serious nature of the research taking place within.

Periodicals

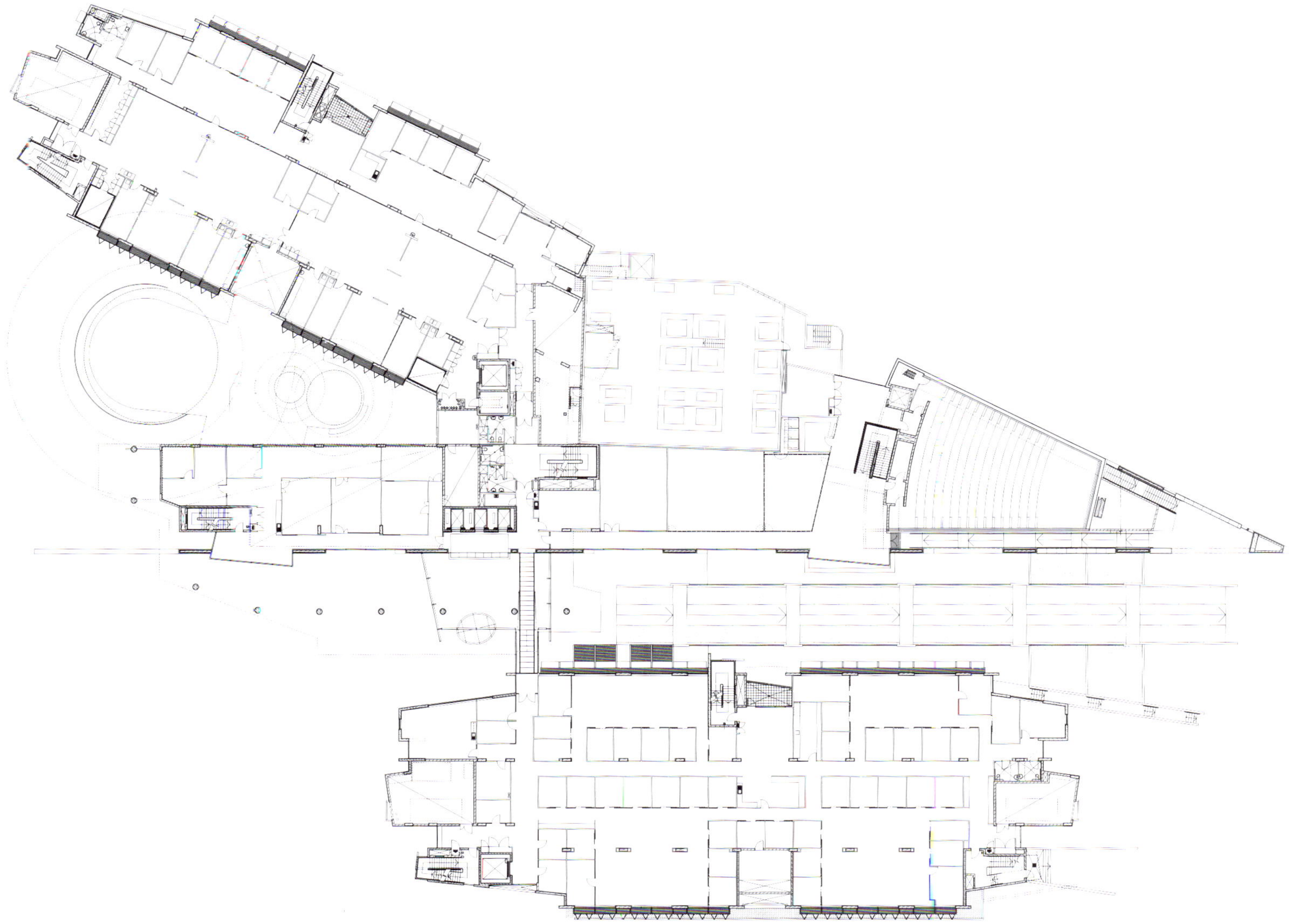

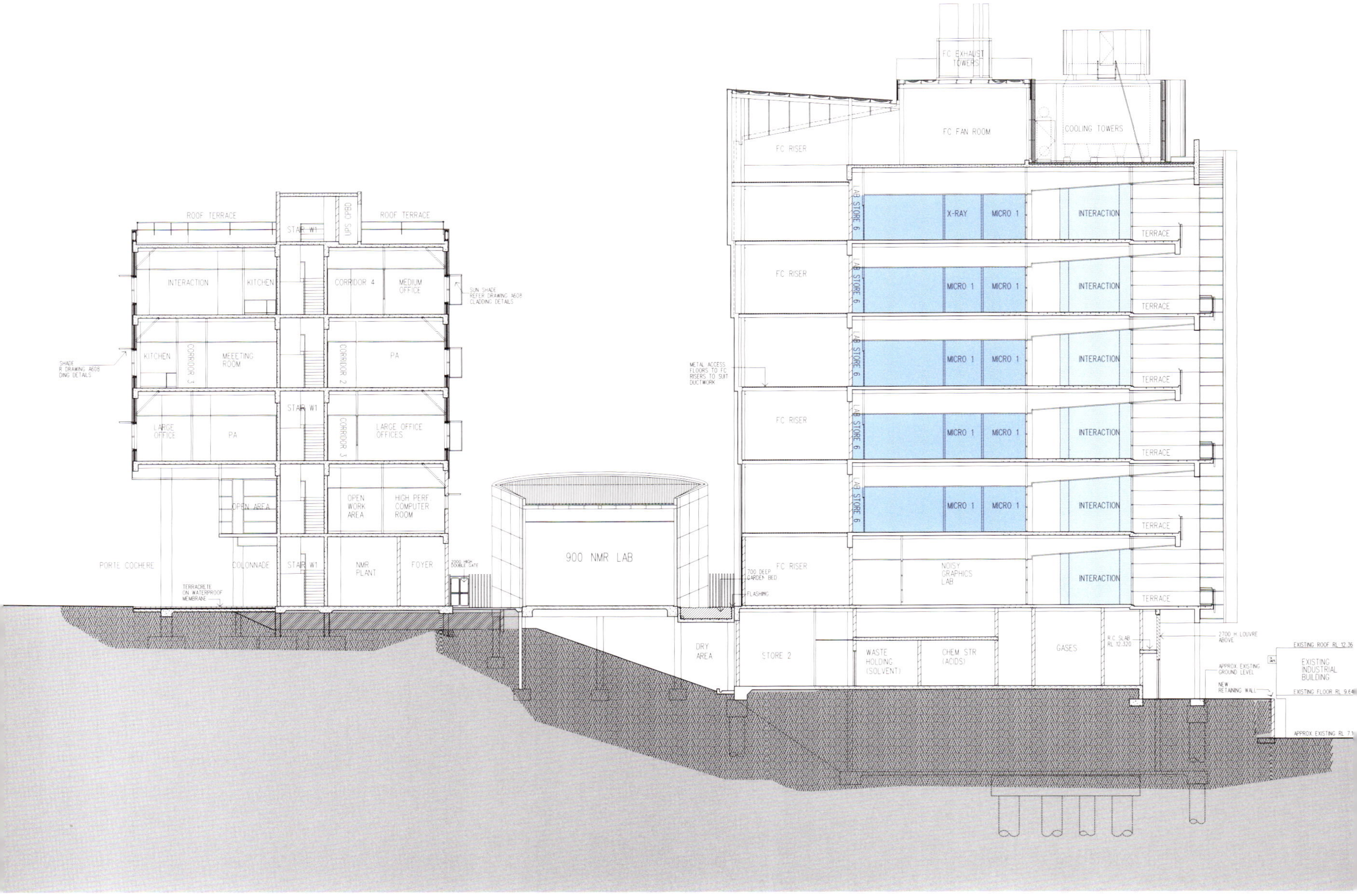

ROOF TERRACE
STAIR W1
ROOF TERRACE
INTERACTION
KITCHEN
CORRIDOR 4
MEDIUM OFFICE
KITCHEN
MEETING ROOM
PA
LARGE OFFICE
PA
STAIR W1
LARGE OFFICE OFFICES
OPEN AREA
OPEN WORK AREA
HIGH PERF COMPUTER ROOM
PORTE COCHERE
COLONNADE
STAIR W1
NMR PLANT
FOYER
900 NMR LAB
FC EXHAUST TOWERS
FC FAN ROOM
COOLING TOWERS
FC RISER
X-RAY
MICRO 1
INTERACTION
TERRACE
NOISY GRAPHICS LAB
DRY AREA
STORE 2
WASTE HOLDING (SOLVENT)
CHEM. STR (ACIDS)
GASES
EXISTING INDUSTRIAL BUILDING

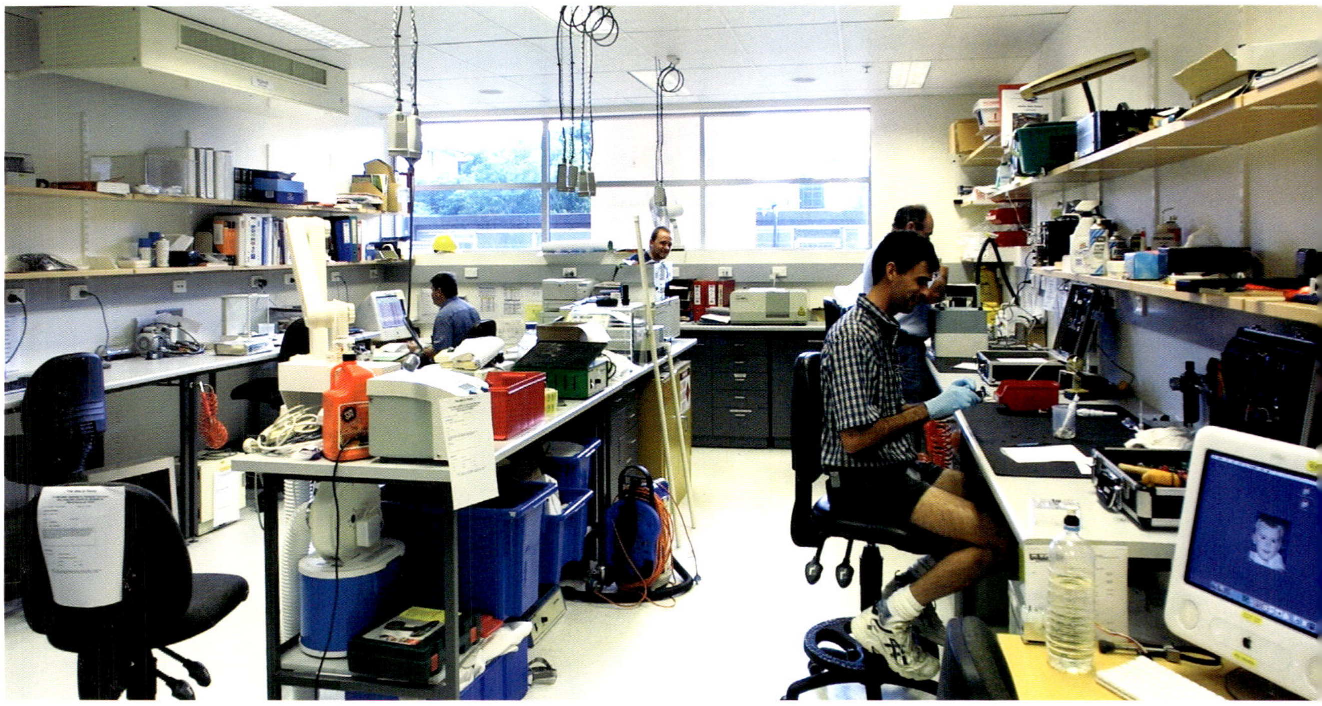

AVANCE

EXIT
DANGER

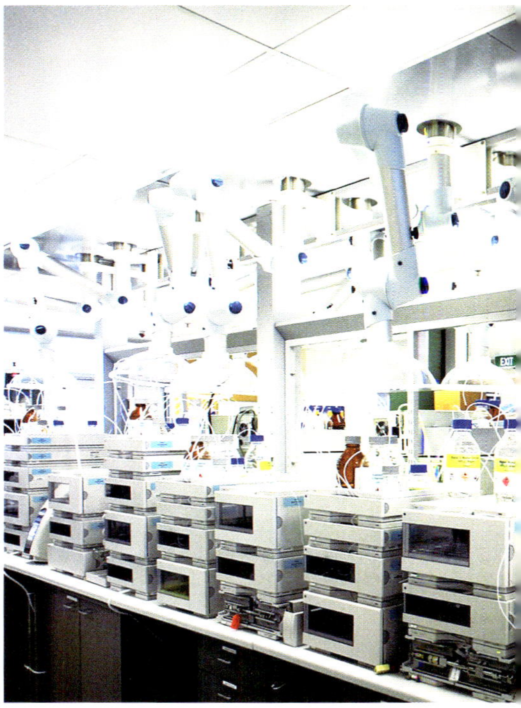

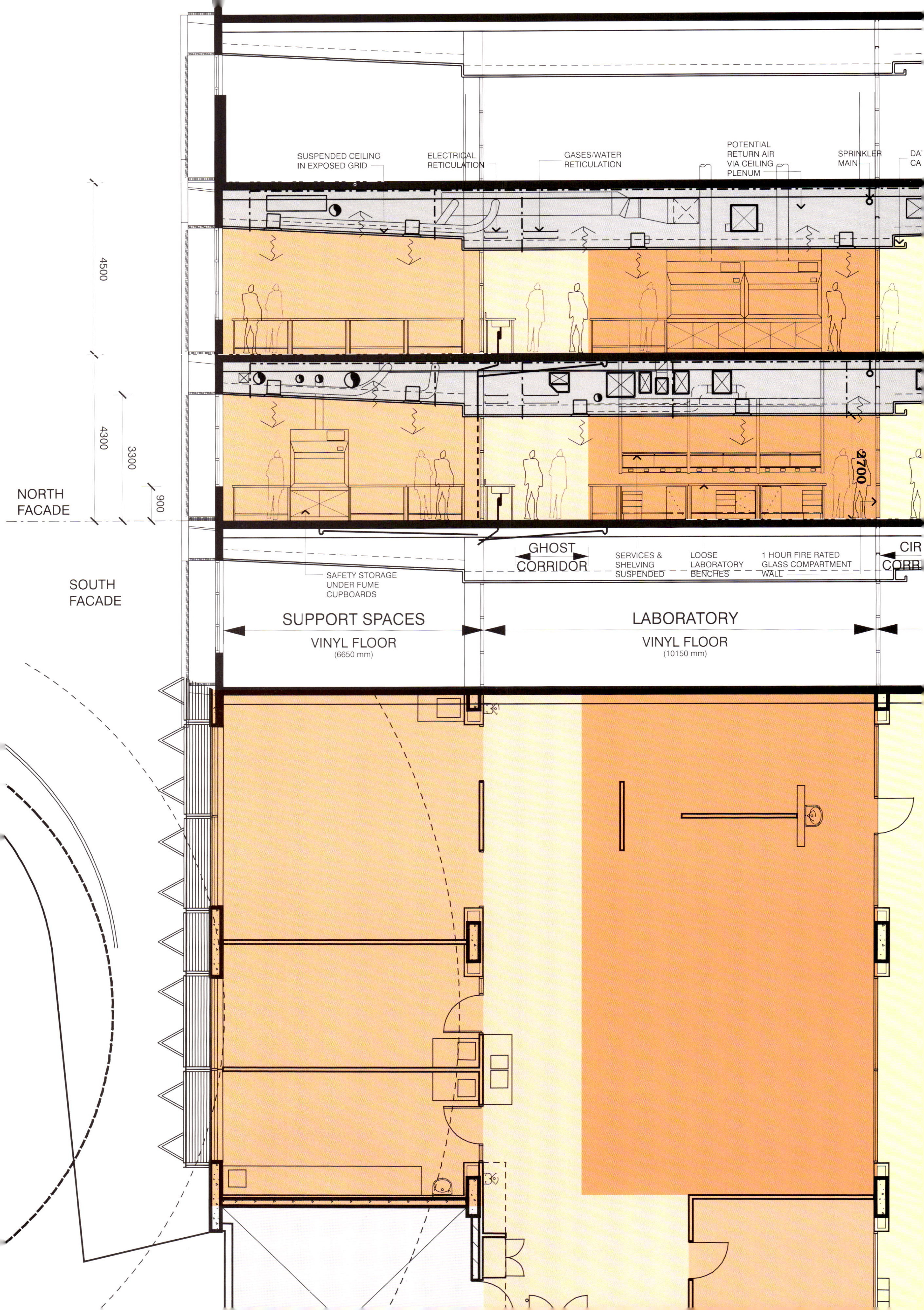
SUSPENDED CEILING IN EXPOSED GRID
ELECTRICAL RETICULATION
GASES/WATER RETICULATION
POTENTIAL RETURN AIR VIA CEILING PLENUM
SPRINKLER MAIN
4500
4300
3300
900
2700
NORTH FACADE
SOUTH FACADE
GHOST CORRIDOR
SERVICES & SHELVING SUSPENDED
LOOSE LABORATORY BENCHES
1 HOUR FIRE RATED GLASS COMPARTMENT WALL
SAFETY STORAGE UNDER FUME CUPBOARDS
SUPPORT SPACES
VINYL FLOOR
(6650 mm)
LABORATORY
VINYL FLOOR
(10150 mm)

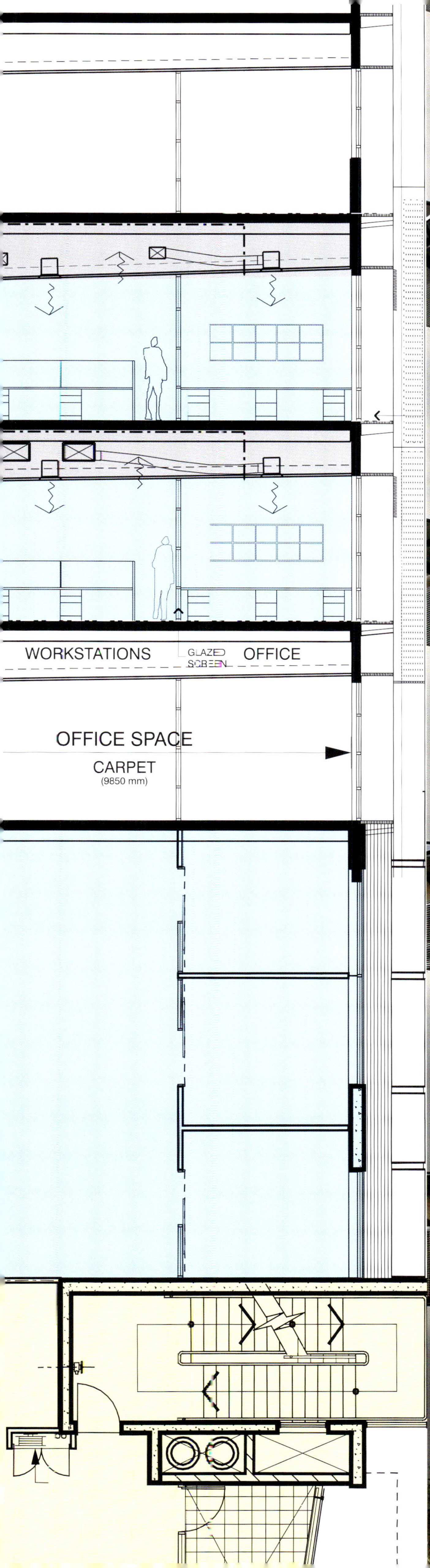
WORKSTATIONS
GLAZED SCREEN
OFFICE
OFFICE SPACE
CARPET
(9850 mm)

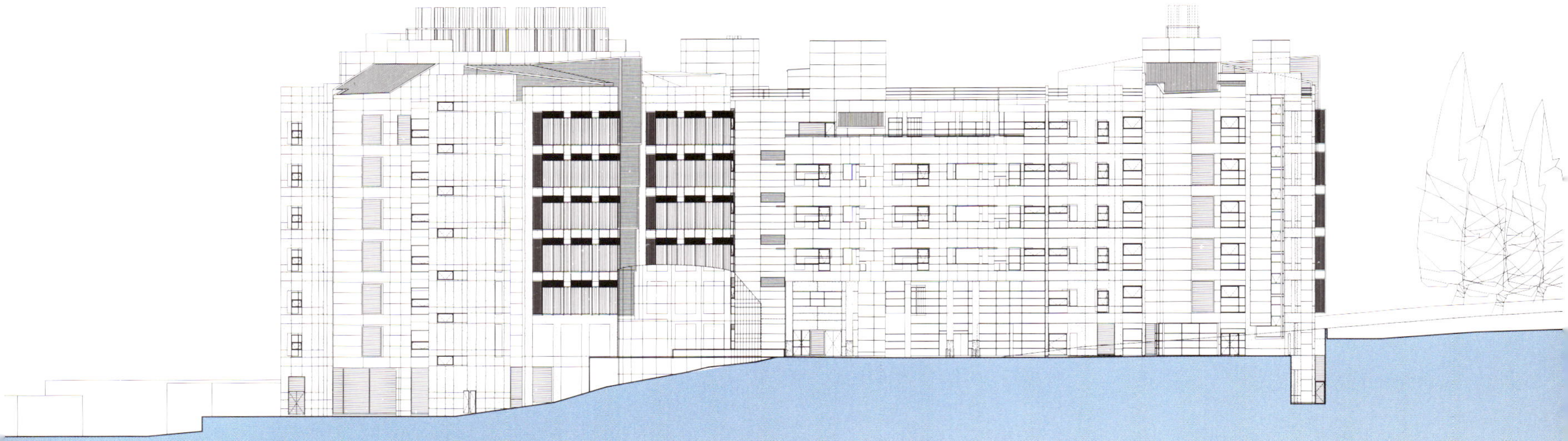

Singapore Library is a design created for a competition. Rescued here from a bottom drawer, it is a piece of work that established a position and was subsequently pursued for its ideas. It was applied elsewhere as a continuing exploration.

The idea of the city block, cut into and eroded to present a variety of inner volumes, with a double shade skin for the tropics on the exterior, remains valid. Air movement, outer balconies and recreation levels add to the comfort of the interior and complement the serious study of the occupants.

Stacks, readers, IT, conference areas, individual working realms, public theatres and communal spaces constitute the programme.

The response was to lift the mass above the street, undercut it and excavate into a basement, with floors going down as well as up to the mass above. The folded form of a street level plaza drops gently into the lower-level theatres and conference areas. Lift stacks take the readers to a number of identifiable levels for

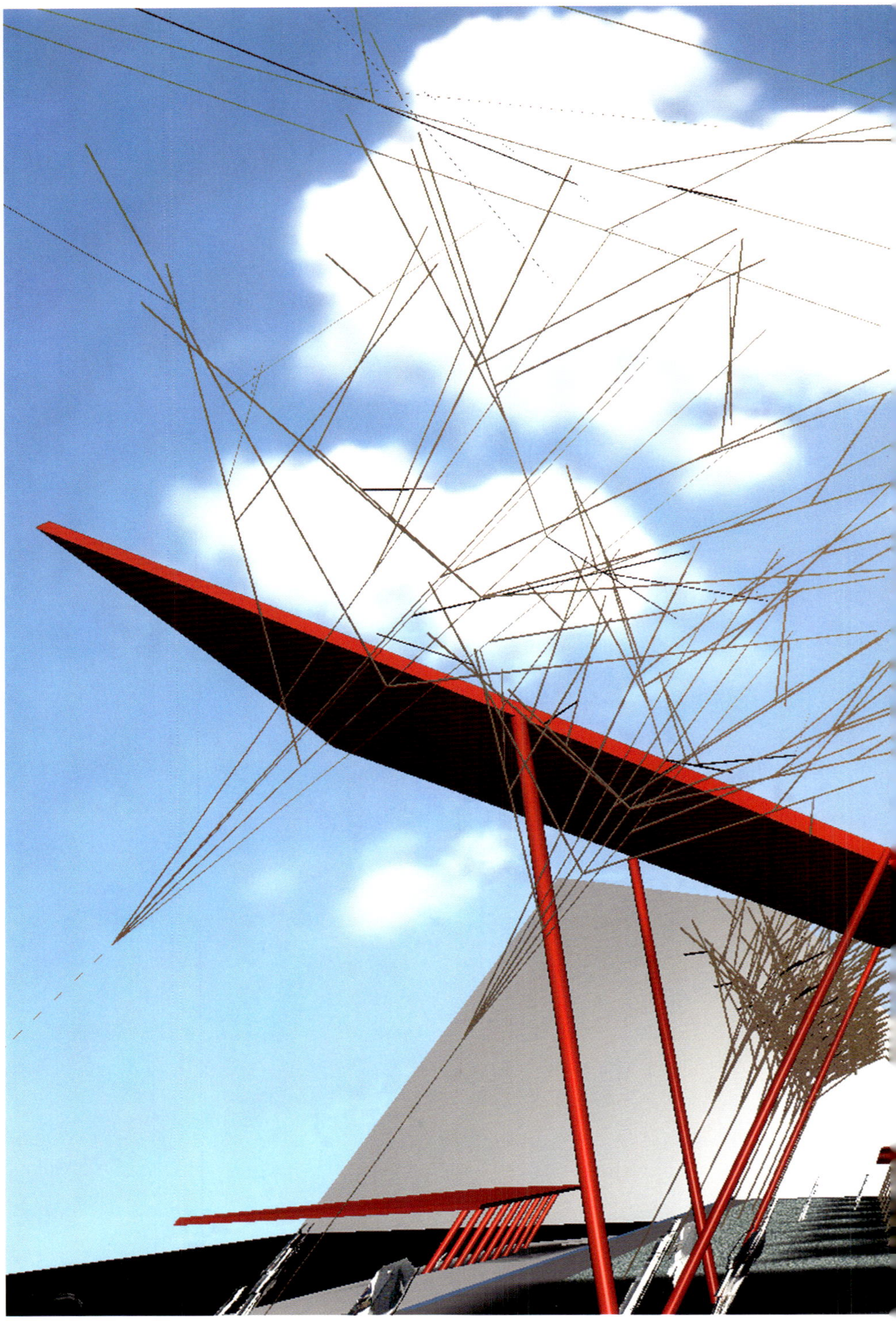

SINGAPORE LIBRARY

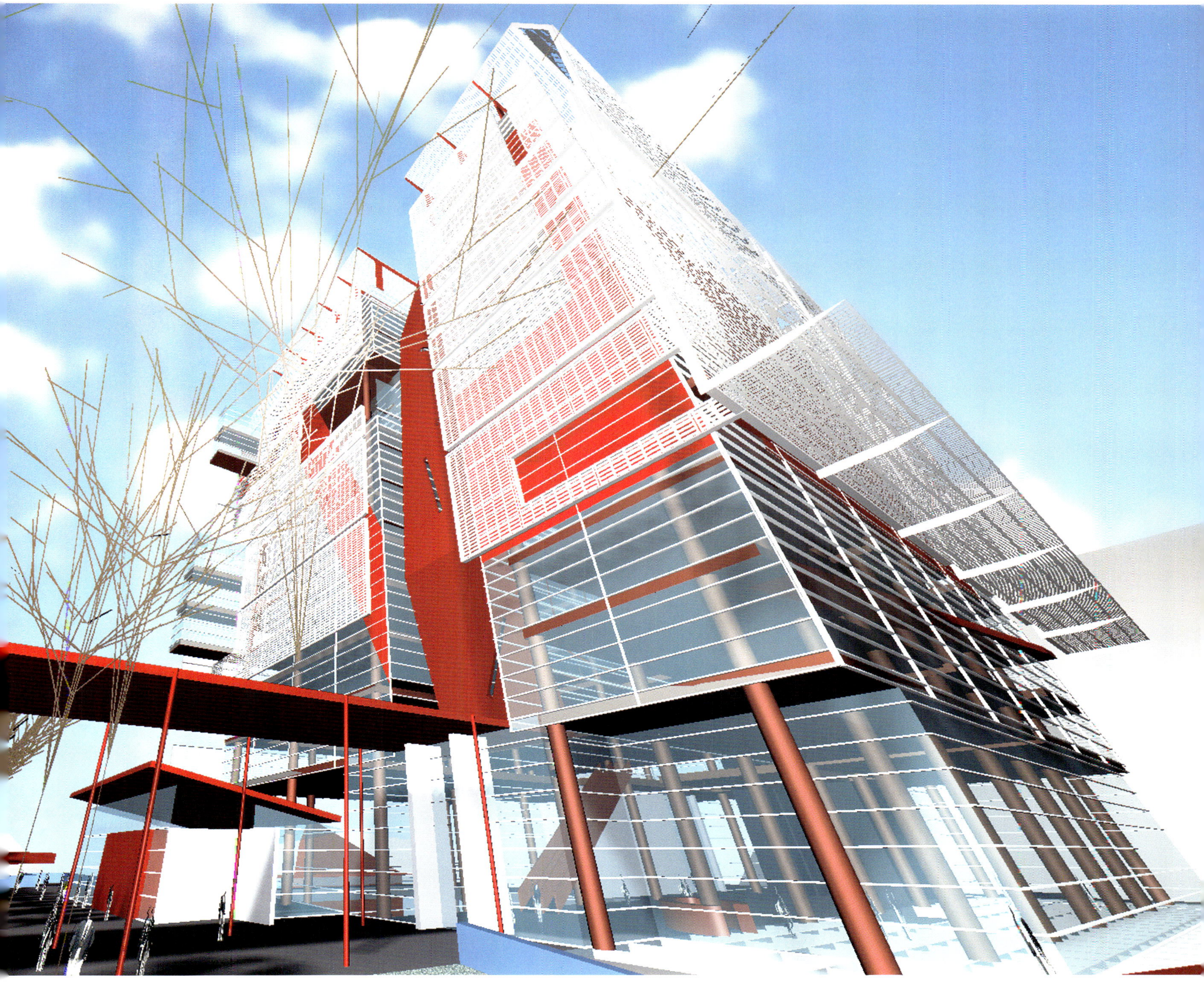

specific topics, with 'free', stratified and undesignated interstitial floor levels. Vertical cpen slots allow light to penetrate the mass with open stair connections making the three-level assembly of space apparent to users and visitors.

The shading device consists of a fabric of metal louvres stretched across the glass enclosure as a second skin. The colour red is a symbol of the culture; the tautness and folded forms are devices subsequently deployed elsewhere.

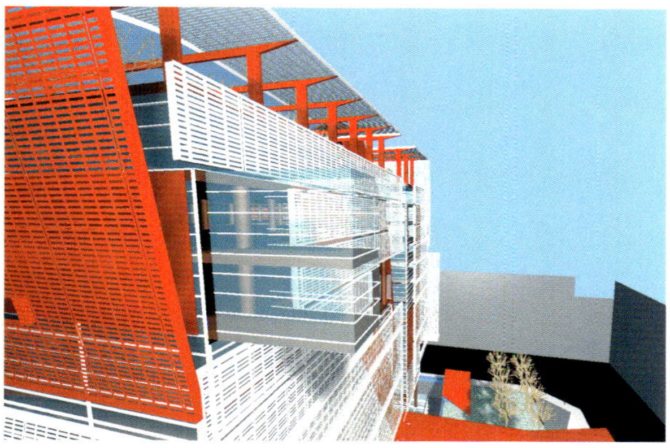

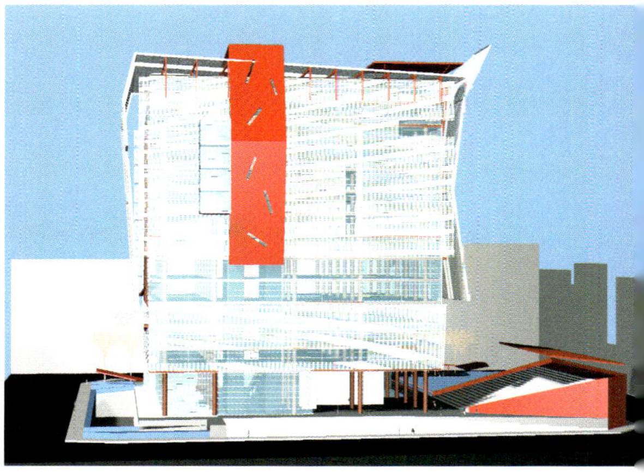

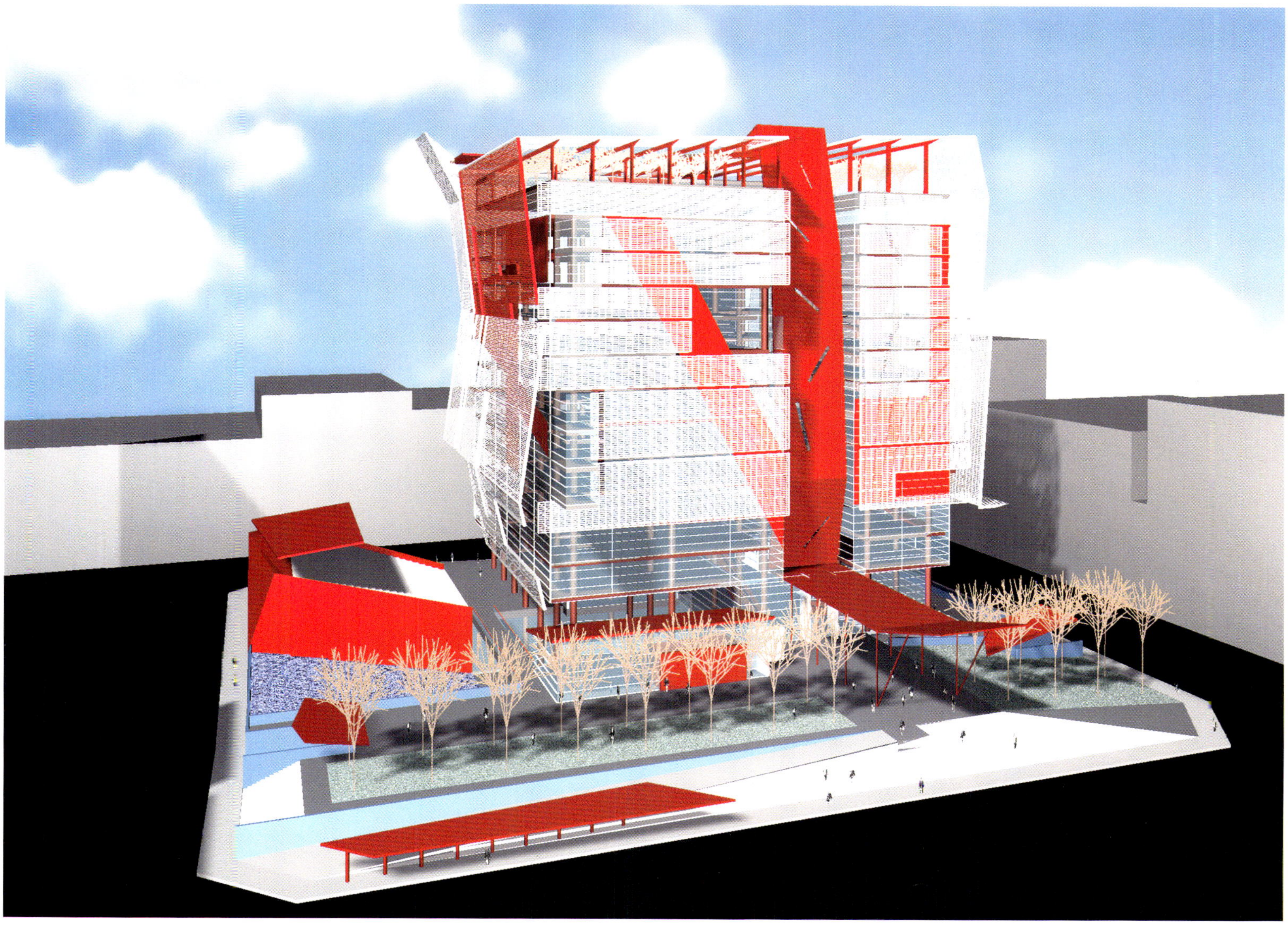

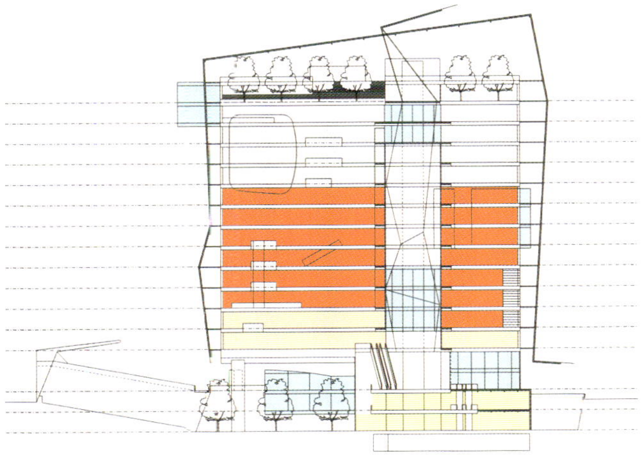

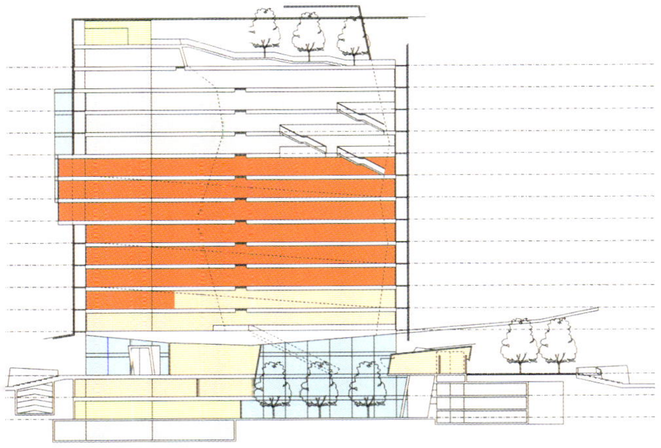

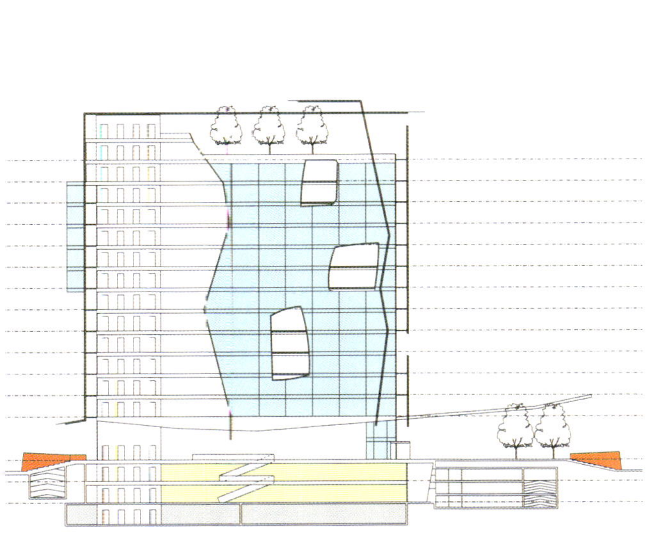

A
PUBLIC CARPARK EXIT
COVERED DROP OFF AREA
RAMP
WATERFALL
OUTDOOR PERFORMANCE AREA
GRASSED FORECOURT
CAFE
COURTYARD BELOW
LIBRARY BOOKSHOP
RAMP
B
VOID
VOID
ENTRANCE
LIBRARY FOYER
LOBBY
C
REFERENCE POINT
COURTYARD BELOW
COURTYARD BELOW
PUBLIC CARPARK ENTRANCE
SERVICE ENTRY RAMP DOWN
A

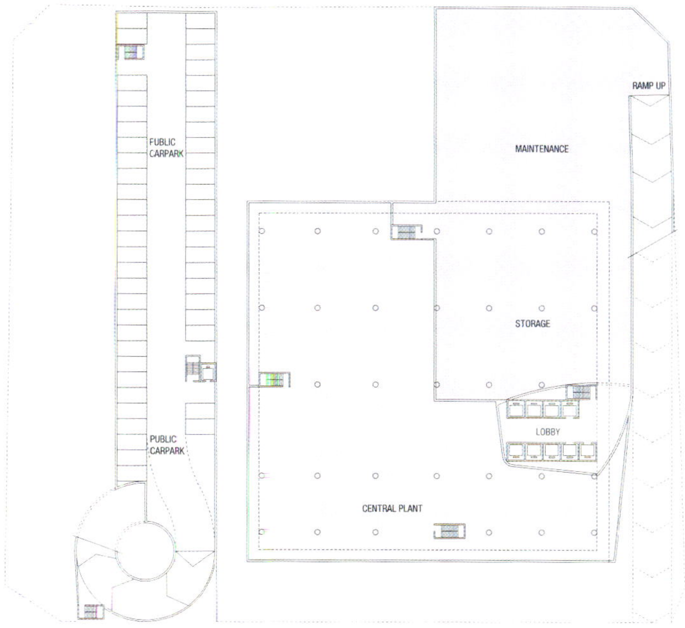
RAMP UP
PUBLIC CARPARK
MAINTENANCE
STORAGE
LOBBY
PUBLIC CARPARK
CENTRAL PLANT

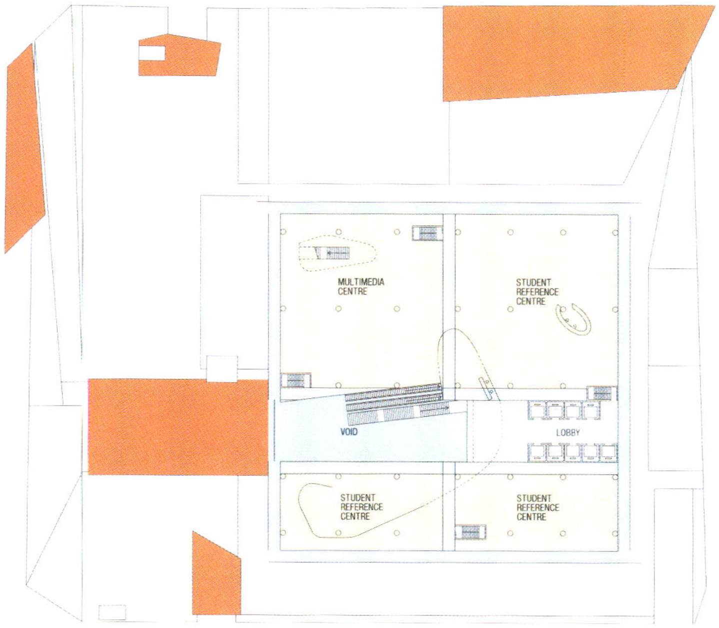
MULTIMEDIA CENTRE
STUDENT REFERENCE CENTRE
VOID
LOBBY
STUDENT REFERENCE CENTRE
STUDENT REFERENCE CENTRE

STAGE
CHANGE ROOMS
STORE
RESERVE LINE BELOW
PUBLIC CARPARK
COURTYARD
CENTRAL LIBRARY
PUBLIC CARPARK
CENTRAL LIBRARY
CENTRAL LIBRARY
LOBBY
CENTRAL LIBRARY
CENTRAL LIBRARY
COURTYARD
COURTYARD

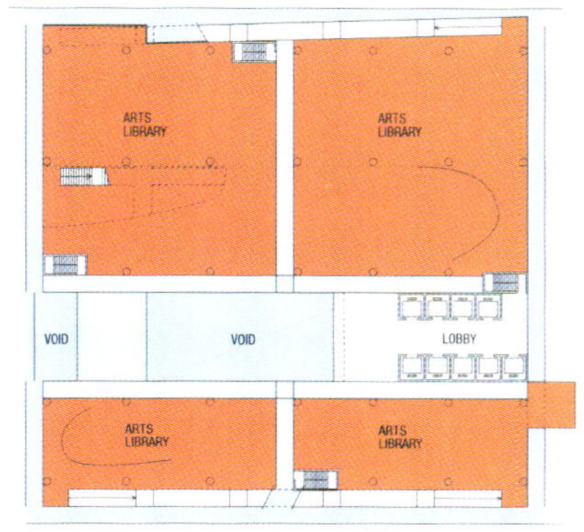
ARTS LIBRARY
ARTS LIBRARY
VOID
VOID
LOBBY
ARTS LIBRARY
ARTS LIBRARY

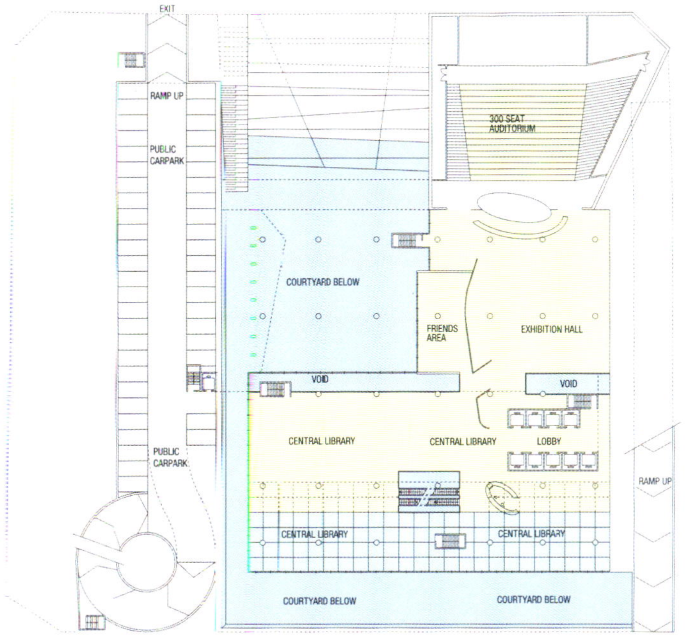
EXIT
RAMP UP
PUBLIC CARPARK
300 SEAT AUDITORIUM
COURTYARD BELOW
FRIENDS AREA
EXHIBITION HALL
VOID
VOID
PUBLIC CARPARK
CENTRAL LIBRARY
CENTRAL LIBRARY
LOBBY
RAMP UP
CENTRAL LIBRARY
CENTRAL LIBRARY
COURTYARD BELOW
COURTYARD BELOW

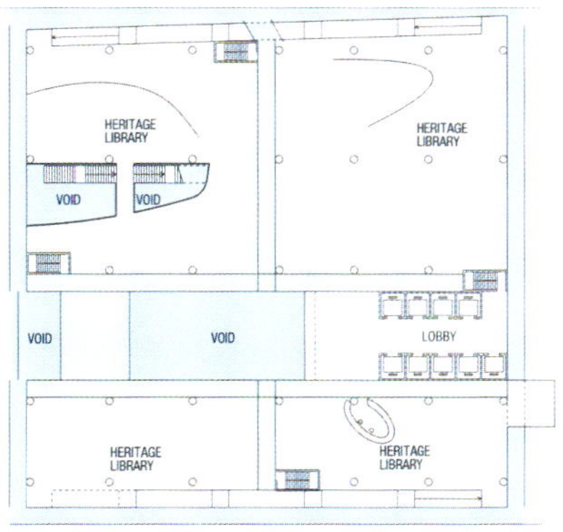
HERITAGE LIBRARY
HERITAGE LIBRARY
VOID
VOID
VOID
VOID
LOBBY
HERITAGE LIBRARY
HERITAGE LIBRARY

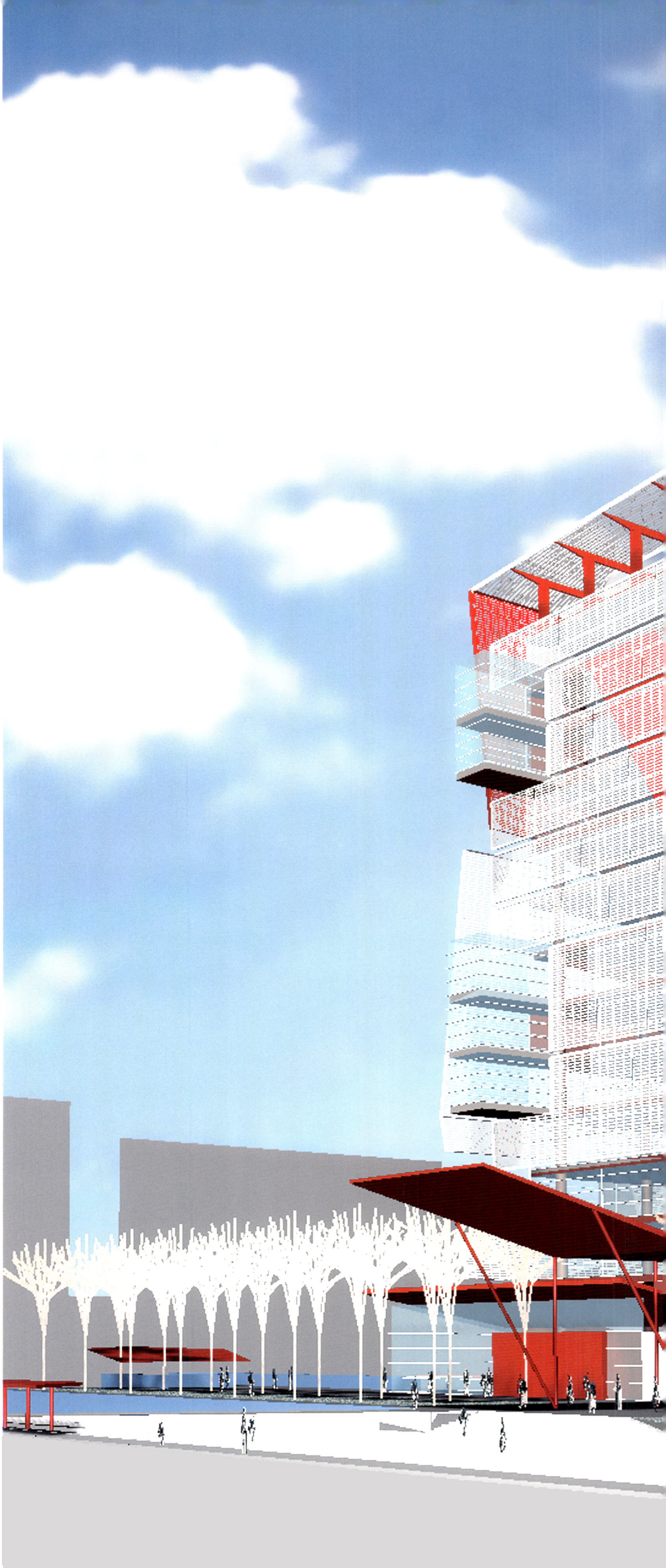

City courts are a rare modern building type. The new Victorian County Court in Melbourne occupies a significant corner of the city grid plan, with viewlines protecting the dome of the 19th-century Supreme Court, located on the opposite corner. The new building mass reflects the four-storey plinth height of the existing Supreme Court, addressing planning and urban design considerations and ensuring its dome remains visible in the long views of William Street offered as one enters this sector of the city.

The lower-level four/five-storey plinth building reinforces the street edges at pedestrian level while the central tower, containing jury rooms, court spaces and public galleries, is stepped back (and above) into the site. In so doing, a distinguishing folded form in zinc cladding is achieved. The courts are situated in this modern metal ten-storey shaft, allowing a precinct identity, while the Justices' chambers occupy the masonry base below.

The tower is a metal and glass sculpted container, juxtaposed with the higher buildings of the CBD and contrasting with the lower plinth; a punched-opening box of white concrete with window reveals of folded aluminium adds depth and density to the urban base.

VICTORIAN COUNTY COURT

Within the building a number of vertical slots, in the form of deeply cut access corridors or laneways, allow top light to enter the lower mass. The slices are placed to reinforce the segregation of judges from jurors, and both jurors and judges from the public. These main corridors, penetrating the four-level plinth, are lined with a brilliant blue colour or zinc and mirror skins that are folded to catch the daylight and make contact with their exterior counterpart that is visible above.

At first-floor level, a triple-height public gallery overlooking the city receives visitors and appellants and directs them to escalators or lifts for vertical access to courts. It serves as a critical 'lobby area' as well as a ceremonial foyer or grand hall that precedes the largest court used for special jurisdiction.

The formal ceremonial hall is distinguished by a timber-lined sawtooth flying stair. Folded timber wall panels and the metallic planes of the escalator void characterise the interior surfaces and bring light down to this space from above.

All courts receive natural light either through a central lightwell that penetrates the tower form or through perimeter windows.

Handsomely crafted with sloping blackwood veneer wall panels and matching furniture elements, the interiors offer a formal and modern elegance, demonstrating a sense of respect and esteem for the judicial system. Here lighting is concealed to enhance the coved ceiling.

Externally, the architectural skin is represented as a series of folded etched zinc, anodised aluminium or white polished precast concrete forms, creased to allow light to enter or, on the William Street face of the Judges' Chambers, to take the eye from street level up towards the dome of the Supreme Court. This gesture ends with the cantilevered entrance canopy and vertical signature valence, suspended some four levels above the corner pavement. This front canopy is known by the wits at the bar as 'la guillotine'.

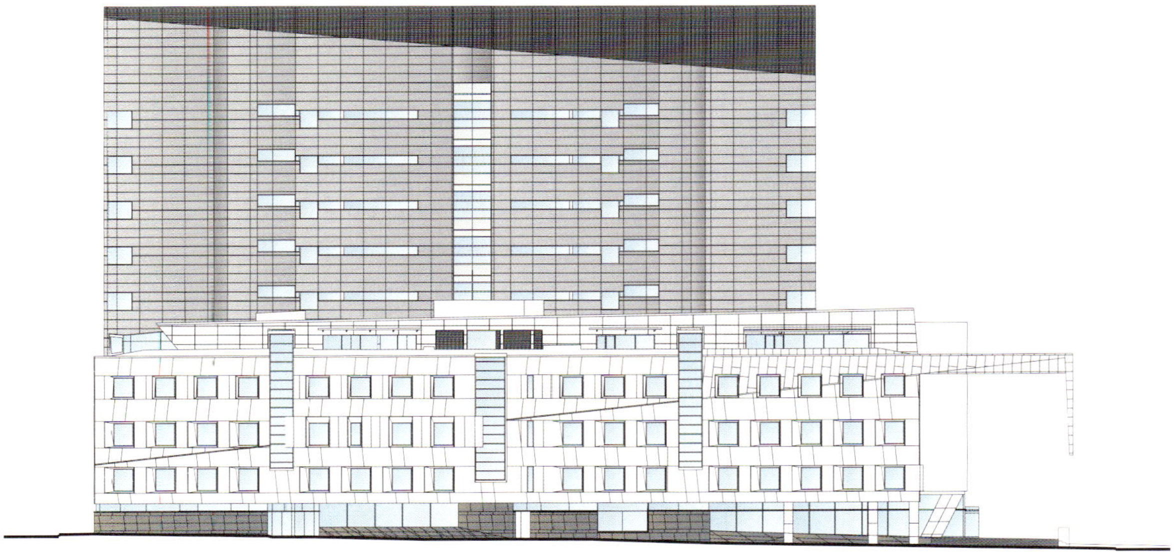

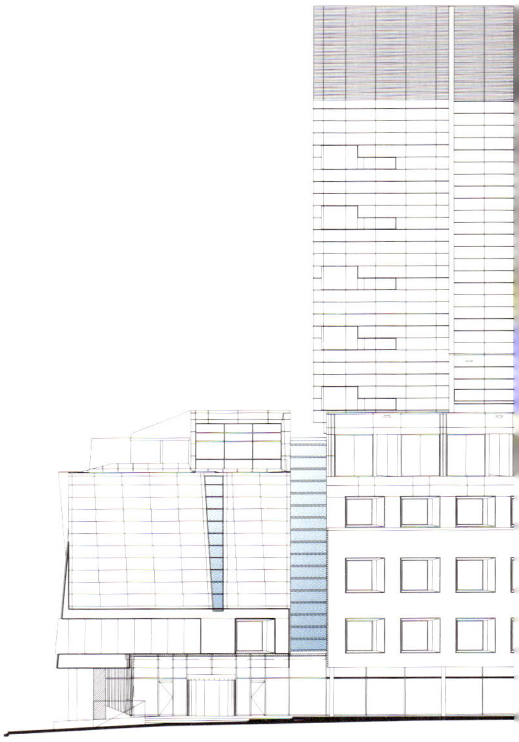

CountyCourt
Victoria
250
William Street

EXIT

COURT ZONE
JUDICIAL ZONE
PUBLIC ZONE
JURY ZONE
ADMINISTRATION ZONE

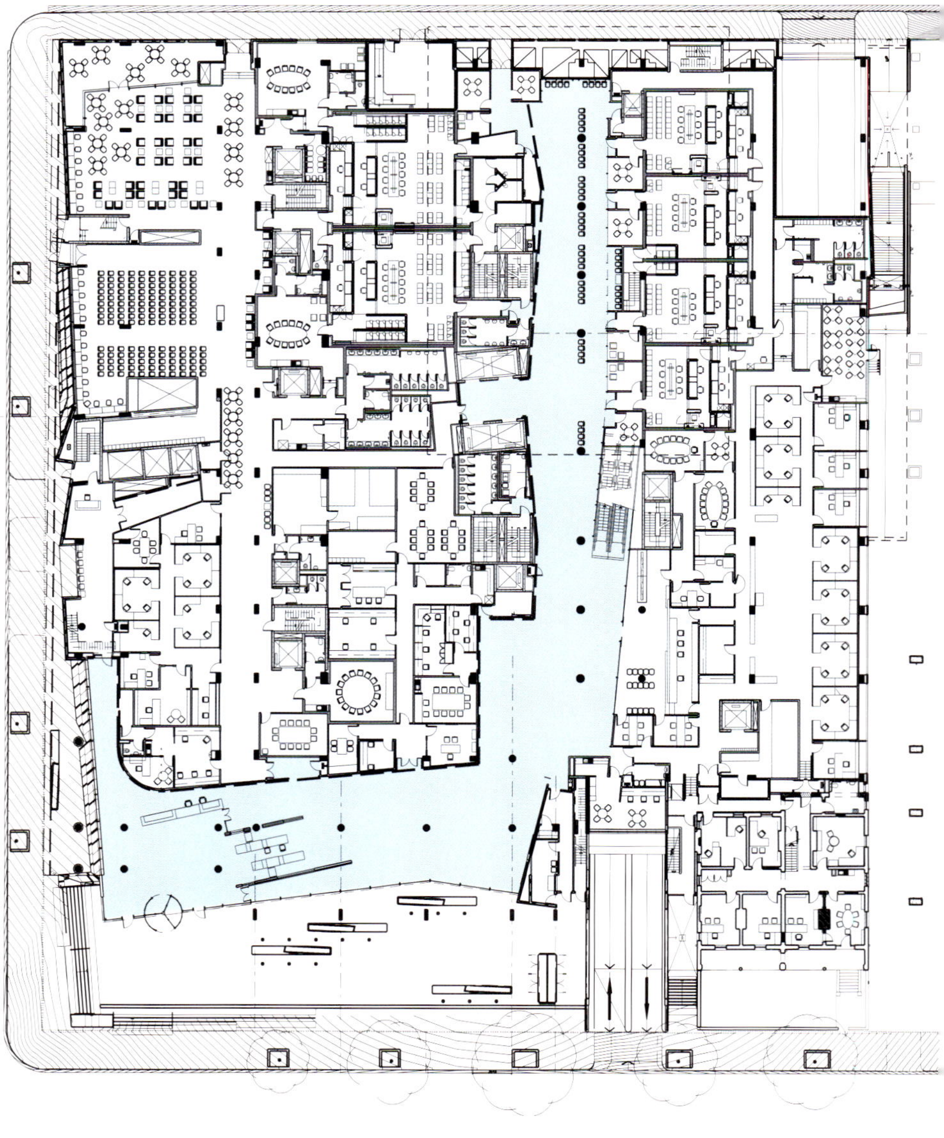

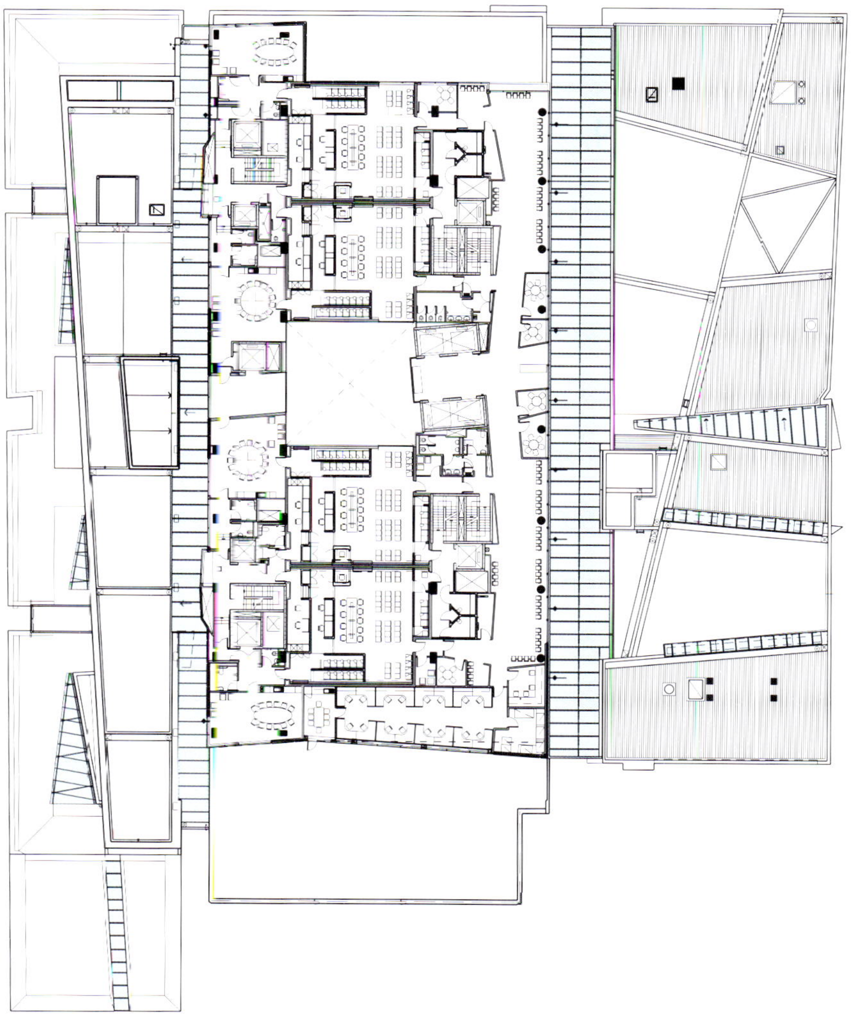

1.4
1.5

3.3
1.6
1.7

This school educates children of all ages, from early childhood to year twelve and students are customarily from expatriate resident, diplomatic and business families posted in Hanoi.

The curriculum is broad, focused upon the International Baccalaureate. Special emphasis is on high competency in the English language.

The student body comprises boys and girls from various nationalities with varying talents and academic experiences. Contact between young and old is encouraged as children of similar nationality offer mutual support and friendship.

This is not a large school; the present school is designed for 800, with growth projected to double over the next ten years. The school's courtyard plan forms are placed each side of a central stem of core facilities. Incremental growth is possible for each age group precinct as well as for the central areas.

The school is organised into discrete learning units, each with specific identity and form pertinent to the age of the students and their activities.

Students work in 'home' based class areas of 25 students from preparatory to year six, with a more mobile school population using key facilities for the arts and sciences in the middle and senior high years. Everyone gets to use the library and the canteen, the central courtyards and the sports areas, but each 'school' is clustered around a courtyard form to give precinctual definition, identity and a particular sense of habitation or home.

UNITED NATIONS INTERNATIONAL SCHOOL

Two major pedestrian avenues act as spines of the campus, with a cross axis narrower pedestrian walkway located at a mid point. This structure binds the campus together and provides access to all learning and support facilities. Each sub-school precinct has an in-school address point on the pedestrian spine. These face towards the centre of the campus where the canteen, library and auditorium are located. A covered way, created by the overhang of the upper levels of surrounding buildings and by linking canopies, protects from sun and rain and links these address points.

A central covered court is placed at the intersection of the pedestrian spines; this serves the canteen and library, and acts as a central, shared recreational space and gathering area for school functions. From here, covered walkway areas extend into the sub-school courtyards, allowing undercover circulation to all precincts.

The sub-school territorial definition is important in offering smaller, focused groups of students a sense of belonging, and assists everyone in getting to know each other.

This feeling is heightened through the design of paving, landscaping and play equipment suitable to the particular age group. Views into the courtyard from the precinct learning areas are maximised through glazing, with indoor/outdoor programmes achieved through verandahs and outdoor play areas.

Hanoi's hot and humid climate is a key factor for the design response and architectural expression. Large roof overhangs, and wall shading devices provide fundamental covered outdoor play areas allowing both air circulation in the hot, wet summers, and protection from the cold northwest wind in winter.

In this location, concrete frame structures may be economically built by the existing labour force, while fabricated steel is expensive. The architecture relies on solid, cement-rendered brick walls for thermal protection in both summer and winter, with an emphasis on natural air movement in the more temperate periods.

The use of double-skin pitched roofs for insulation and to shed water in the wet informs the massing, the clustering of elements and the character of the courtyard forms. Roof planes incline towards the centre, bringing the interior verandah edges down into the 'outdoor' room established for play areas.

Above the courtyard stairs, a large elliptical acrylic umbrella adds further protection and a distinctive form.

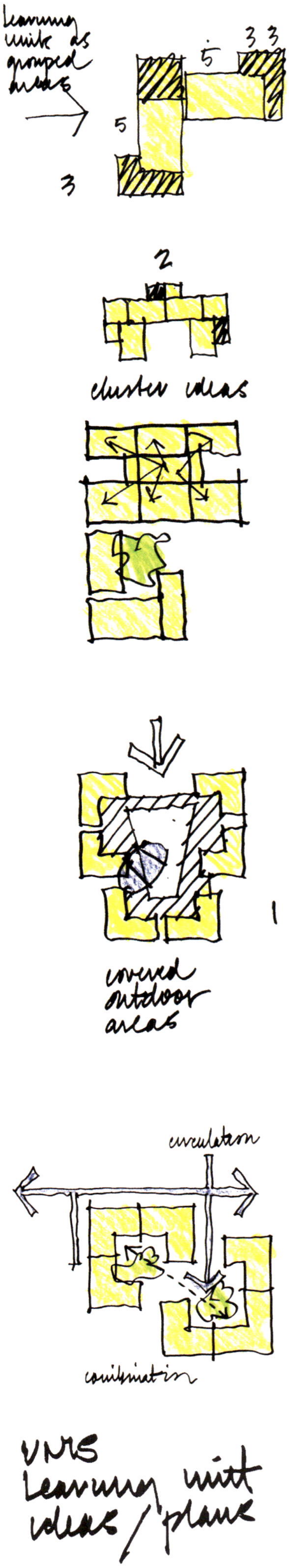

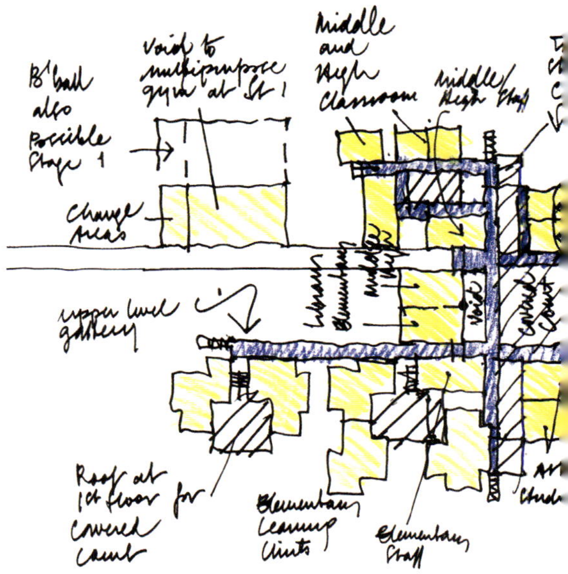

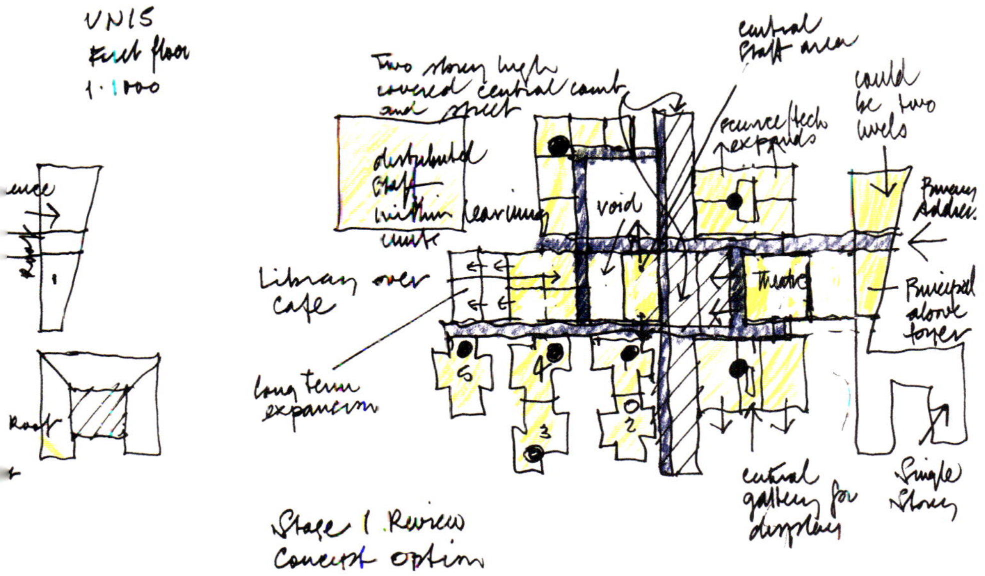
UNIS
First floor
1:1000
Two storey high covered central court and street
central staff area
could be two levels
distributed staff within learning units
void
science/tech expands
Primary Address
Library over cafe
Theatre
Principal above foyer
long term expansion
central gallery for display
Single storey
Stage 1 Review
Concept option

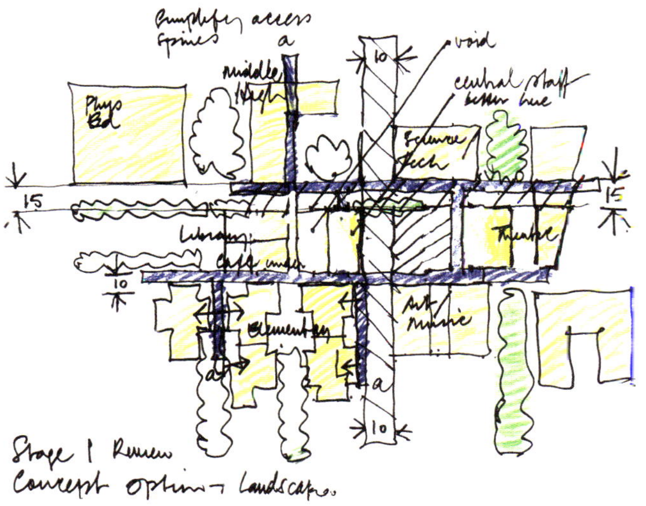
void
Phys Ed
Theatre
Art/music
UNIS
Stage 1 Review
Concept option – Landscape

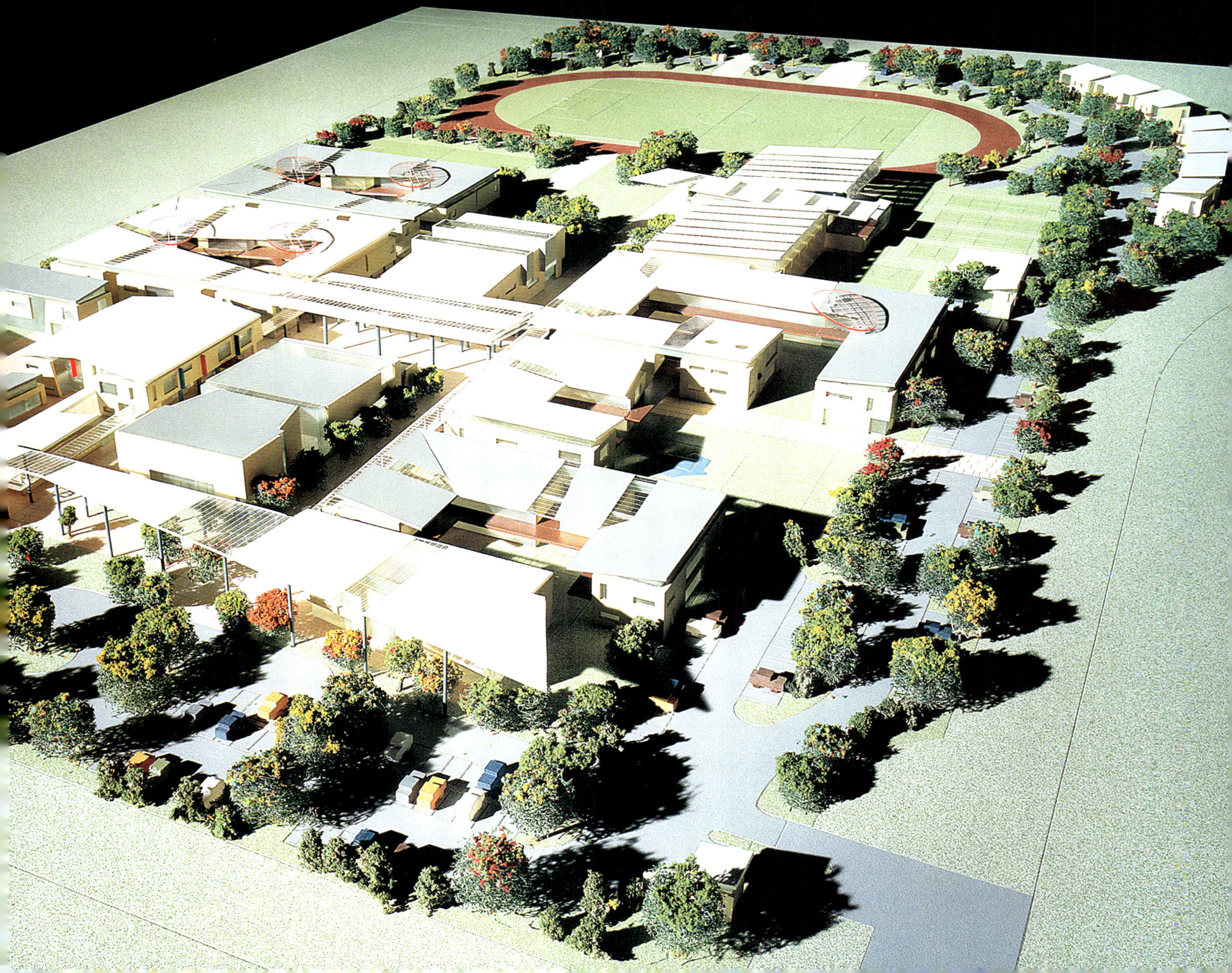

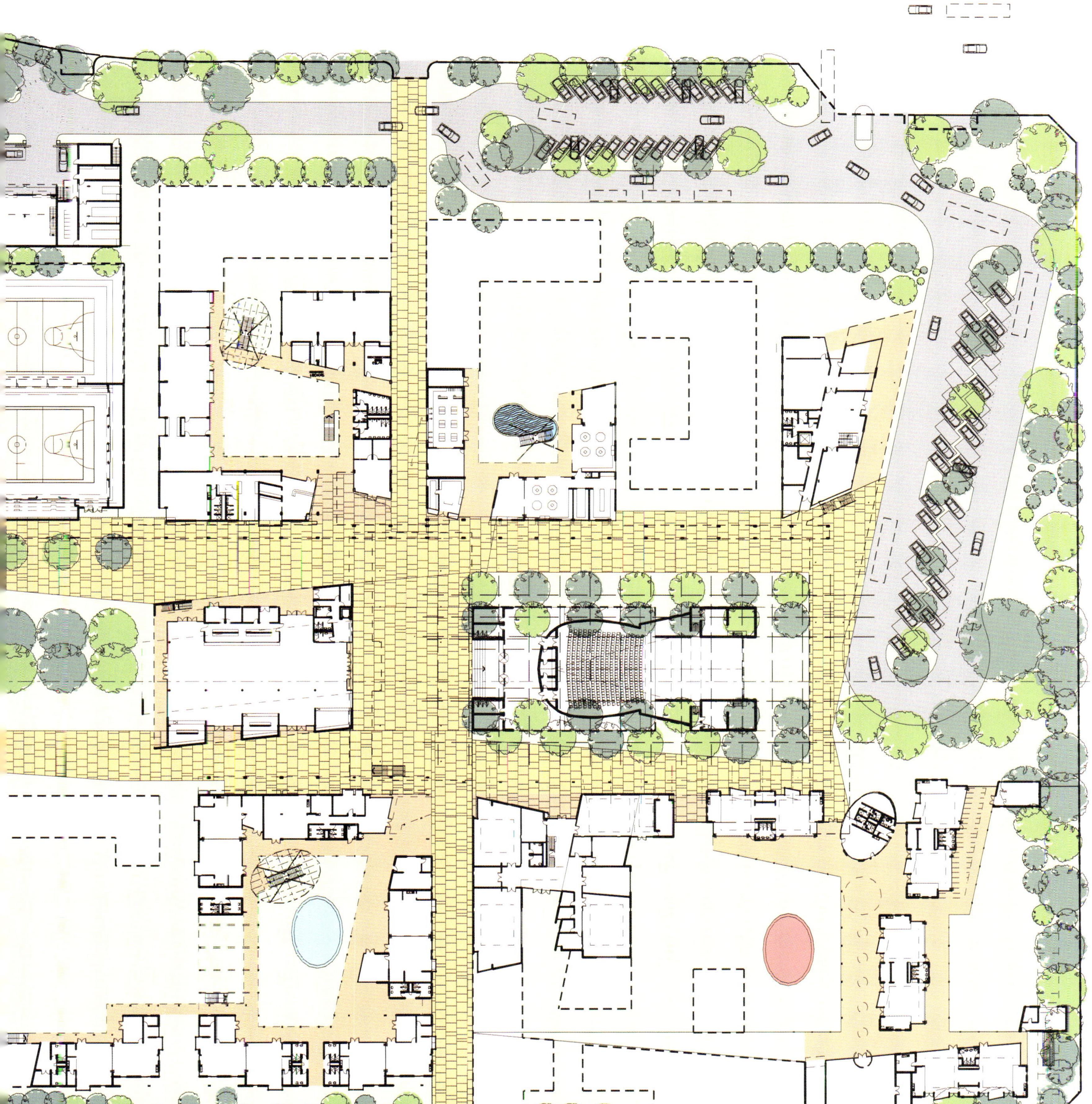

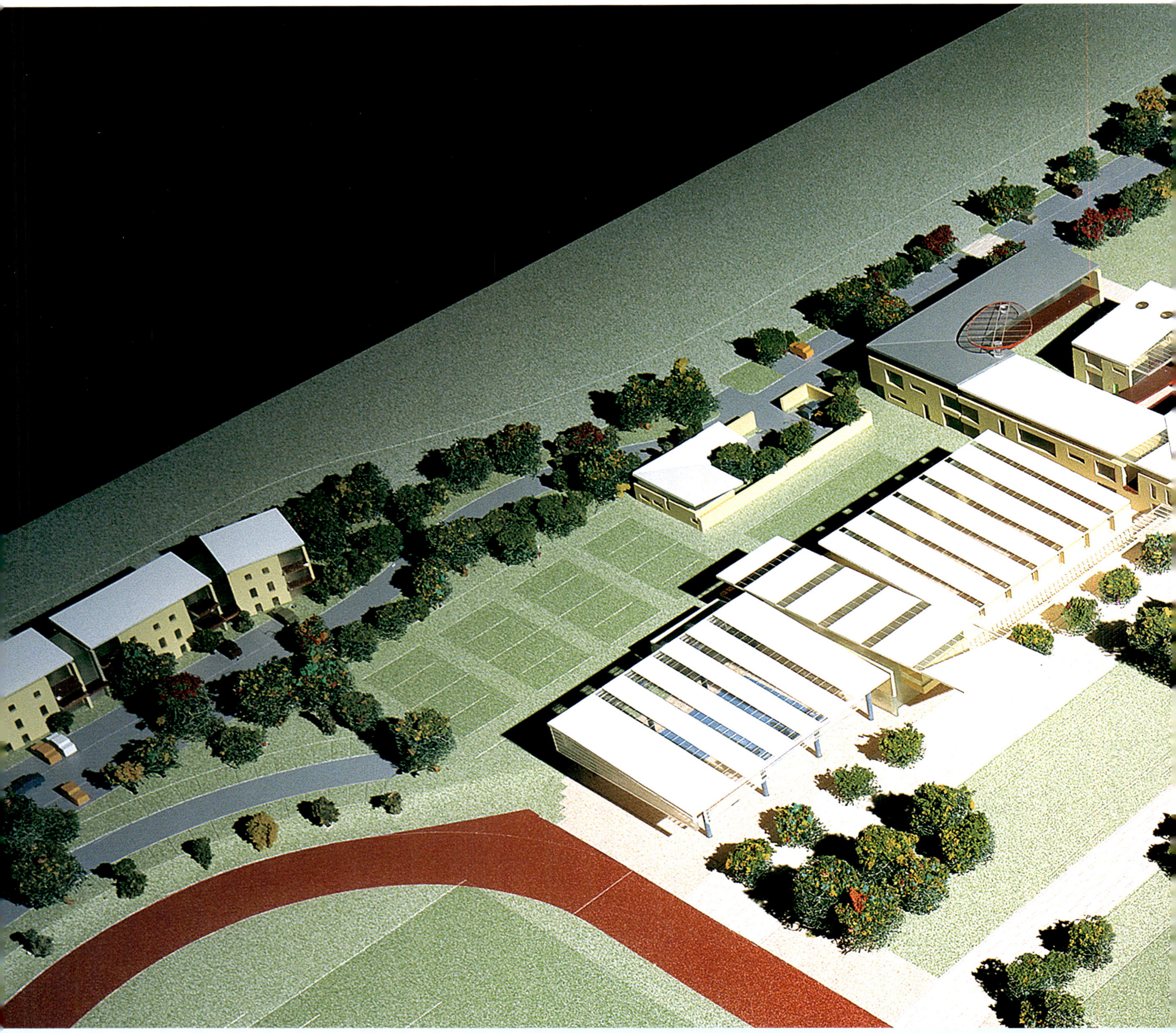

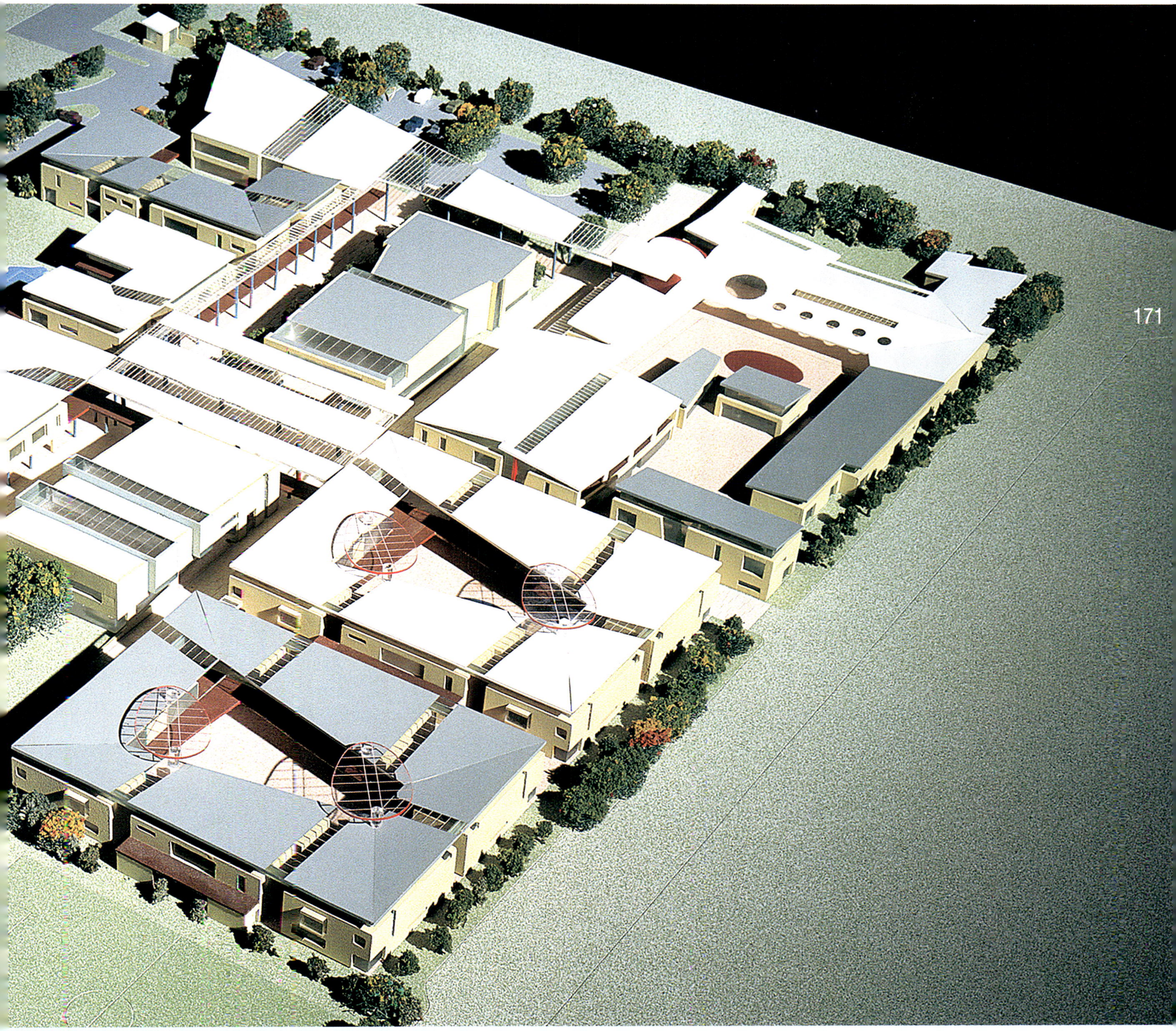

In a school, educational ideas and architectural expression are brought together. Both these aspects of human endeavour are important components of an environment where the programme intent is to inform, encourage and stimulate enquiry and learning as a lifelong skill.

Educational psychologists are more aware now than ever before of how the young learn, and of how the need to stimulate and encourage the emotional and intellectual capability of particular age groups changes as they develop.

Wanting to learn becomes a critical value for students, with a mixture of exchanges: students to teachers; spaces to programmes; indoor curriculum and outdoor experiences. Comprehension and appreciation, self esteem and confidence, coordination and challenge are further measures for determining the developmental phases attached to children's abilities, and to their natural desire to understand, express themselves, and form concepts.

It is in this area of the educational encounter that most educators seek an architecture of colour and form, human scale and object recognition, a built form of spaces and shape-making that may be seen to match the aspirations of the school and engage the senses of the students.

Young children enjoy sunlit playgrounds towards the east and north, and all workspaces for all age groups open towards the east, where wide verandahs offer protection as well as a mediating environment between inside and outside. Further opportunities to create light-filled, lively rooms exist via the use of skylights along the interior gallery.

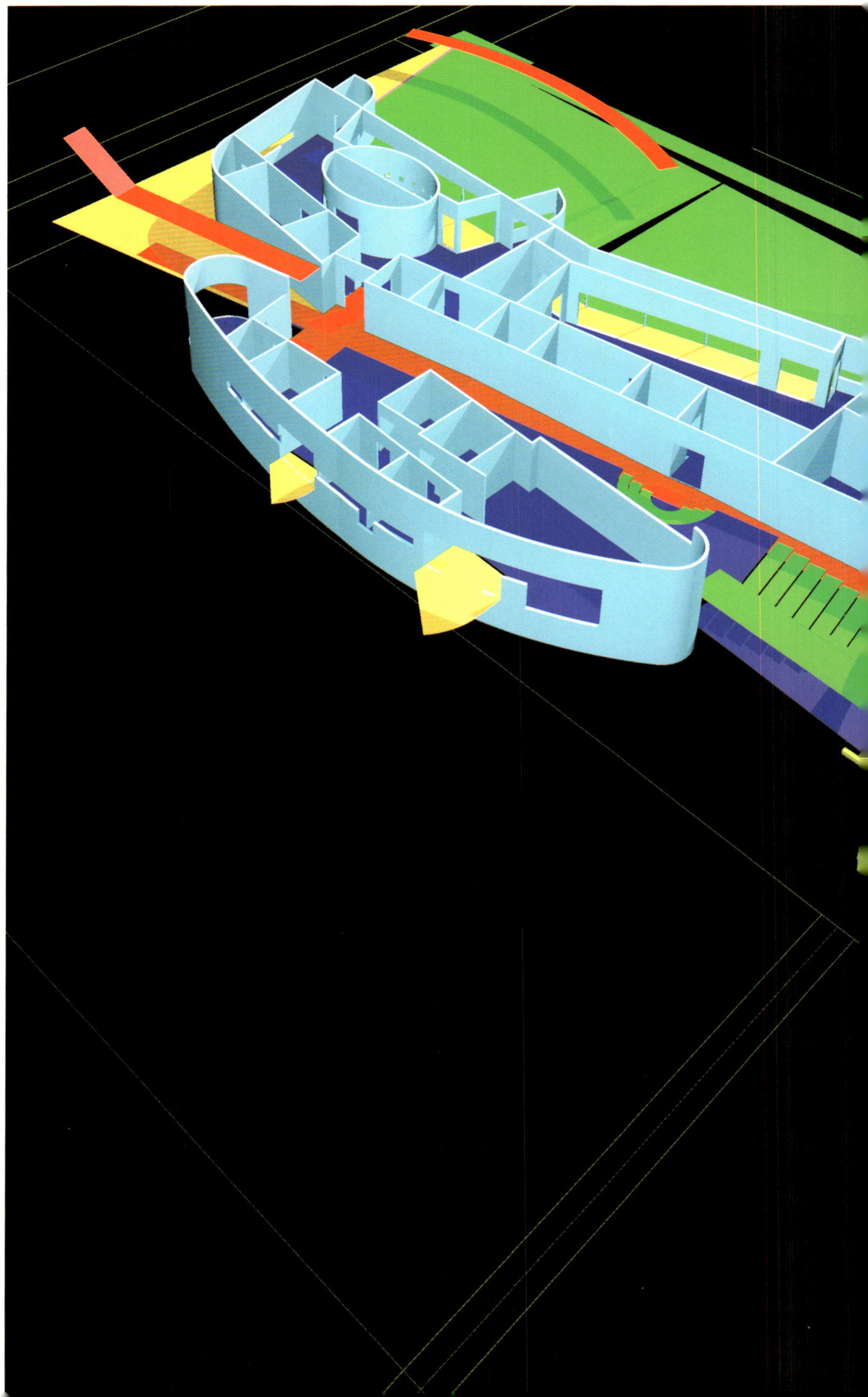

XAVIER PREPARATORY SCHOOL

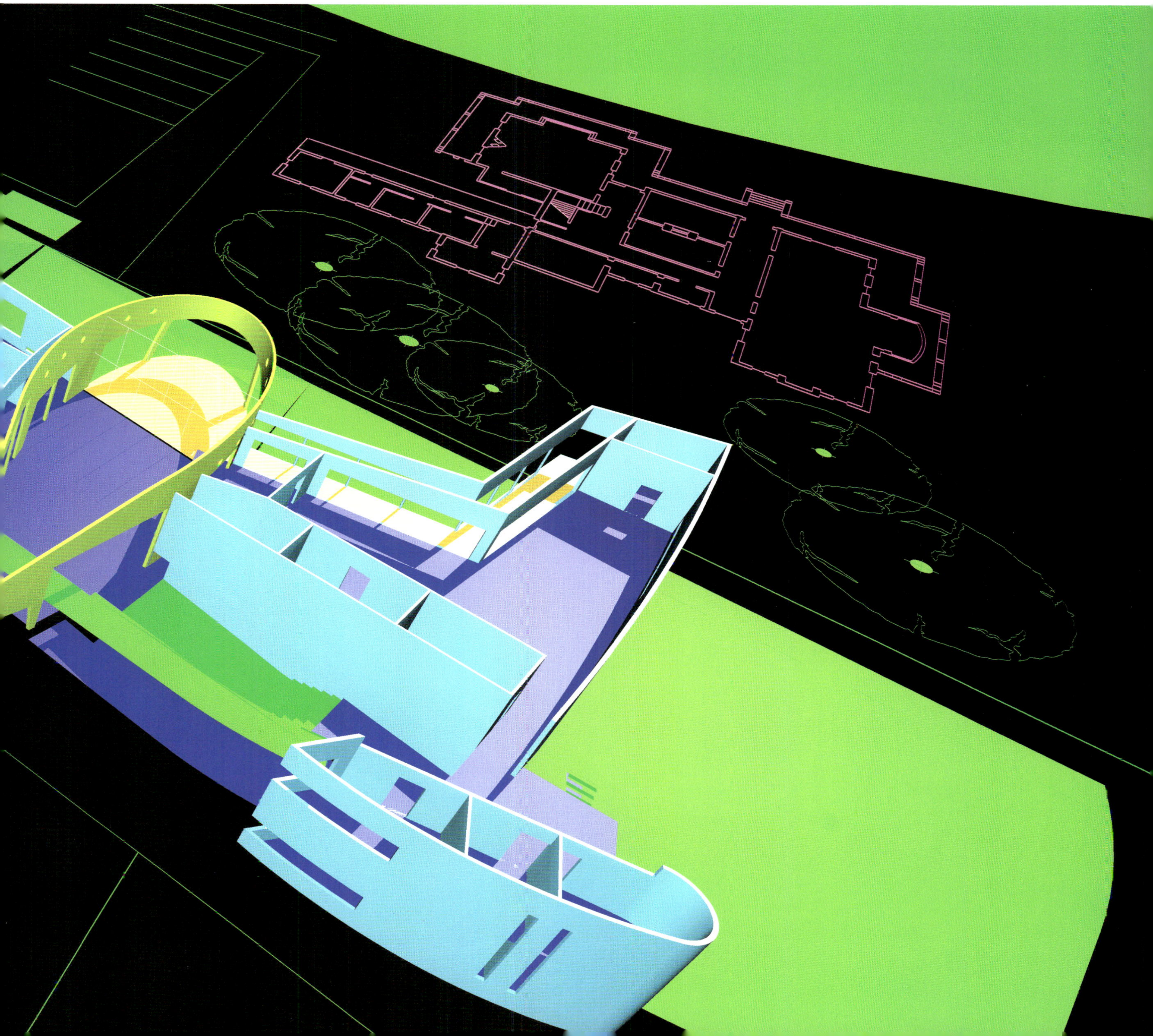

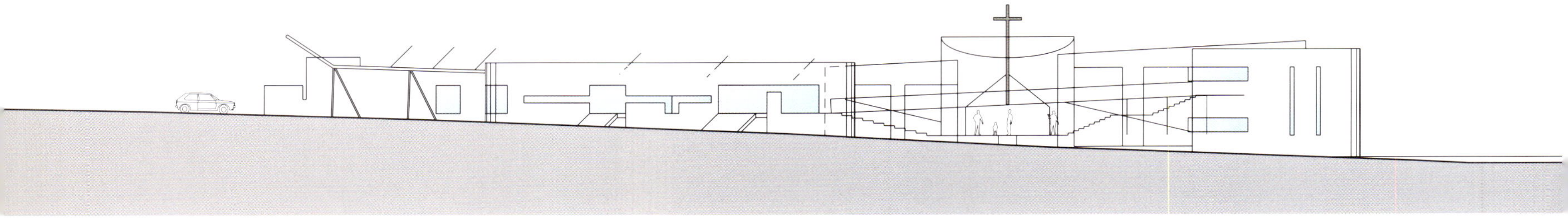

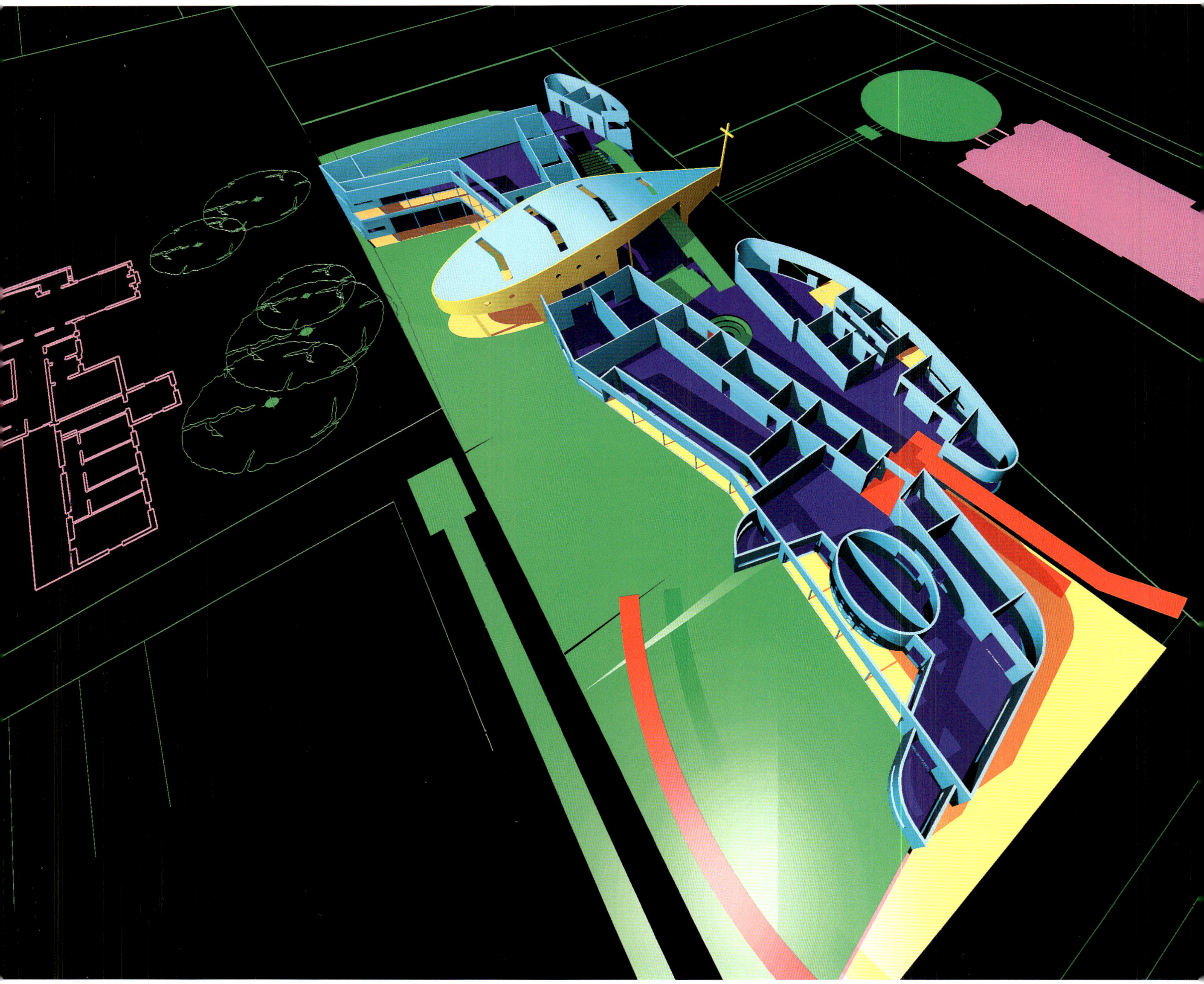

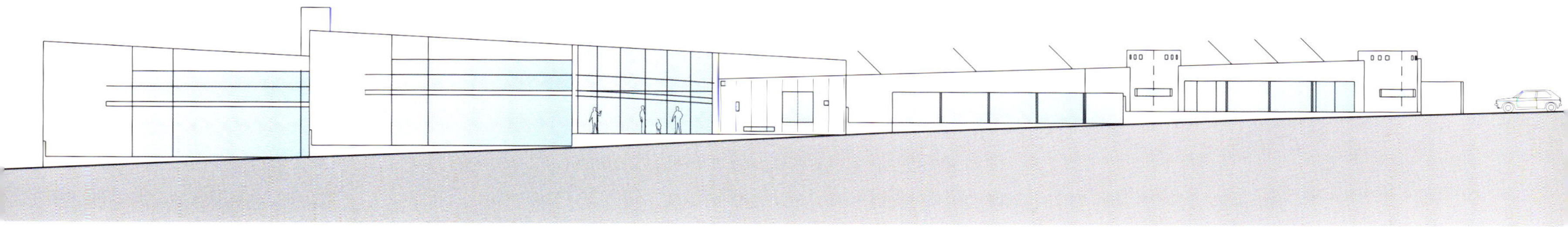

NOLAN AVENUE
STORE
ELC 1
QUIET ROOM
STAFF
KITCHEN
WC
LOCKER
ELC PLAY AREA
HEAD
FOYER
MEETING
SICK BAY
RECEPTION
LAUNDRY
ELC 2
QUIET ROOM
WAITING
STORE
STAFF WC
STAFF
PREP
PREP PLAY AREA
VILLA ALBA
SHARED GARDEN
LOCKER
COMMON AREA
STAFF ROOM
PREP STAGE TWO
ATELIER
LIBRARY
ARK
GRADE 1
COMMON AREA
GRADE 2
WREN HOUSE
STAGE TWO
LANDSCAPED BUFFER ZONE

The planning of the new Xavier Preparatory School is structured around a dynamic circulation gallery that follows the fall of the site to connect with the view to the south over the Yarra River valley. A sequence of flexible learning spaces is presented to the east, addressing the existing campus.

From the arrival hall visitors are offered a sculptured view through the primary exhibition gallery to the Great Space and beyond. This circulation space is an area of adventure and exploration. Levels rise and fall, with access choices between stairs and ramps, between bridges and ground planes, offering students an adventurous pathway from one area to another.

The Great Space, thought of by us as an 'Ark', is a fluid area designed to be evocative, yet abstract enough to allow students to develop their own responses and imaginings about its ellipsoidal form: a boat, a cubby, a church or a spaceship; all is dependent upon the game at hand. The Ark is biblical analogy, a place where all living things may be considered safe.

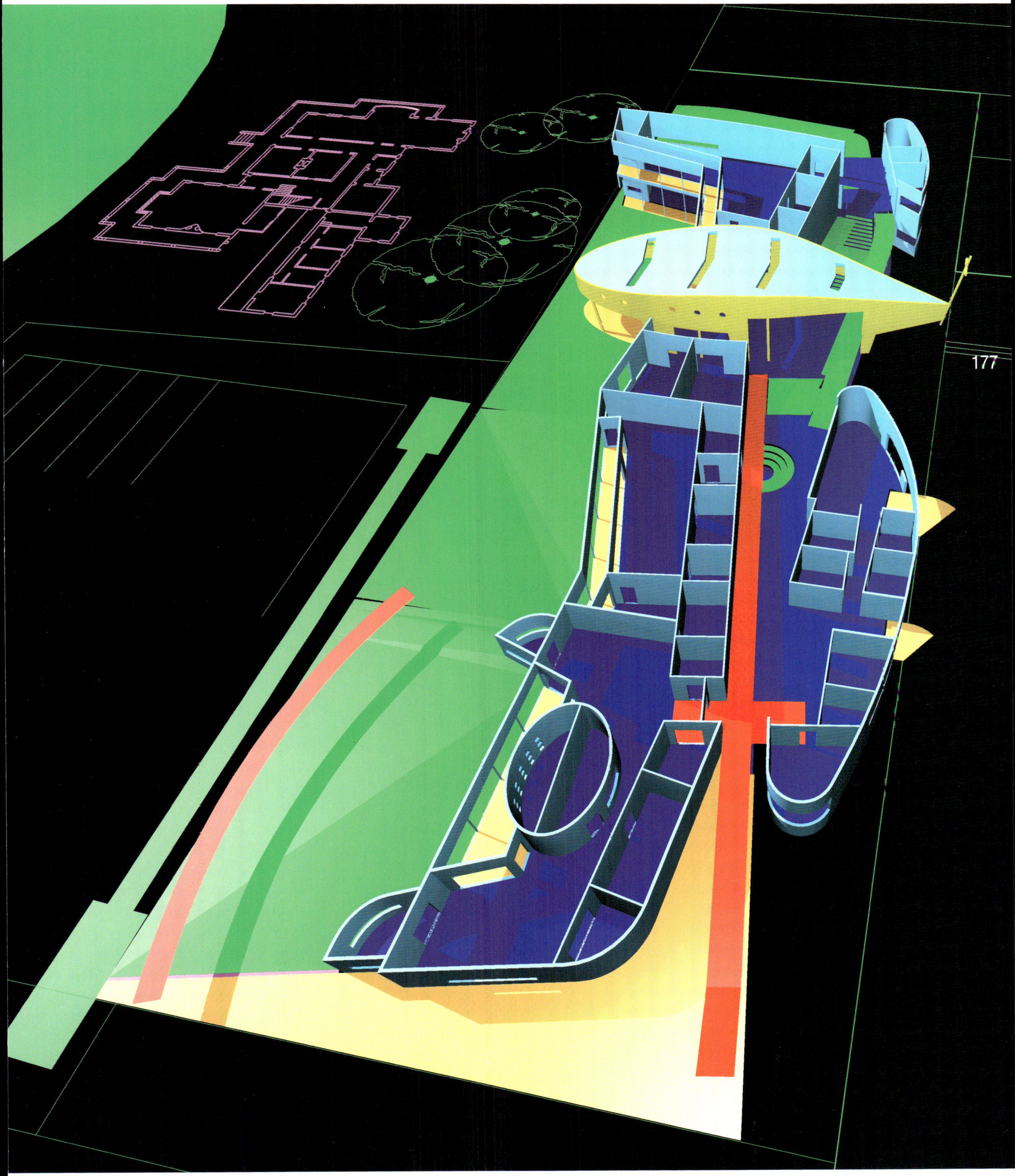

Swinburne is an urban university; its buildings edge the surrounding streets and form an open interface with the adjacent neighbourhood. Three levels hold one corner of the precinct to present a face of weathered and folded zinc, leaning into the urbis, yet anchored to the ground by a solid white masonry base.

The School of Management contains conference facilities, a lecture theatre, classrooms, function rooms, staff offices and student facilities. The plan allows student access to parts of the buildings at all hours, while limited-access rooms are easily secured. The simple plan layout makes use of angled walls in both horizontal and vertical planes to create dynamic spaces.

A central opening leads to an atrium where slots of light are cut into the rendered skin to reveal the inner circulation system and a terrace cut into the overall form.

Material edges are sharply defined, developing a pattern of openings that appear as though cut into the overall mass.

The inner face reveals a larger 'open frame' glass wall and the interior gallery access.

SWINBURNE UNIVERSITY GRADUATE SCHOOL OF MANAGEMENT

ROOF BELOW
STAFF LOUNGE 70 M2
MALE TOILETS
FEMALE TOILETS
CLNR
VOID
LMR
LIFT
STAIR
VOID
ESCAPE STAIR
CORRIDOR
ESCAPE STAIR
CCMMS
STAFF 33
STAFF 32
STAFF 31
CORR
STAFF 30
STAFF 29
STAFF 28
CORR
MEETING ROOM 40 M2
STORE
COPY
WAIT AREA 2
WAIT AREA 1
SEC
STAFF 27 HEAD OF SCHOOL
SEC
STAFF 26
STAFF 25
STAFF 24
ROOF TERRACE
STAFF 23
STAFF 22
STAFF 21
STAFF 20
CORR.
STORE
STAFF 9
CORR.
STAFF 18
STAFF 17
PHOTOCOPY
CORR.
STAIR
POST GRAD RESEARCH
RESEARCH
STAFF 10
SEC
WAIT AREA
STORE
STAFF 19
STAFF 16
STAFF 15
STAFF 14
STAFF 13
STAFF 36
STAFF 12
STAFF 11

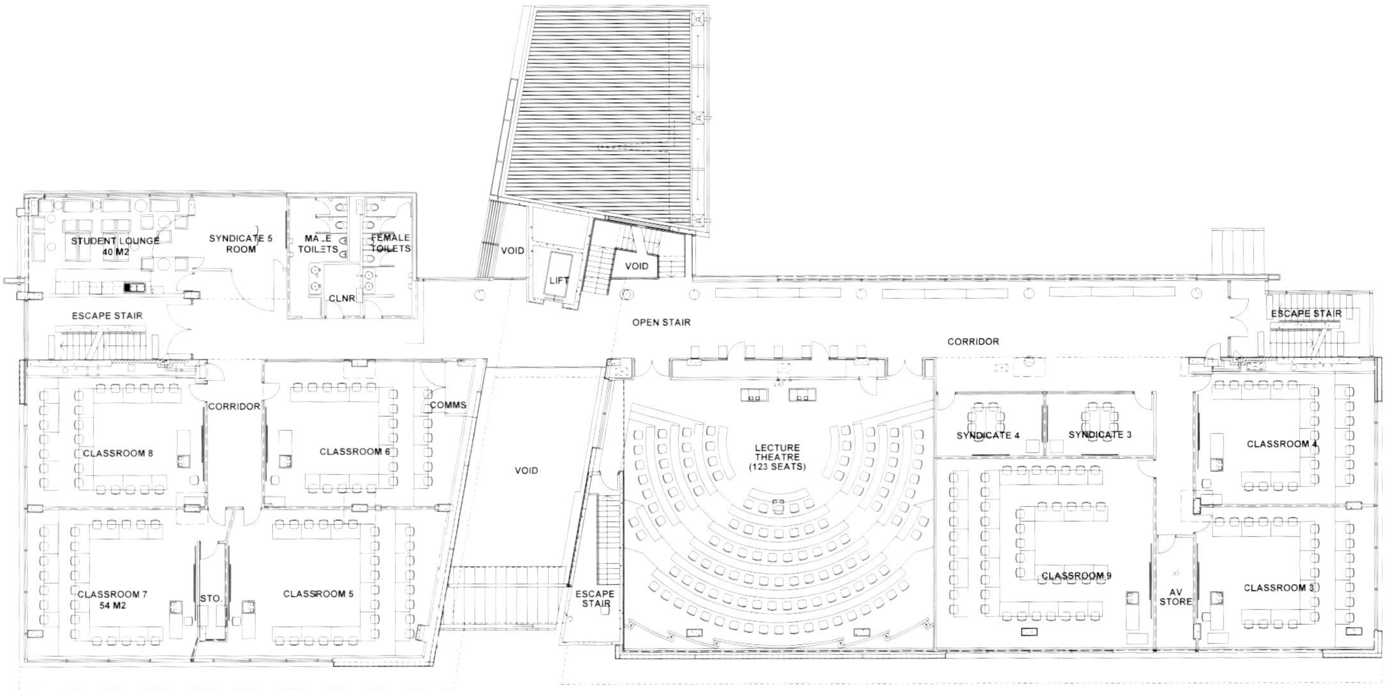
STUDENT LOUNGE 40 M2
SYNDICATE 5 ROOM
MALE TOILETS
FEMALE TOILETS
CLNR
VOID
LIFT
VOID
ESCAPE STAIR
OPEN STAIR
CORRIDOR
ESCAPE STAIR
CORRIDOR
COMMS
CLASSROOM 8
CLASSROOM 6
VOID
LECTURE THEATRE (123 SEATS)
SYNDICATE 4
SYNDICATE 3
CLASSROOM 4
CLASSROOM 7 54 M2
STO.
CLASSROOM 5
ESCAPE STAIR
CLASSROOM 9
AV STORE
CLASSROOM 3

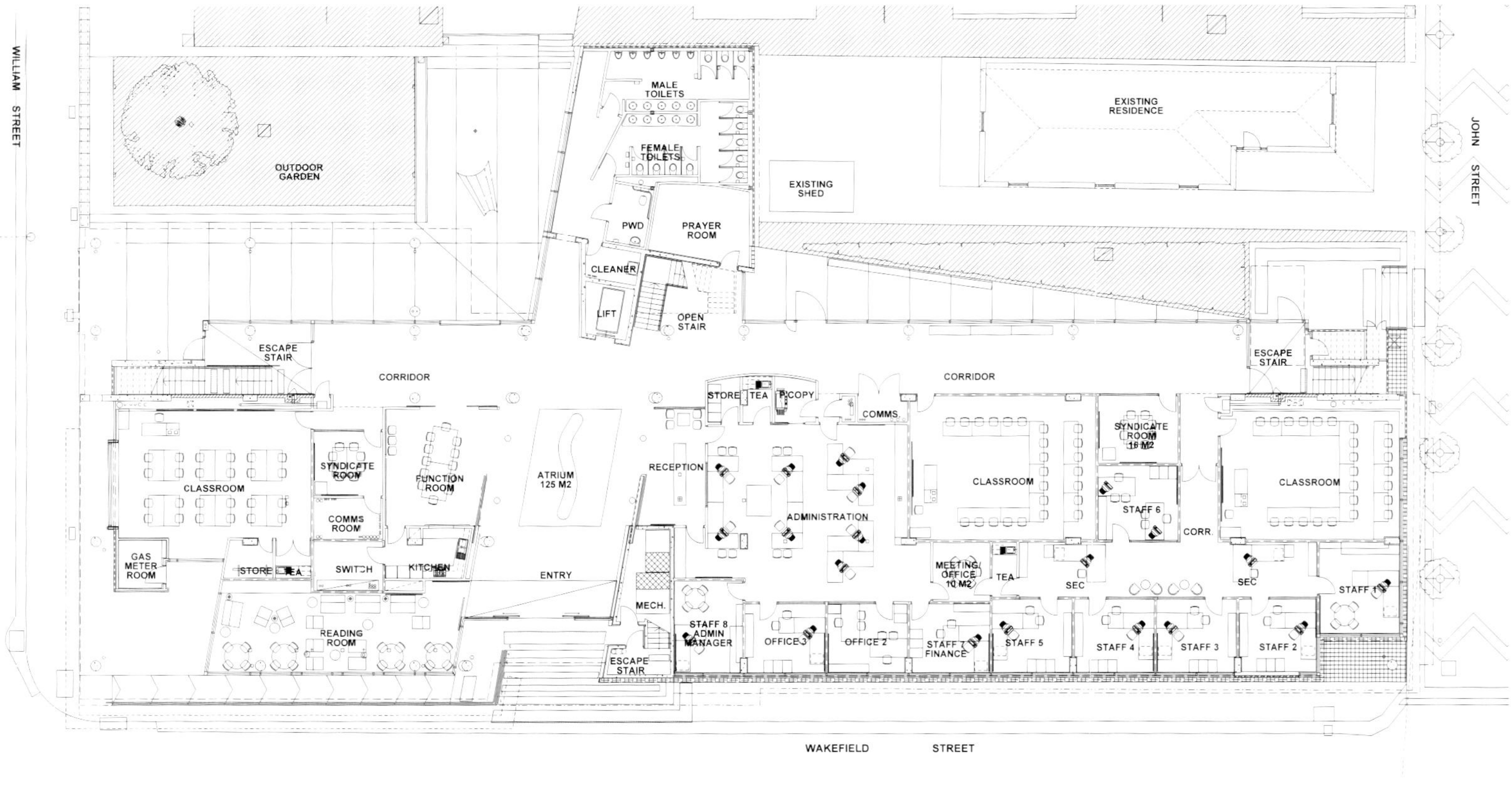
WILLIAM STREET
OUTDOOR GARDEN
MALE TOILETS
FEMALE TOILETS
PWD
PRAYER ROOM
CLEANER
LIFT
OPEN STAIR
EXISTING SHED
EXISTING RESIDENCE
JOHN STREET
ESCAPE STAIR
CORRIDOR
CORRIDOR
ESCAPE STAIR
STORE
TEA
PCOPY
COMMS
CLASSROOM
SYNDICATE ROOM
FUNCTION ROOM
ATRIUM 125 M2
RECEPTION
ADMINISTRATION
CLASSROOM
SYNDICATE ROOM 18 M2
STAFF 6
CLASSROOM
CORR
COMMS ROOM
GAS METER ROOM
STORE
TEA
SWITCH
KITCHEN
ENTRY
MEETING OFFICE 10 M2
TEA
SEC
SEC
STAFF 1
READING ROOM
MECH.
STAFF 8 ADMIN MANAGER
OFFICE 3
OFFICE 2
STAFF 7 FINANCE
STAFF 5
STAFF 4
STAFF 3
STAFF 2
ESCAPE STAIR
WAKEFIELD STREET

BOOSTER CONNECTION POINT LOCATED IN JOHN STREET →

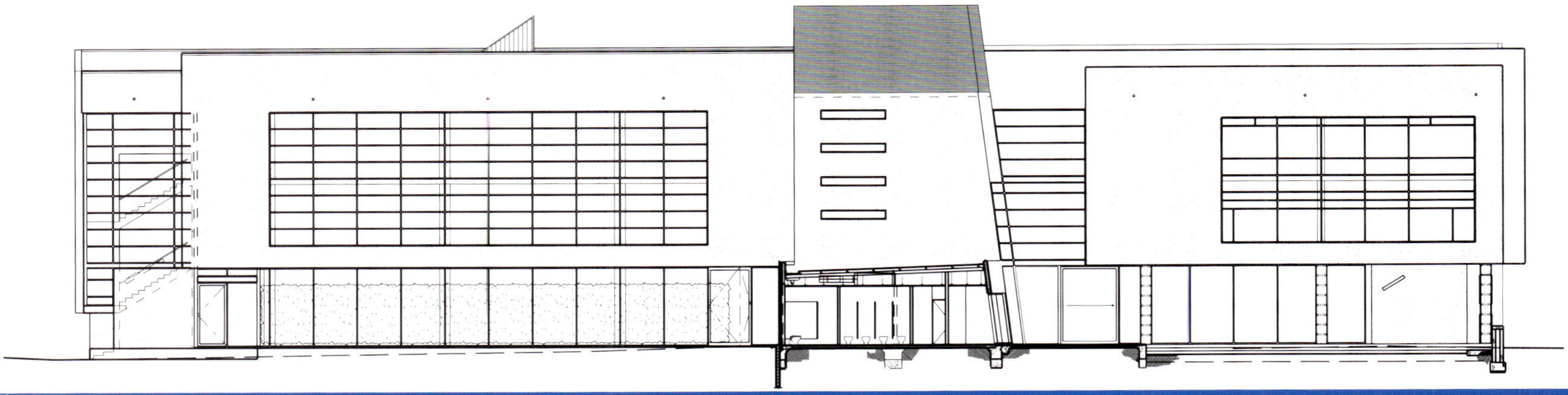

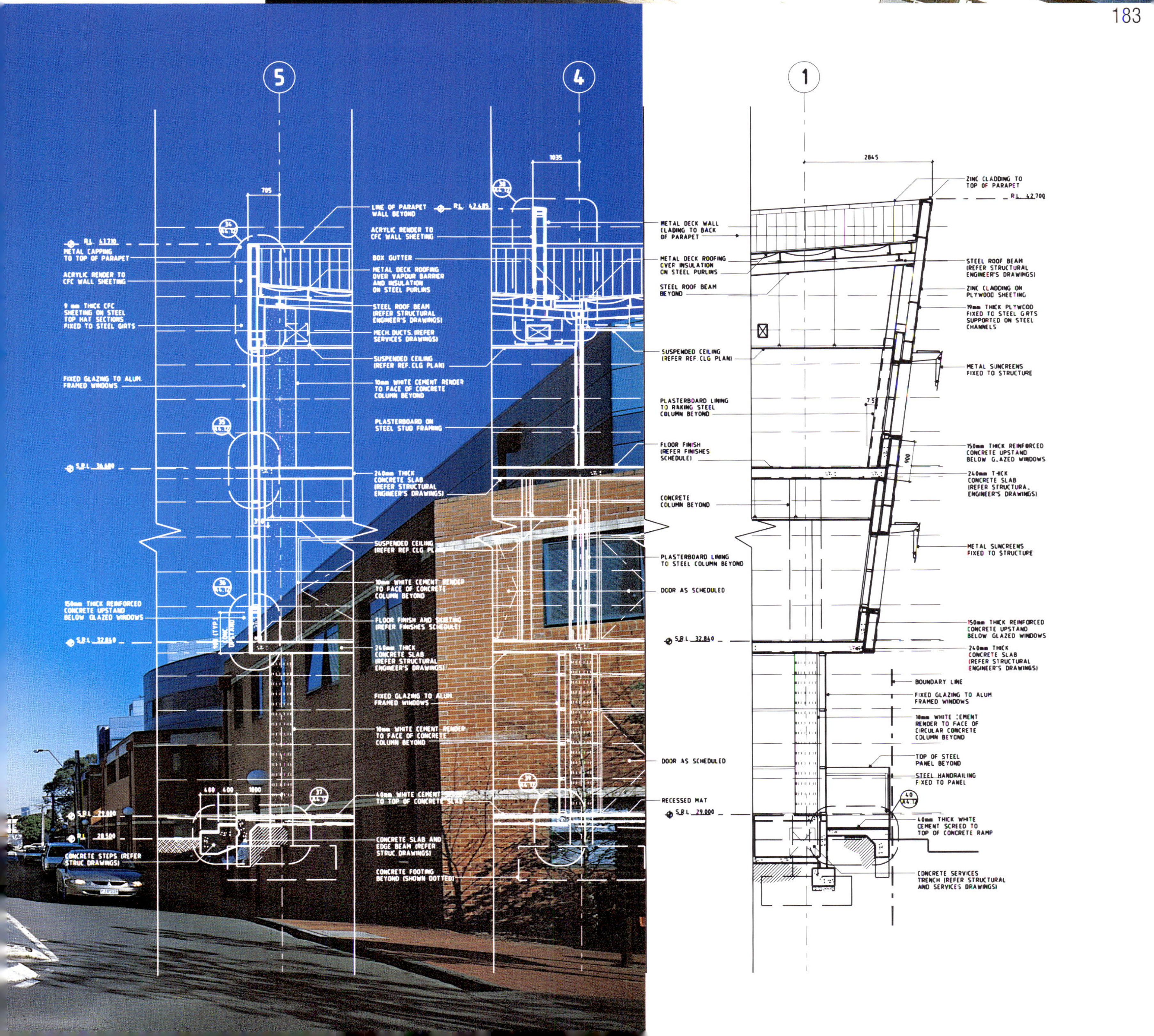
5
4
1
705
1035
2845
R.L. 41.710
METAL CAPPING TO TOP OF PARAPET
ACRYLIC RENDER TO CFC WALL SHEETING
9 mm THICK CFC SHEETING ON STEEL TOP HAT SECTIONS FIXED TO STEEL GIRTS
FIXED GLAZING TO ALUM. FRAMED WINDOWS
S.R.L. 36.600
150mm THICK REINFORCED CONCRETE UPSTAND BELOW GLAZED WINDOWS
S.R.L. 32.860
S.R.L. 29.000
R.L. 28.500
CONCRETE STEPS (REFER STRUC. DRAWINGS)
LINE OF PARAPET WALL BEYOND
R.L. 42.685
ACRYLIC RENDER TO CFC WALL SHEETING
BOX GUTTER
METAL DECK ROOFING OVER VAPOUR BARRIER AND INSULATION ON STEEL PURLINS
STEEL ROOF BEAM (REFER STRUCTURAL ENGINEER'S DRAWINGS)
MECH. DUCTS (REFER SERVICES DRAWINGS)
SUSPENDED CEILING (REFER REF. CLG PLAN)
10mm WHITE CEMENT RENDER TO FACE OF CONCRETE COLUMN BEYOND
PLASTERBOARD ON STEEL STUD FRAMING
240mm THICK CONCRETE SLAB (REFER STRUCTURAL ENGINEER'S DRAWINGS)
SUSPENDED CEILING (REFER REF. CLG PLAN)
10mm WHITE CEMENT RENDER TO FACE OF CONCRETE COLUMN BEYOND
FLOOR FINISH AND SKIRTING (REFER FINISHES SCHEDULE)
240mm THICK CONCRETE SLAB (REFER STRUCTURAL ENGINEER'S DRAWINGS)
FIXED GLAZING TO ALUM. FRAMED WINDOWS
10mm WHITE CEMENT RENDER TO FACE OF CONCRETE COLUMN BEYOND
400 400 1000
40mm WHITE CEMENT SCREED TO TOP OF CONCRETE SLAB
CONCRETE SLAB AND EDGE BEAM (REFER STRUC. DRAWINGS)
CONCRETE FOOTING BEYOND (SHOWN DOTTED)
METAL DECK WALL CLADDING TO BACK OF PARAPET
METAL DECK ROOFING OVER INSULATION ON STEEL PURLINS
STEEL ROOF BEAM BEYOND
SUSPENDED CEILING (REFER REF. CLG PLAN)
PLASTERBOARD LINING TO RAKING STEEL COLUMN BEYOND
FLOOR FINISH (REFER FINISHES SCHEDULE)
CONCRETE COLUMN BEYOND
PLASTERBOARD LINING TO STEEL COLUMN BEYOND
DOOR AS SCHEDULED
S.R.L. 32.860
DOOR AS SCHEDULED
RECESSED MAT
S.R.L. 29.000
ZINC CLADDING TO TOP OF PARAPET
R.L. 42.700
STEEL ROOF BEAM (REFER STRUCTURAL ENGINEER'S DRAWINGS)
ZINC CLADDING ON PLYWOOD SHEETING
19mm THICK PLYWOOD FIXED TO STEEL GIRTS SUPPORTED ON STEEL CHANNELS
METAL SUNSCREENS FIXED TO STRUCTURE
900
150mm THICK REINFORCED CONCRETE UPSTAND BELOW GLAZED WINDOWS
240mm THICK CONCRETE SLAB (REFER STRUCTURAL ENGINEER'S DRAWINGS)
METAL SUNSCREENS FIXED TO STRUCTURE
150mm THICK REINFORCED CONCRETE UPSTAND BELOW GLAZED WINDOWS
240mm THICK CONCRETE SLAB (REFER STRUCTURAL ENGINEER'S DRAWINGS)
BOUNDARY LINE
FIXED GLAZING TO ALUM FRAMED WINDOWS
10mm WHITE CEMENT RENDER TO FACE OF CIRCULAR CONCRETE COLUMN BEYOND
TOP OF STEEL PANEL BEYOND
STEEL HANDRAILING FIXED TO PANEL
40mm THICK WHITE CEMENT SCREED TO TOP OF CONCRETE RAMP
CONCRETE SERVICES TRENCH (REFER STRUCTURAL AND SERVICES DRAWINGS)

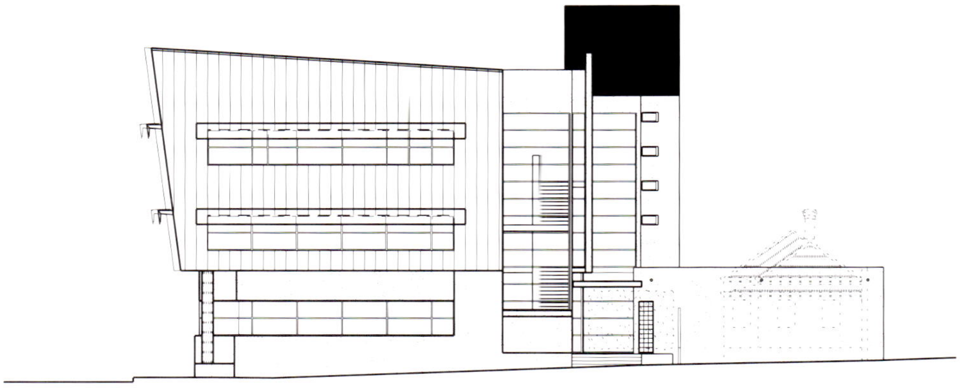

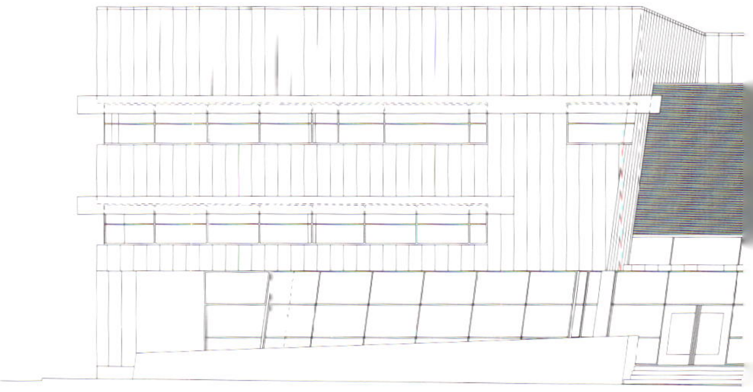

Swinburne
University Of Technology
TOUCH SCREEN TO BEGIN
AMX

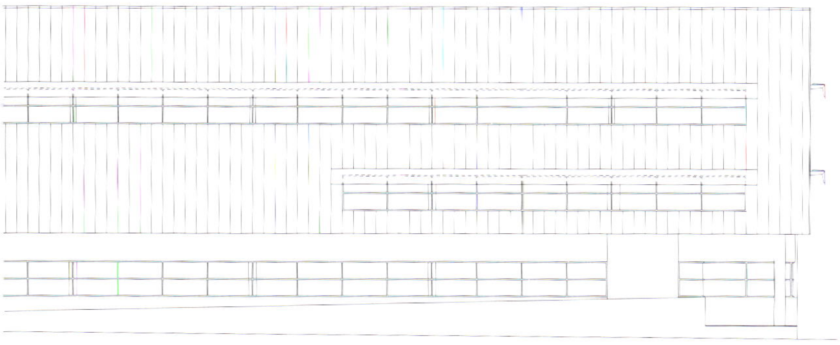

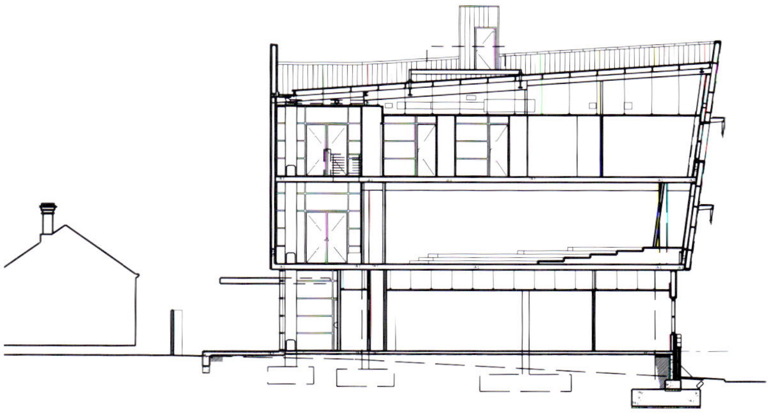

ELMO

The modern office programme demands amenity and flexibility, communication and accessibility.

Teams cluster and regroup continually as personnel come and go, delivering their talents and experiences.

This office park celebrates a new generation of office planning ideals. Large open floor plates, naturally lit perimeter walls, and a spectacular core of central services are separated only by interfloor access stairs, lifts and meeting areas beyond the IT systems and individual work stations.

The design is taut: cut edges of metal model the surface appearance with light penetrating the interior sky-lit voids that separate the paired floor plates. Along the outer edges of the floor, everyone experiences landscape views. Transparency is important and enhances the sense of human exchange taking place on the floor. The circulation core of lifts and stairs is in a dramatic vertical space.

Outside in the park is a range of office areas, although each independent identity is created from a similar vocabulary. Colours, although from a limited palette, are varied and strong.

A central café, childcare centre and tennis club offer further opportunities for human contact. The structured new landscape of walls, water and shade gives a sense of value and a complex edge to the new working environment.

BRINDABELLA BUSINESS PARK

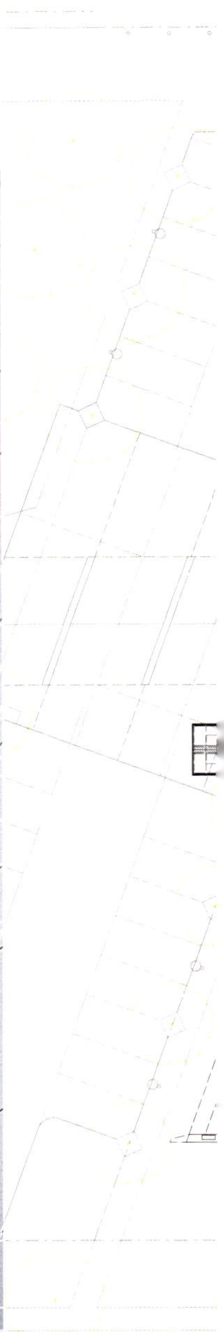

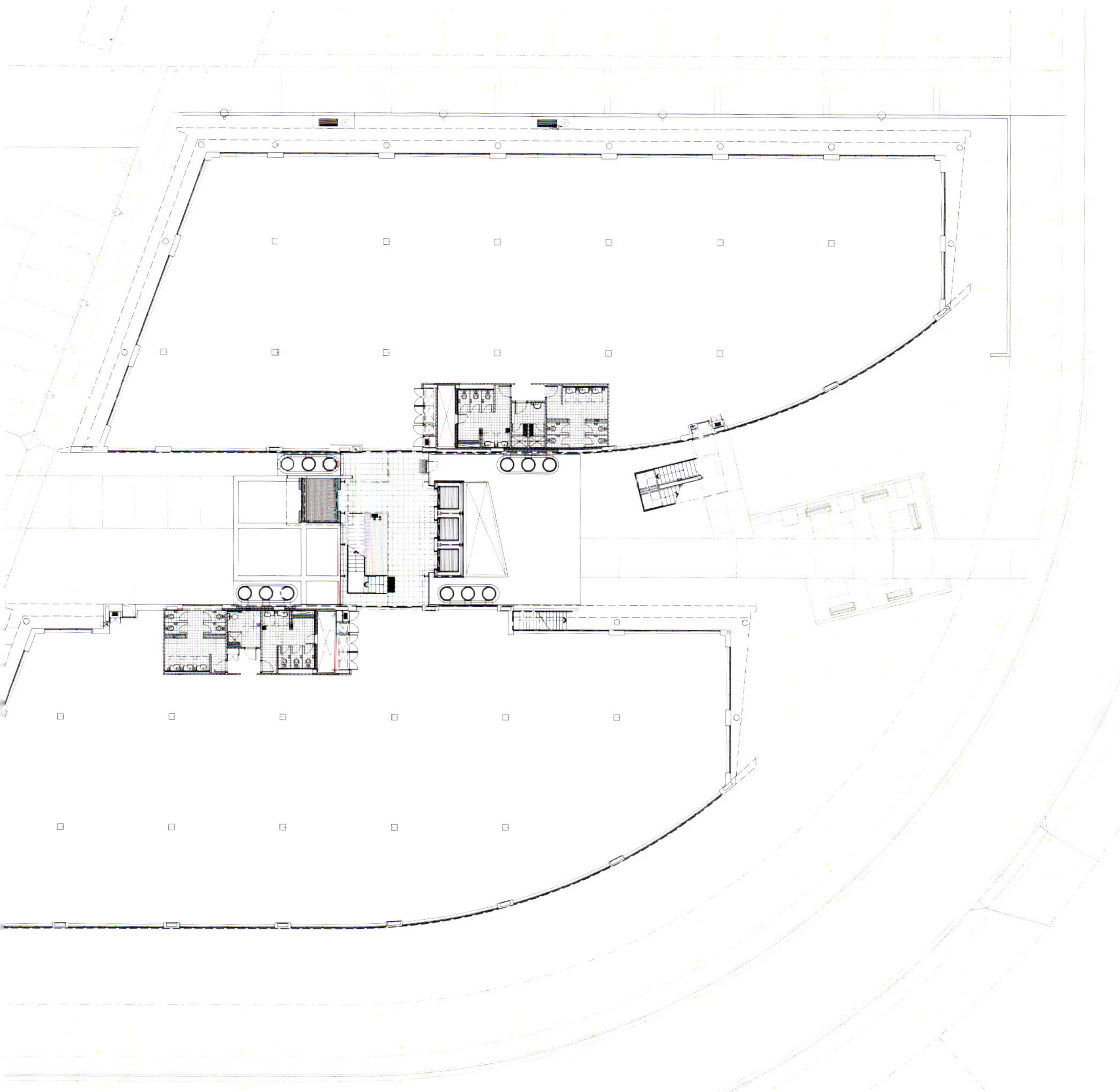

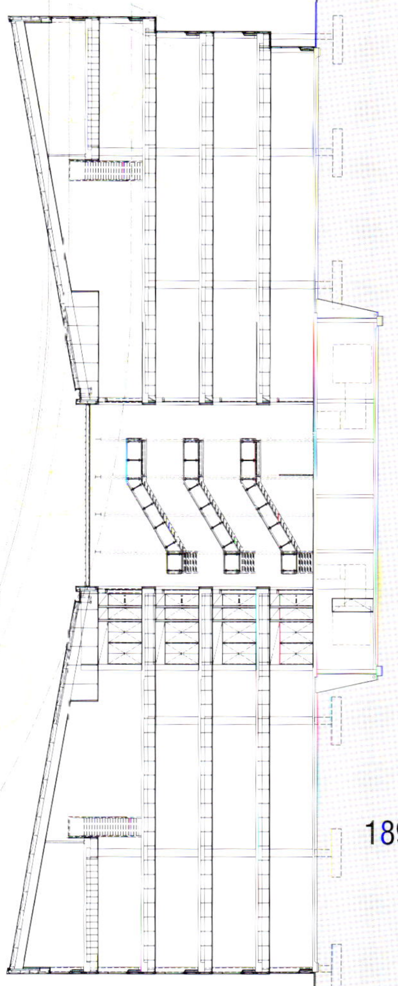

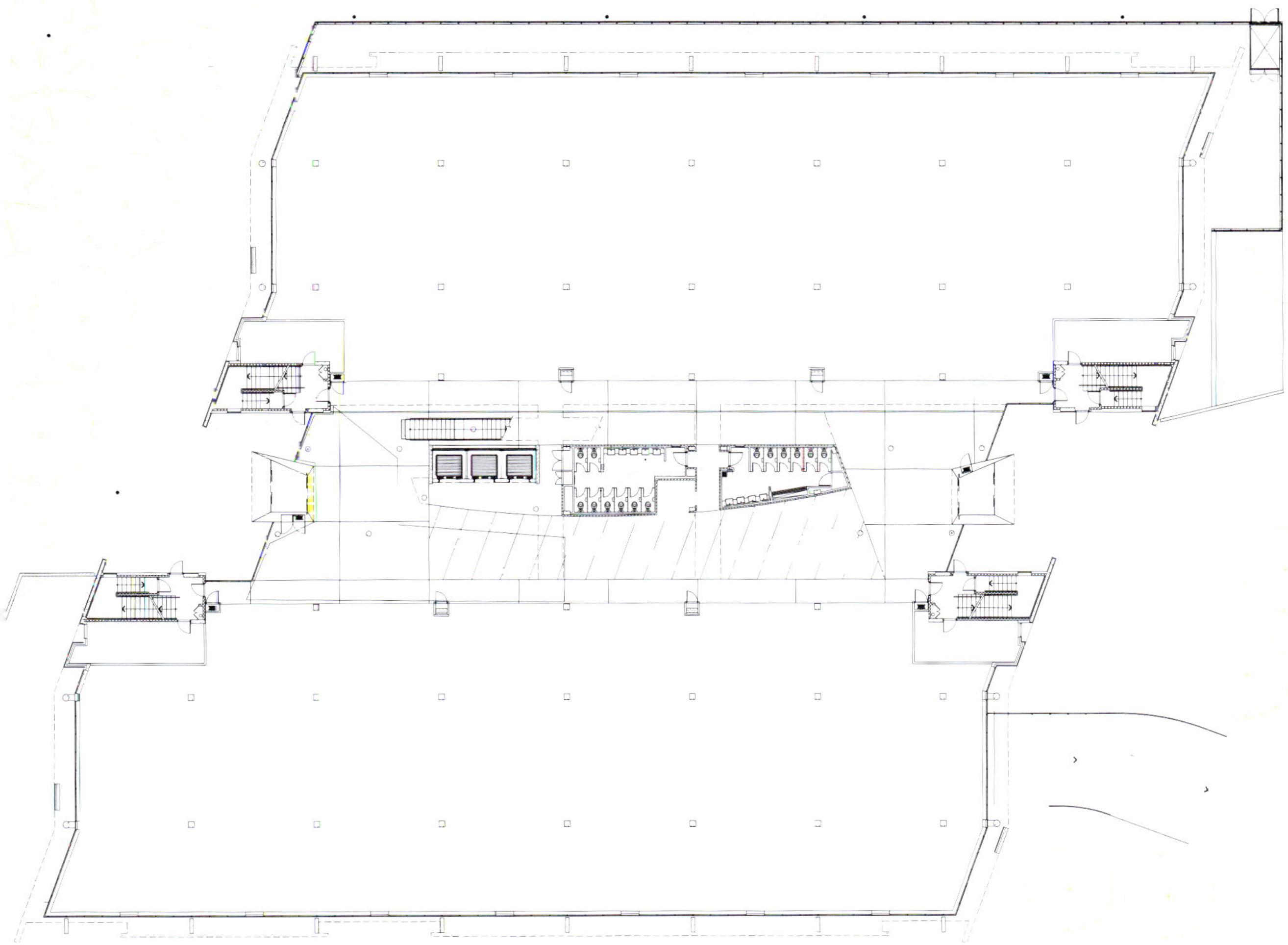

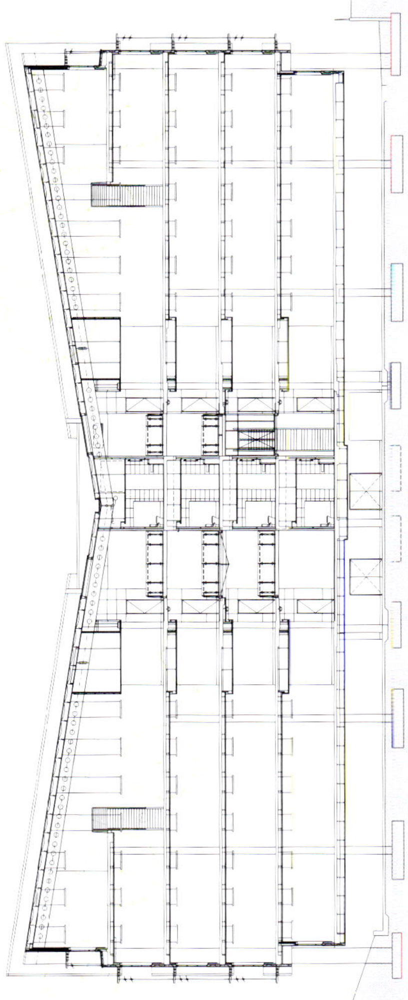

The formal composition is based upon a consolidated, compact massing, split apart by a double-height stair gallery to one side of the arrangement, and counterbalanced by the single-storey mass of the dining and living rooms on the other.

The aim is to conserve mature trees and avoid an excessively heavy two- or three-storey mass stretching across the width of the block. In spite of this square shape overall, the composition appears as a series of narrow slices, given direction and perceived volume by the gallery and by the separated volume of the living room. Both combine to offer view lines into and through the mass.

The added height given to the living room is important for its interior functions, but significantly, results in a balanced massing. It is a grand room for entertaining, with large windows at each end.

A large chimney on the south face anchors the form rotation, and stabilises the resultant dynamic. This sculptural idea has two practical outcomes. First, the building appears narrower at the front and allows trees to be retained. Second, it serves to draw visitors through the rooms to observe or experience the rear terraces and gardens. The garden environment is a highlight of the residence. This plan form, with the separated paved and lawn spaces thrusting out from the house into the natural landscape, offers a unique vision of house and garden integration; one special disposition of Australian architecture at its best.

AUSTRALIAN AMBASSADOR'S RESIDENCE

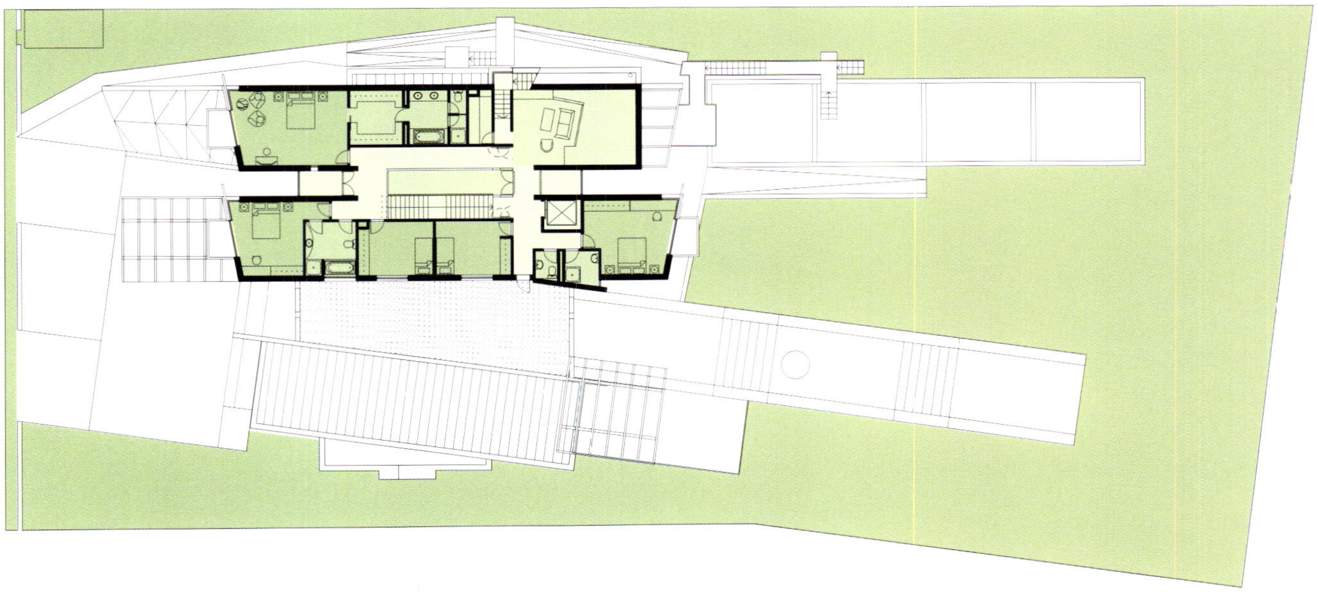

DOUGLASSTRASSE

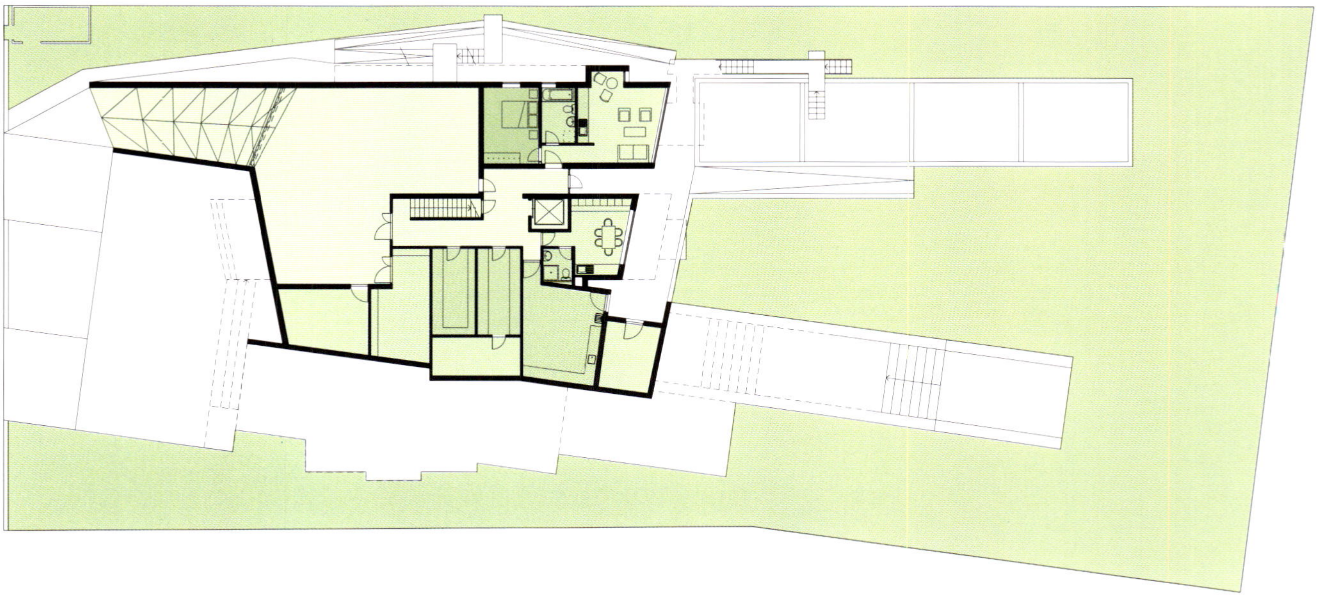

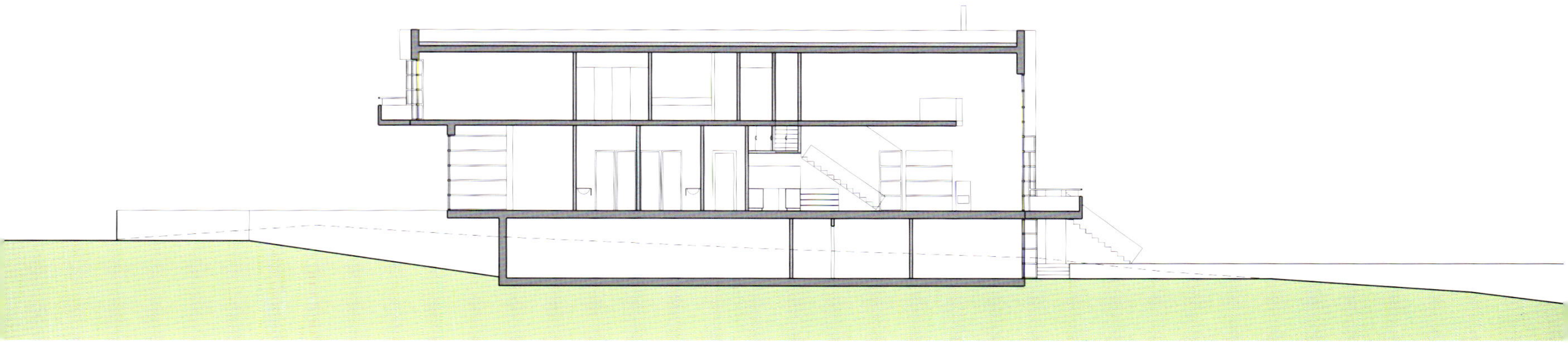

In a modern European setting the content of the interior architecture is as significant as that of the exterior. In this design there is no division between the two, as the exterior space seamlessly flows to the interior. White cement-rendered masonry walls cut through the landscape and carry the eye from outside to inside, and to the outside beyond. This beckoning device relies upon a simple transition between just two key materials: masonry and glass. This project fixes glass in black aluminium frames, defined as horizontal bands that tie the vertical masonry planes together. The extremities of the interior (where the garden/trees/terraces meet) are partially glazed above to allow the tree canopy to be seen. Large sliding glass doors open between the inter or and exterior.

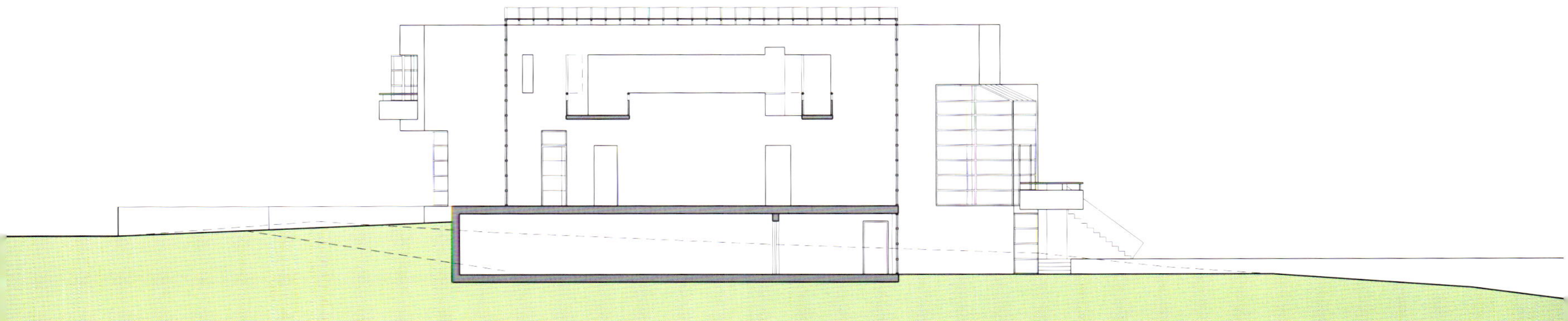

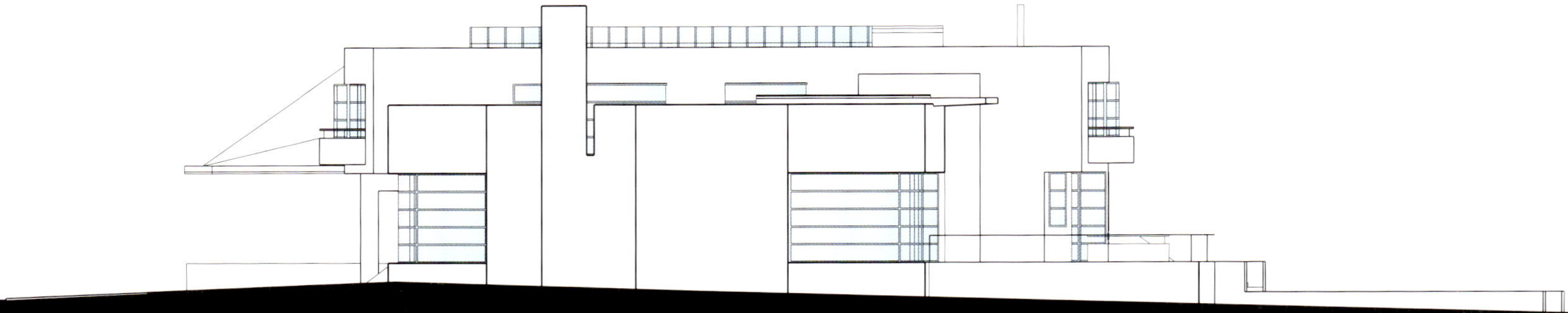

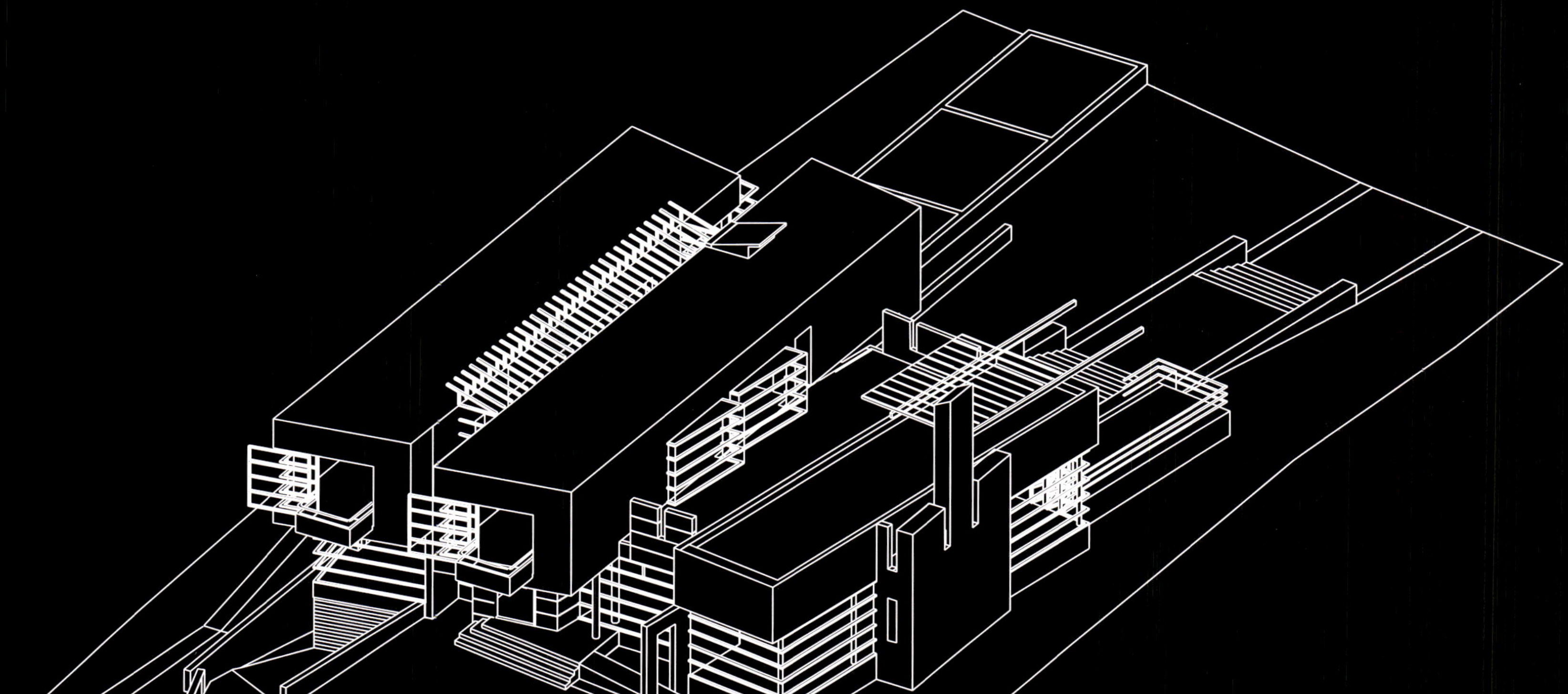

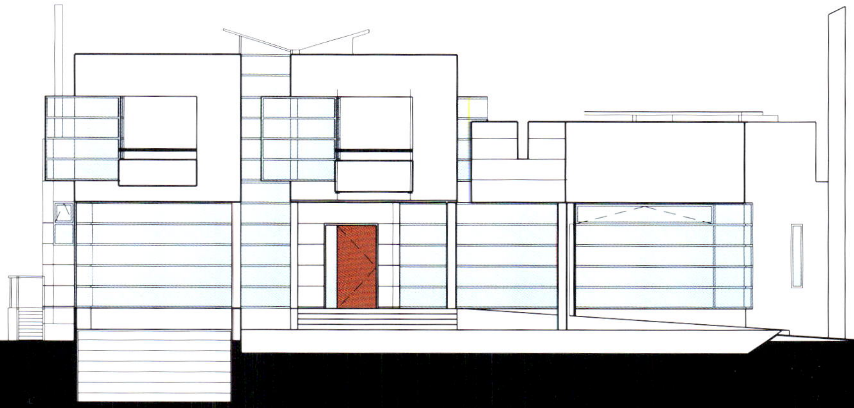

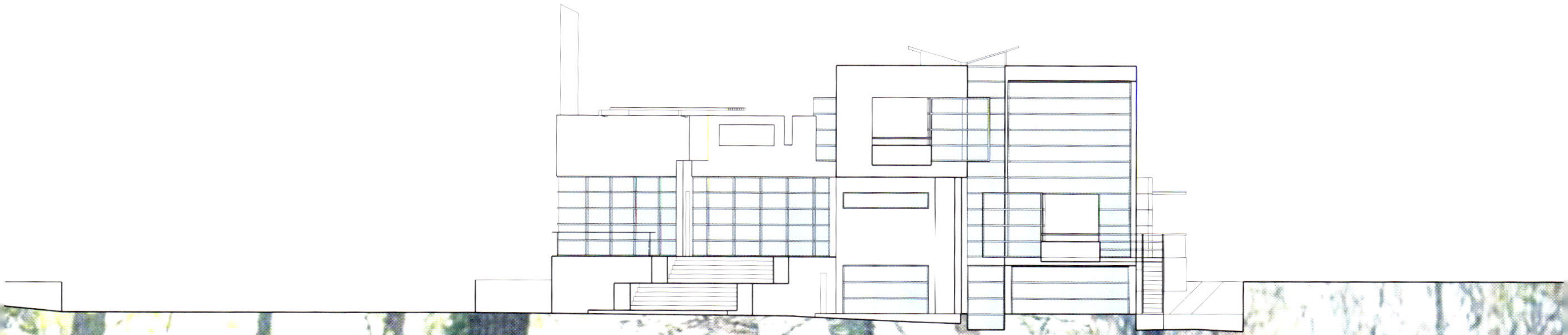

The adaptation of an historic building for use as a museum has the potential to frustrate and confound, resulting in compromise of both the programme and the design. The critical issue was to breathe new life into the existing (but no longer used) Customs House and to integrate new ideas for building and site. Respect and awareness of historic fabric is fundamental; the project is not so much about restoration or reconstruction, as about reinterpretation and overlay: urban transformation.

Museums are rapidly becoming icons of local and world tourism. Today they are about societal change and new understandings of existence, rather than a repository for relics. Interaction with visitors, in the form of cultural instruction and entertainment, is paramount.

The purpose of the Customs House, as a Museum of Immigration and Hellenic Archaeology, is to bring together an understanding of public migration, and to present a new set of ideas and a design resolution that speaks of and symbolises Australia: new world/old world values complemented by an eclectic and rich history.

Importantly, the historic building needs a counterpoint, provided by the architecture of the Museum, as well as its content.

MUSEUM OF IMMIGRATION

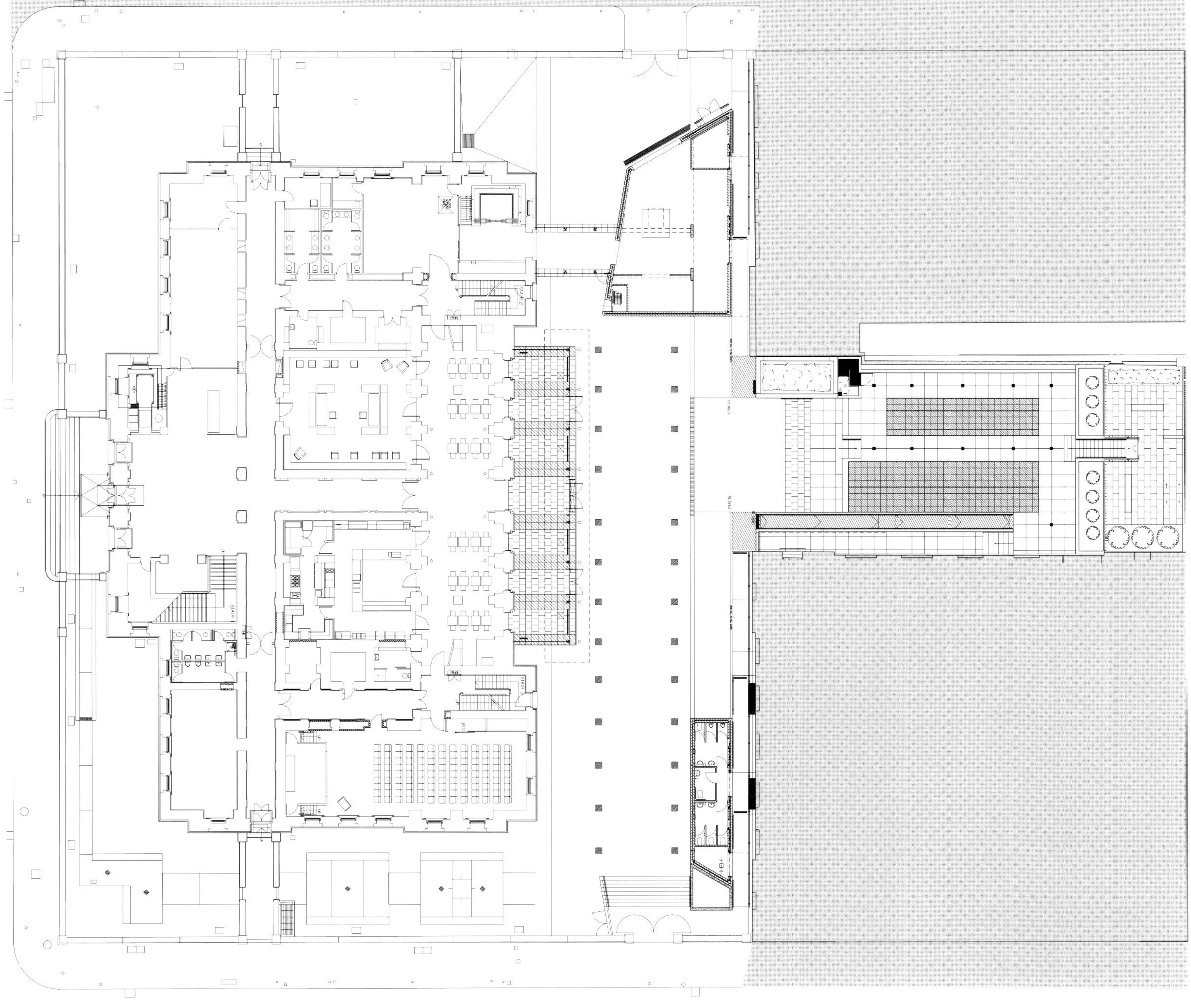

There are three key issues:

- Within the existing building the museum identity is established around rooms, corridors and journeys. Interiors are expressed to enhance the journey, either in an historic or contemporary mode.
- Through the use of exciting and expressed technology the museum conveys an optimism, reflecting on past migration experience, yet with a need to look forward.
- Introduced elements and ideas use a contemporary aesthetic, avoiding pastiche and pseudo-historic references.

All these points led to a perception that the old Customs House needed to become a museum for the new century, capable of bringing fresh and surprising impressions to the Australian circumstance.

Night lighting, markers, and strong graphics are used to give the building renewed presence. At courtyard level a promenade/café overlooks an urban garden, terraced to activate the precinct. This is an important meeting place, accessible to a broader clientele, not just museum visitors, and can be experienced without going into the museum.

The existing vault area at ground level is opened up to join a new 'Courtyard of Names' to the entrance. The new café cut into the plinth of the rear elevation is a tautly expressed assemblage of zinc, steel and glass; light forms opposing the solid masonry original. Zinc panels on the free-standing new mechanical plant room and service centre correspond with the Neo-Classical rustication. Otherwise, old is old and new is new.

On a coastal site 40 kilometres northeast of Qingdao City, this resort, soccer training and club complex comprises housing, parks, recreational water/beach activity, hotels and a commercial centre. It is focused on a site area of 1,790,000 square metres with approximately 1,800 linear metres facing the Yellow Sea.

The structure of the urban design is achieved through a new land/water relationship. Three holding basins or weirs are created to trap the tidal water for prolonged recreational use and visual amenity. The beach is reinstated within the weir to provide a constant water frontage to the nearby houses and public promenade. The layout is characterised by a series of parkland green 'vistas', which connect the water's edge to the site interior.

A hotel at the end of a pier overlooks the central weir. Alongside the hotel are restaurants, cafés and shops, which ensure the area's viability as a waterfront facility through their use by visitors and residents.

A mixed-use town centre is located adjacent to the beach, creating an urban edge with retail and restaurants. The second of the two resort hotels is located above the ground-floor cafés and commercial leases. A fresh fruit and vegetable market enables local farmers to sell their produce, with larger retail stores linked in by the walk-through market stalls, restaurant area, and car parking.

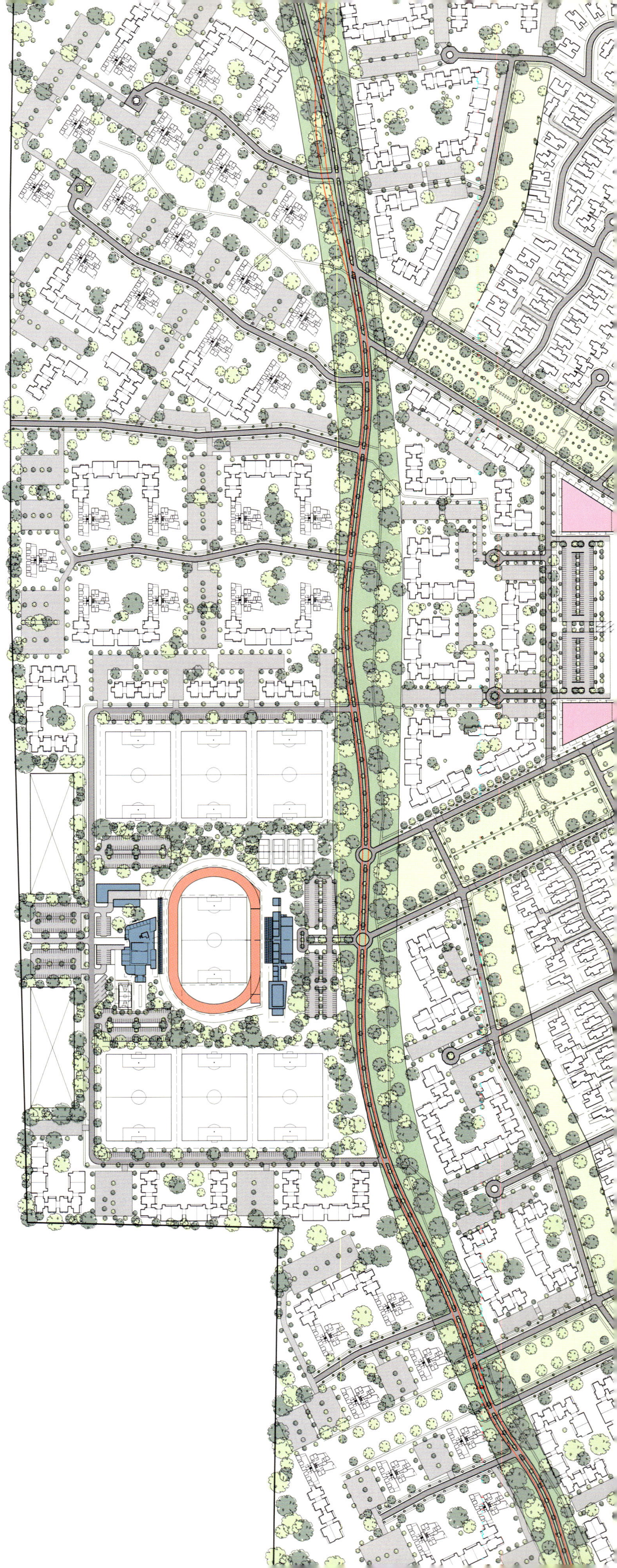

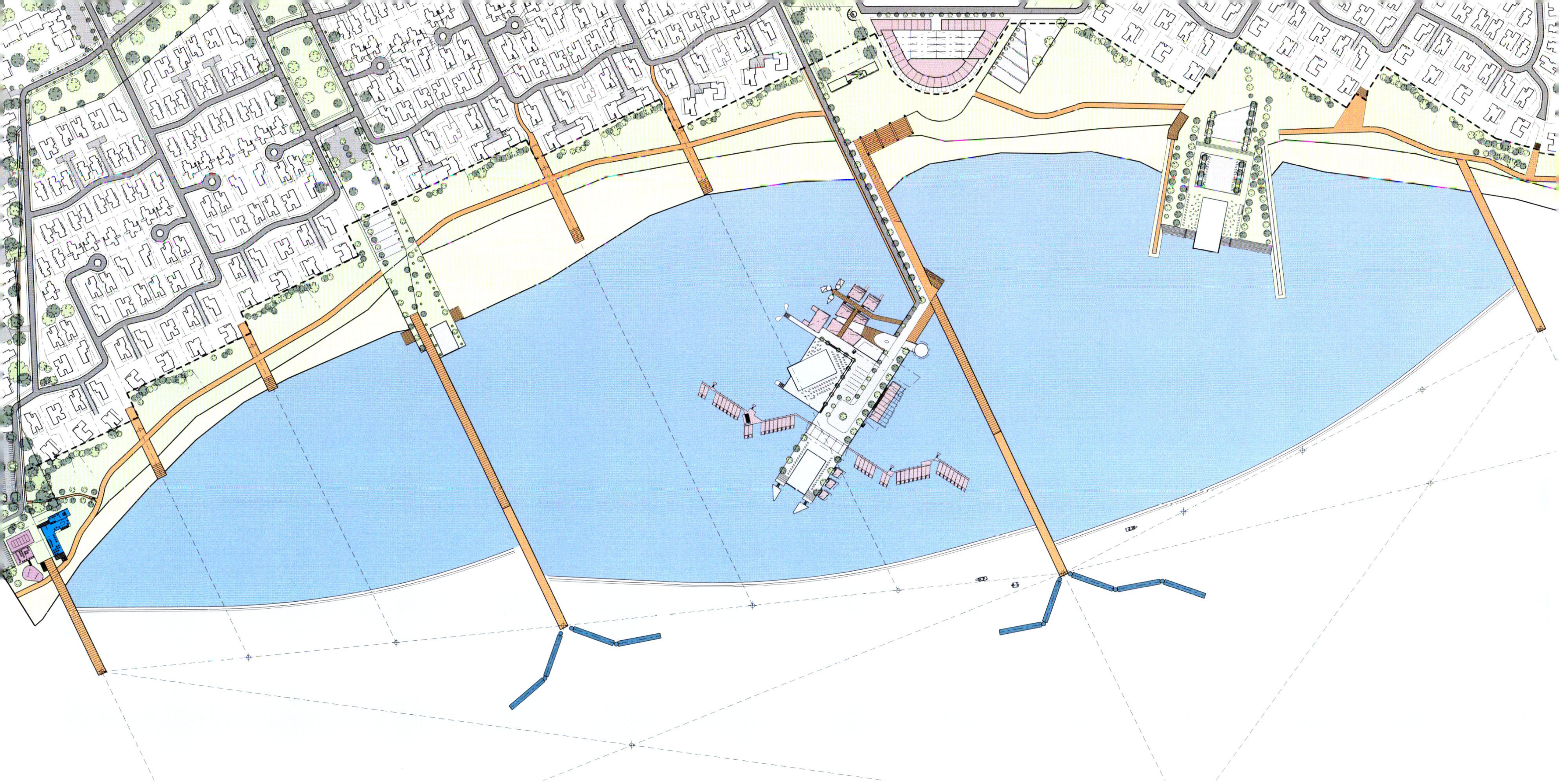

AOSHAN
HOUSING RESORT

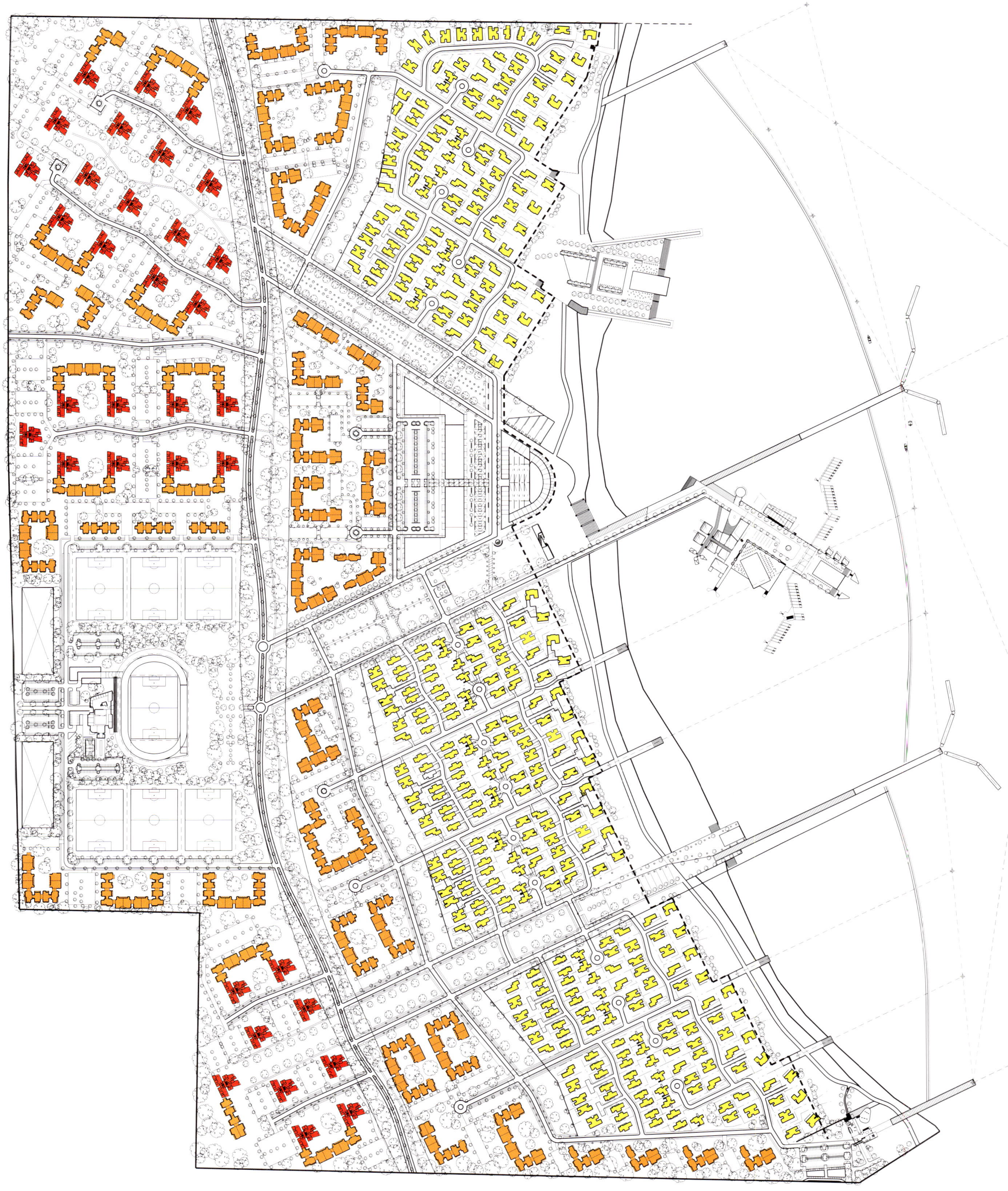

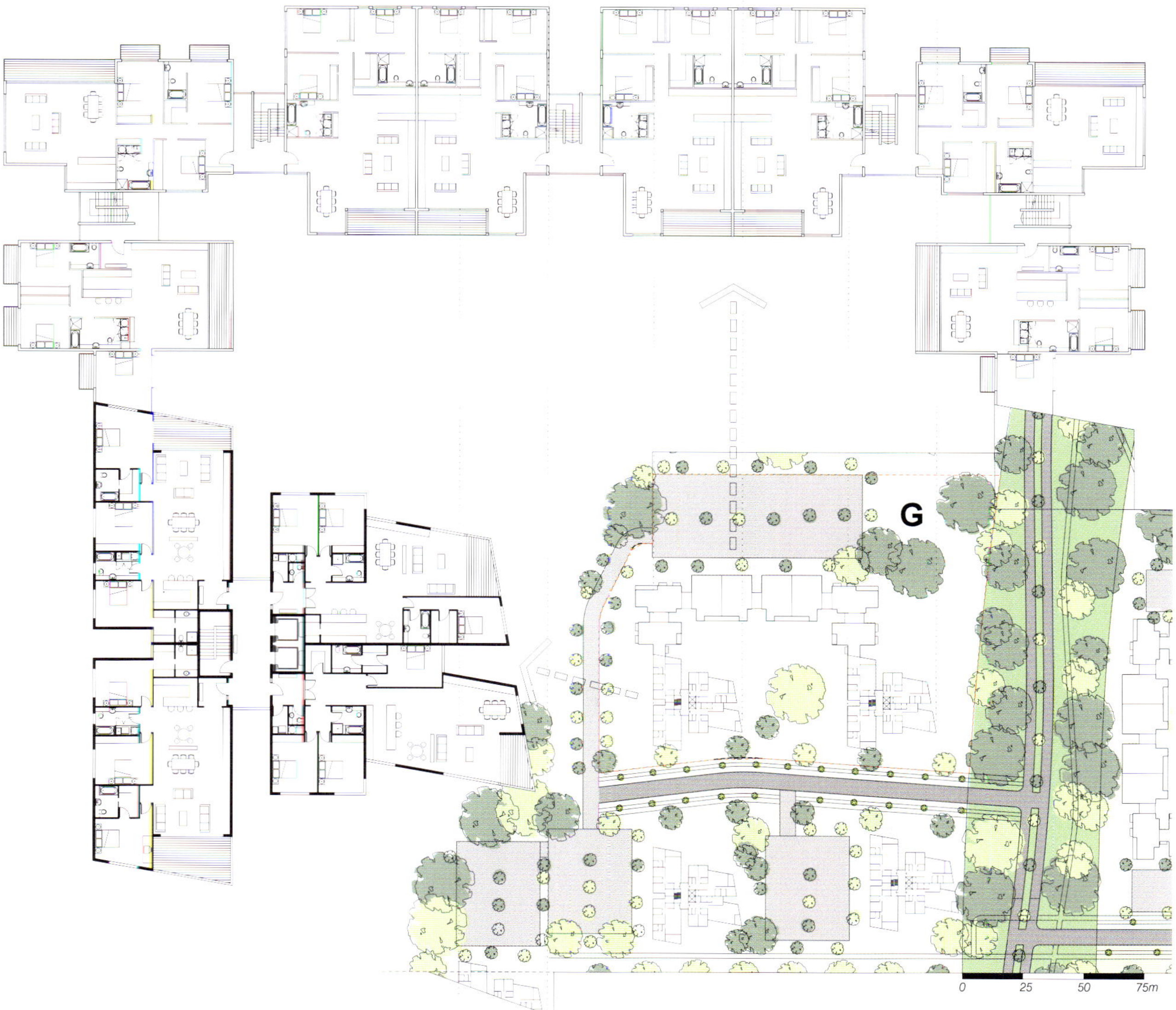
G
0
25
50
75m

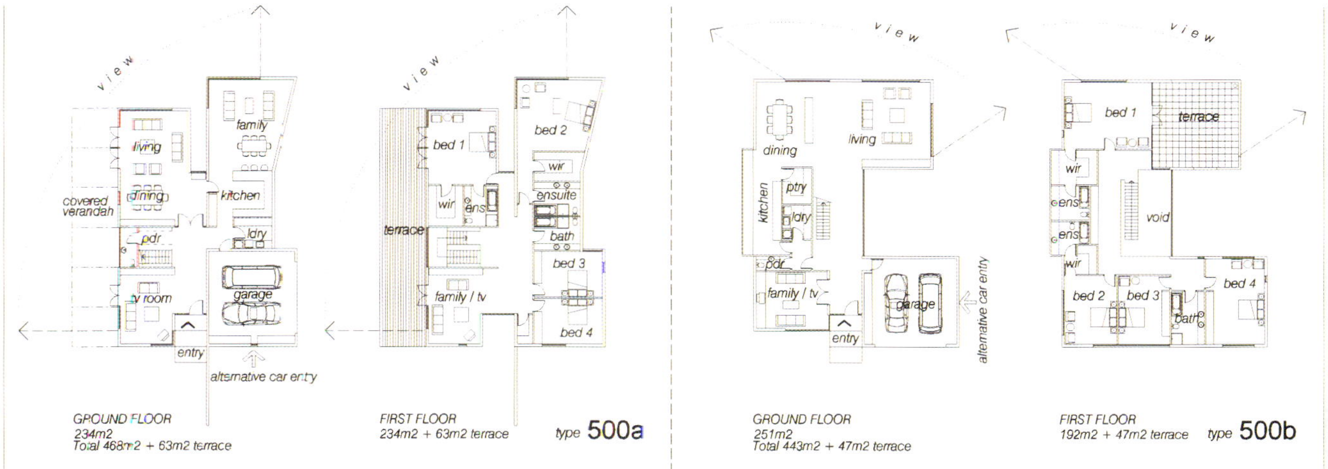
view
living
family
covered verandah
dining
kitchen
pdr
ldry
tv room
garage
entry
alternative car entry
bed 1
bed 2
wir
ensuite
ens
terrace
bath
bed 3
family / tv
bed 4
GROUND FLOOR
234m2
Total 468m2 + 63m2 terrace
FIRST FLOOR
234m2 + 63m2 terrace
type 500a
dining
living
kitchen
ptry
ldry
pdr
family / tv
garage
entry
alternative car entry
bed 1
terrace
wir
ens
void
bed 2
bed 3
bed 4
bath
GROUND FLOOR
251m2
Total 443m2 + 47m2 terrace
FIRST FLOOR
192m2 + 47m2 terrace
type 500b

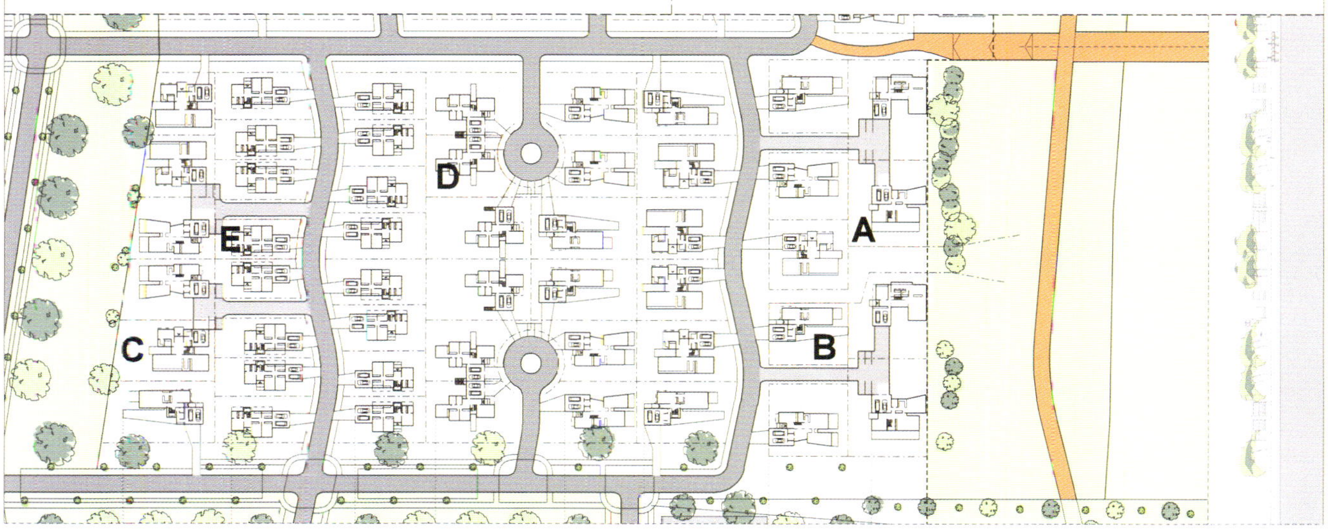
D
E
A
C
B

211

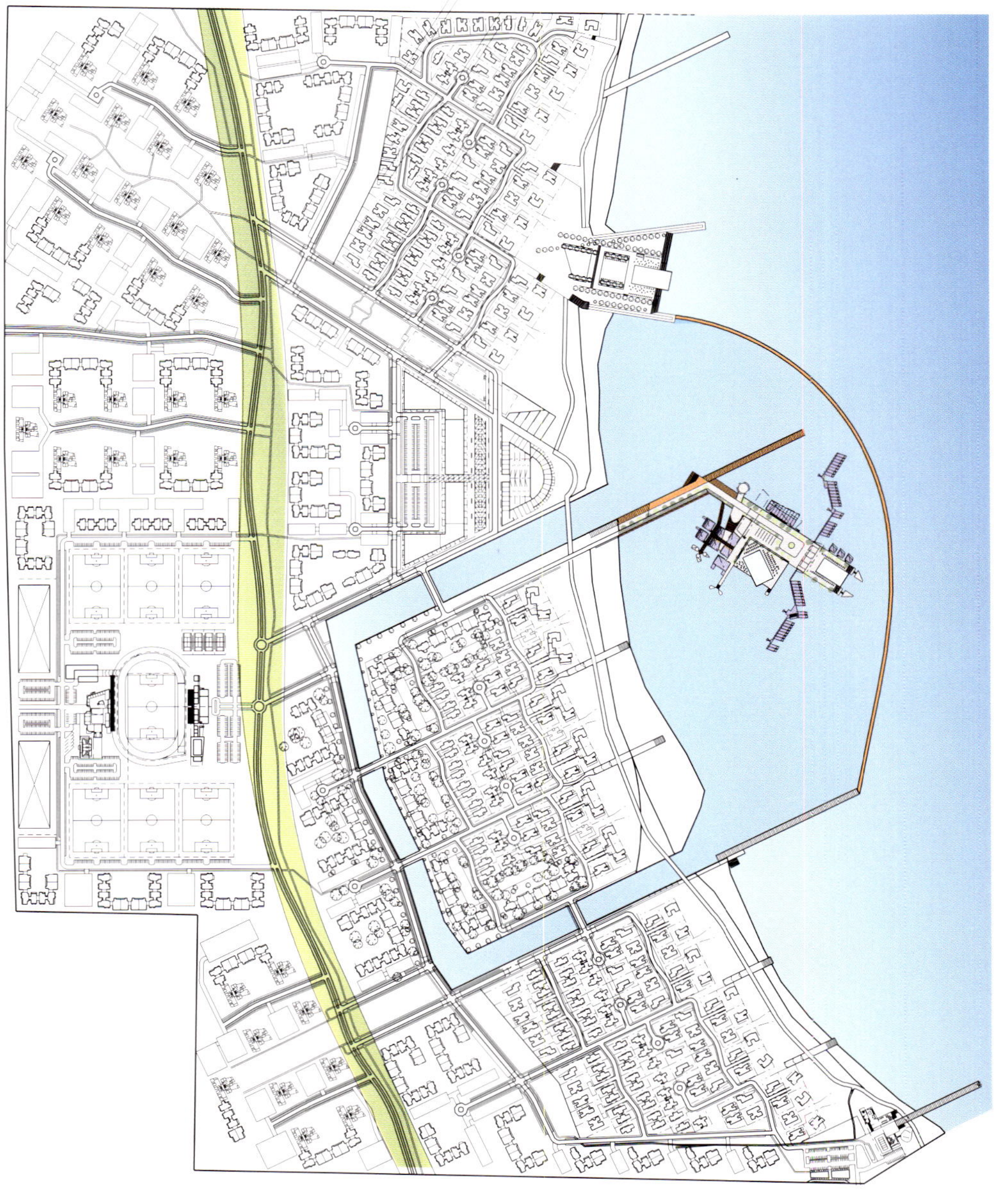

A rich variety of public open space is an integral part of the development. A public promenade runs the entire length of the site at the junction of land and beach, inviting people to observe the waterfront activity. Water's edge 'pocket parks' with public jetties provide places to sit or fish.

All residents and the surrounding community have access to water's edge vantage points, with opportunities for boating, rowing, punting, fishing and sailing an integral part of the landscape and open space system.

All east–west vistas and paths connect to a major (north–south) parkland road link and to the mixed-height tower clusters and the sports facility beyond.

Within the housing precincts so formed, a number of smaller secondary parklands offer houses and apartments both a garden aspect and a pedestrian connection to the centre.

The built-form control places the tallest towers furthest away from the beach (to avoid afternoon shadows) stepping down towards the four-level apartments and finally the two-storey beachfront houses.

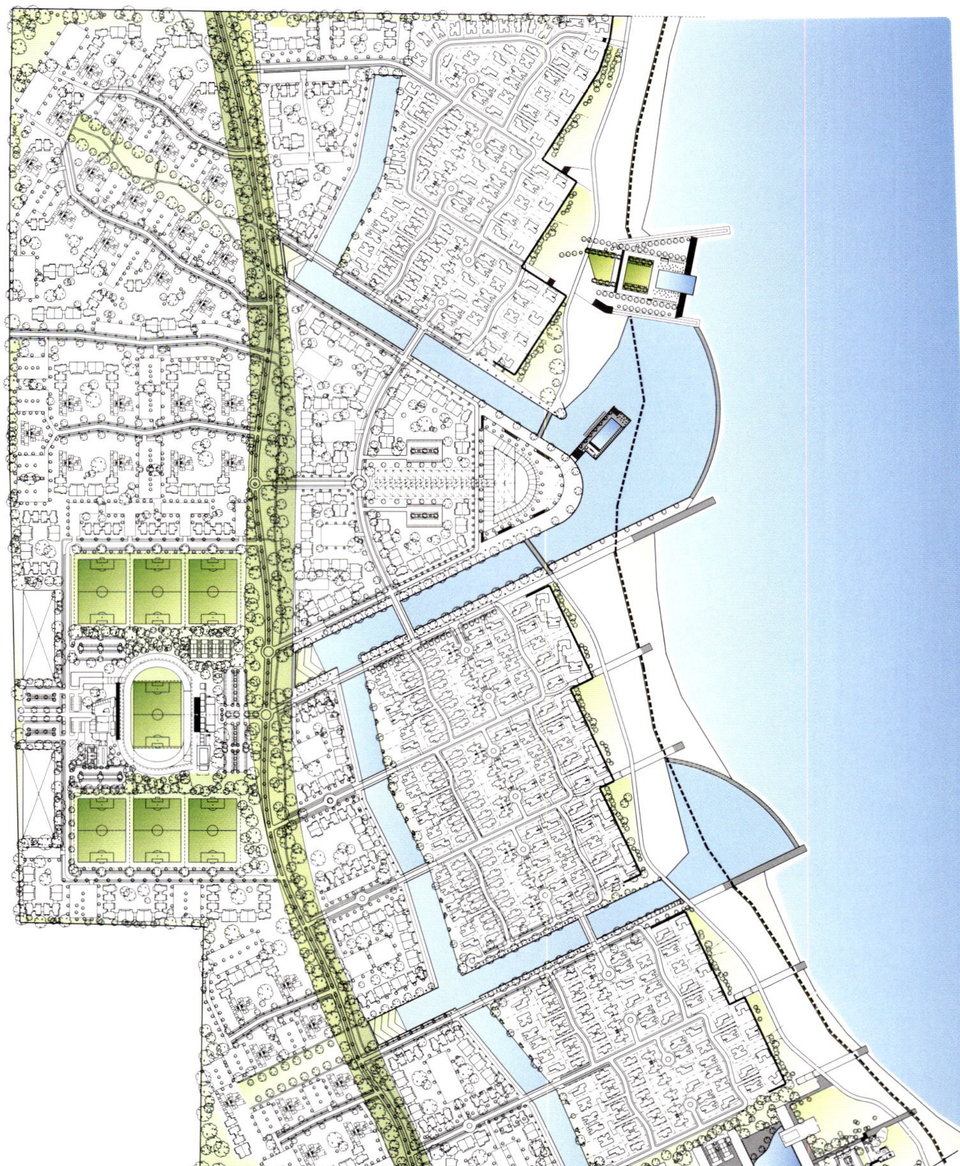

213

Sydney's first architect, the British convict Francis Greenway, was transported for minor embezzlement. He built quite beautiful churches, a lighthouse at the Sydney Heads and a Gothic/Tudor castellated set of stables for the Governor, Lachlan Macquarie, in 1816. In 1915 the NSW Government architect Seymour Wells built a Conservatorium of Music into the stables and filled in the open courtyard with an Arts and Crafts inspired Federation-style concert hall. Over the following 70 years a plethora of lesser buildings embalmed the (by now) historic stables.

Chris Johnson, the NSW State Government architect, initiated design studies with French conservation architect Phillipe Robert, to test the feasibility of rebuilding, essentially below ground, to conserve the concert hall. The brief was to rebuild facilities for a new Conservatorium of Music and Conservatorium High School.

Daryl Jackson Robin Dyke was subsequently appointed to further develop their preliminary ideas. The firm was joined by Kirkegaard Associates (a leading acoustic/architectural practice from Chicago) and by Howard Tanner and Associates, the consultant conservation architect.

Daryl Jackson and Robin Dyke were the principal designers, with Barry McGregor and Alex Kibble key coordinating design project architects.

CONSERVATORIUM OF MUSIC

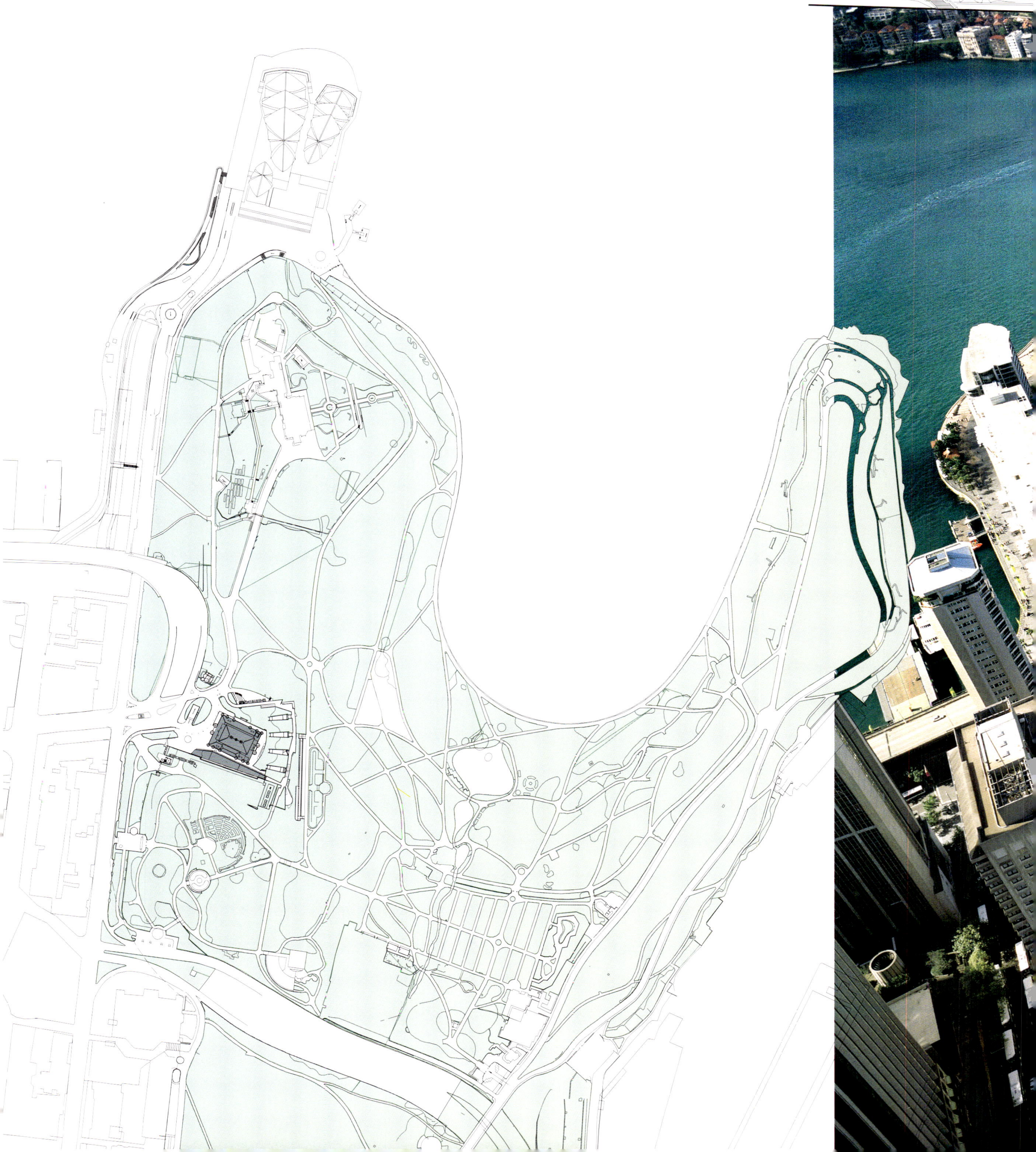

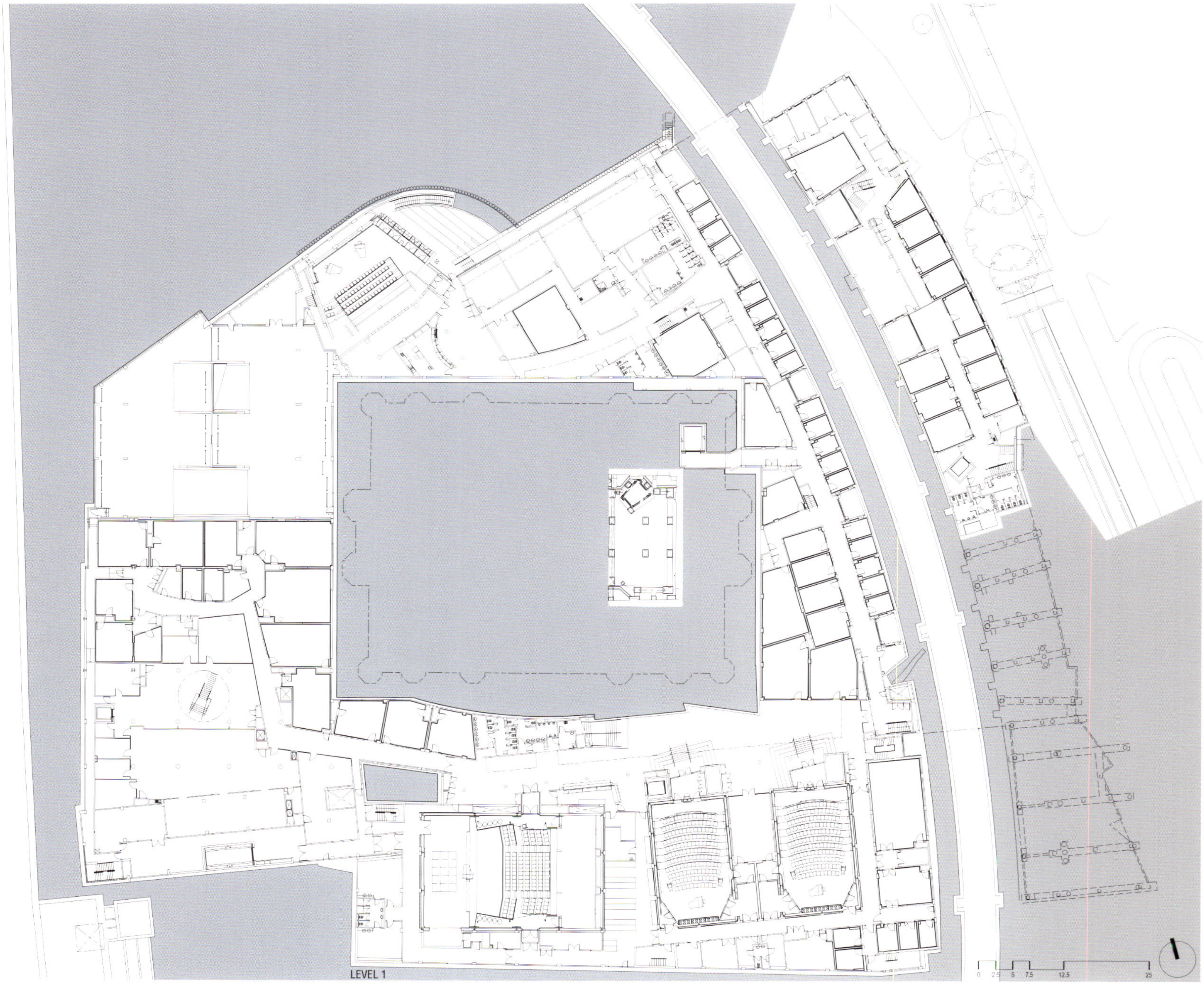

LEVEL 1

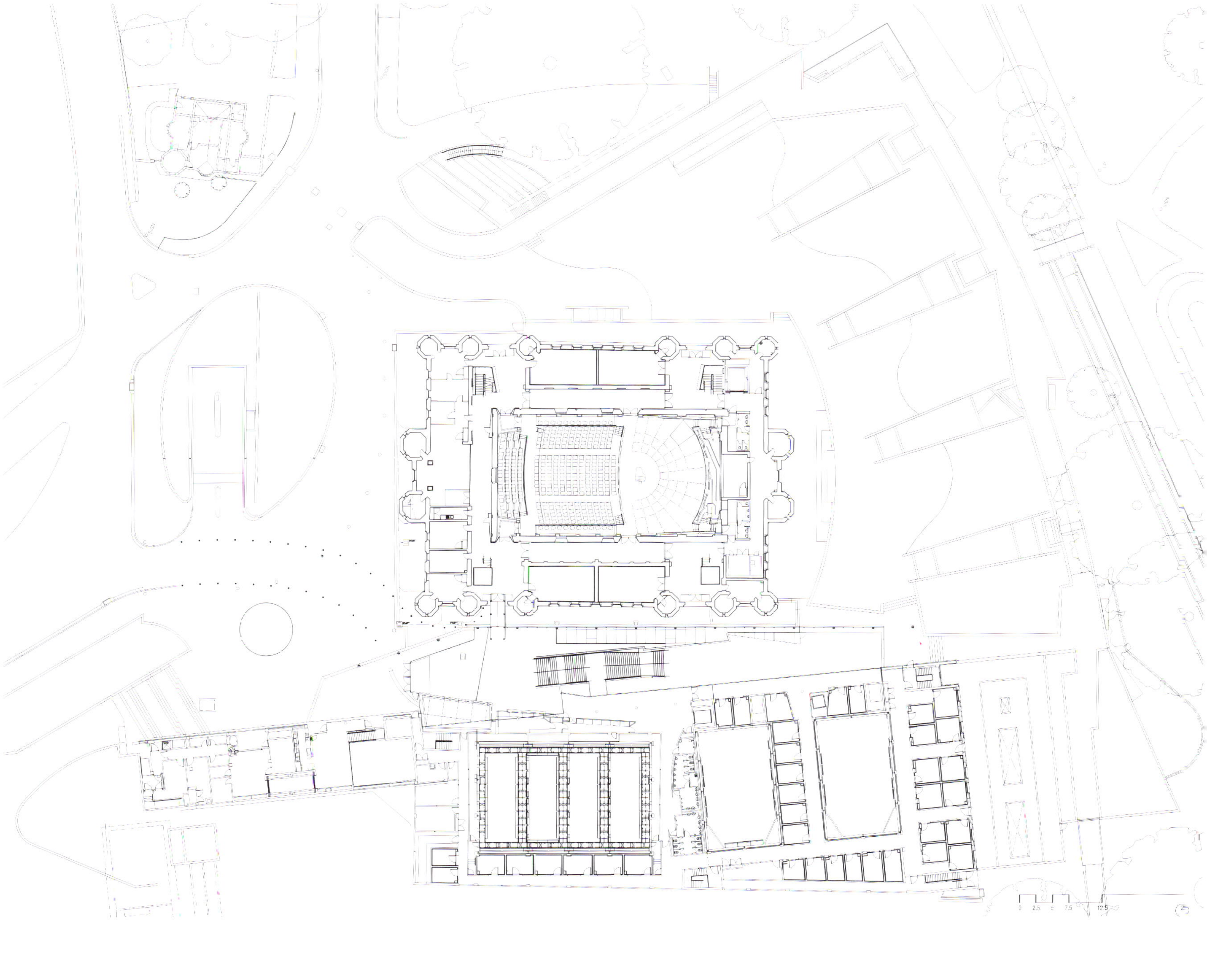

TANK

EXIT

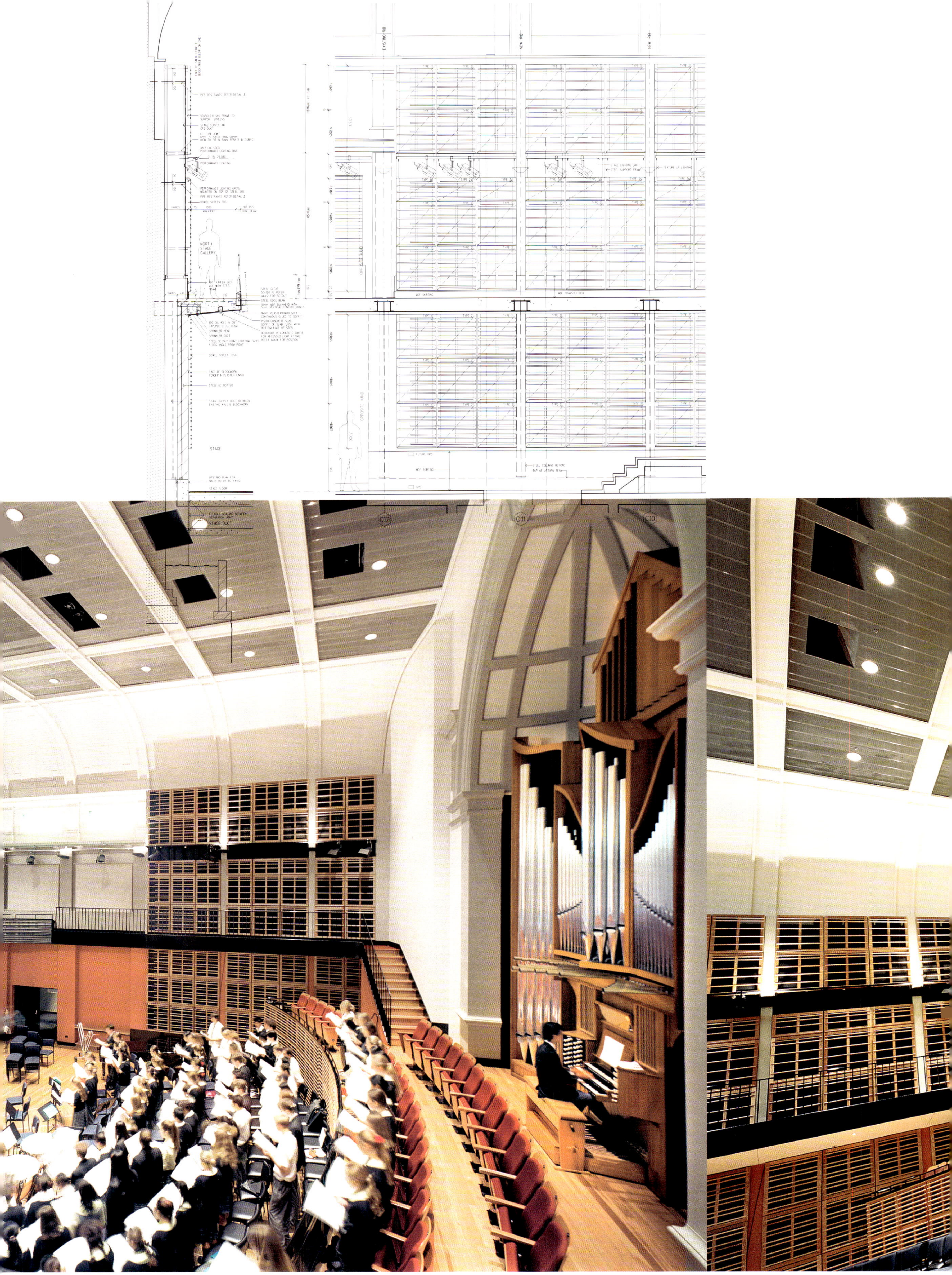

NORTH STAGE GALLERY
STAGE
STAGE DUCT
C12
C11
C10

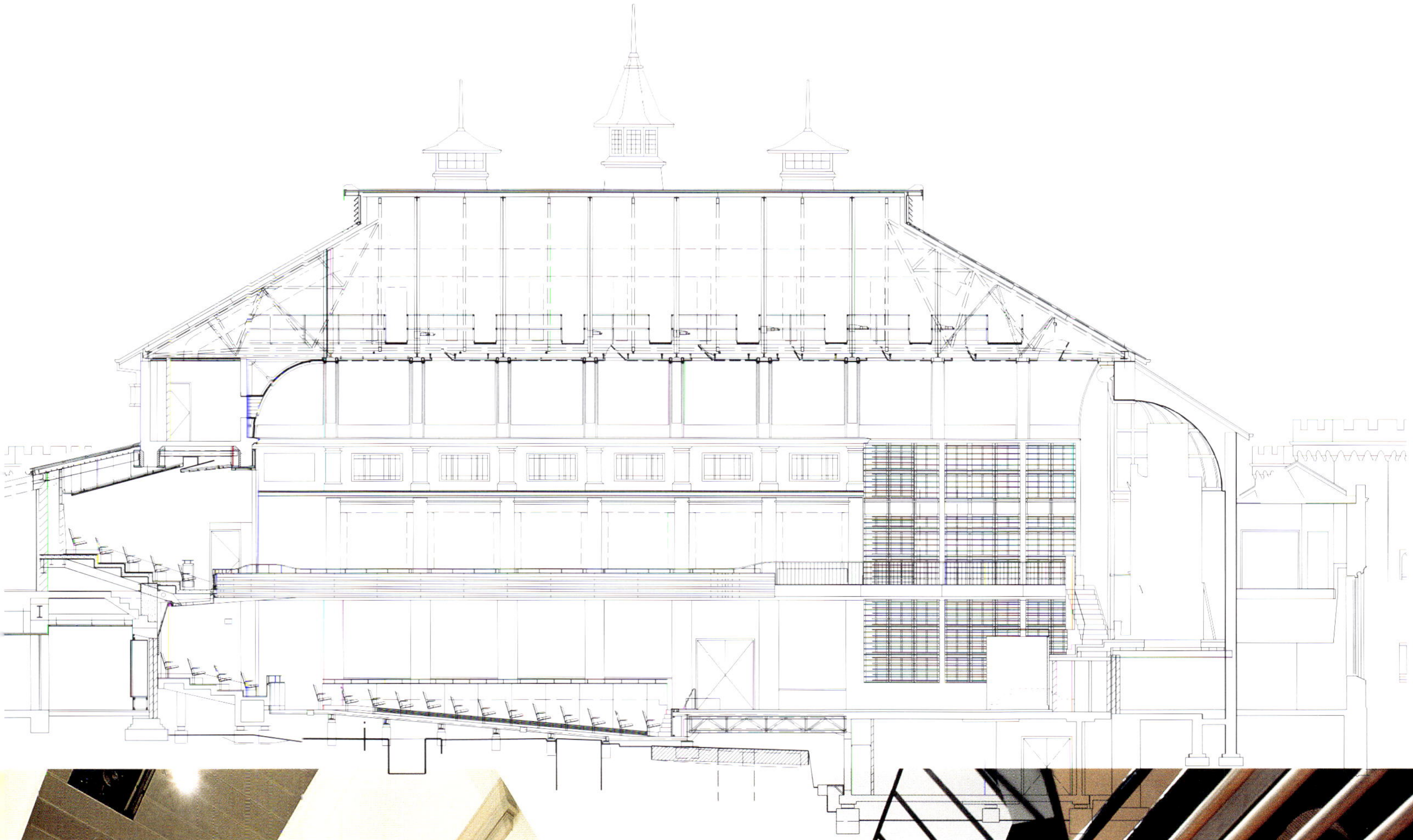

EXIT

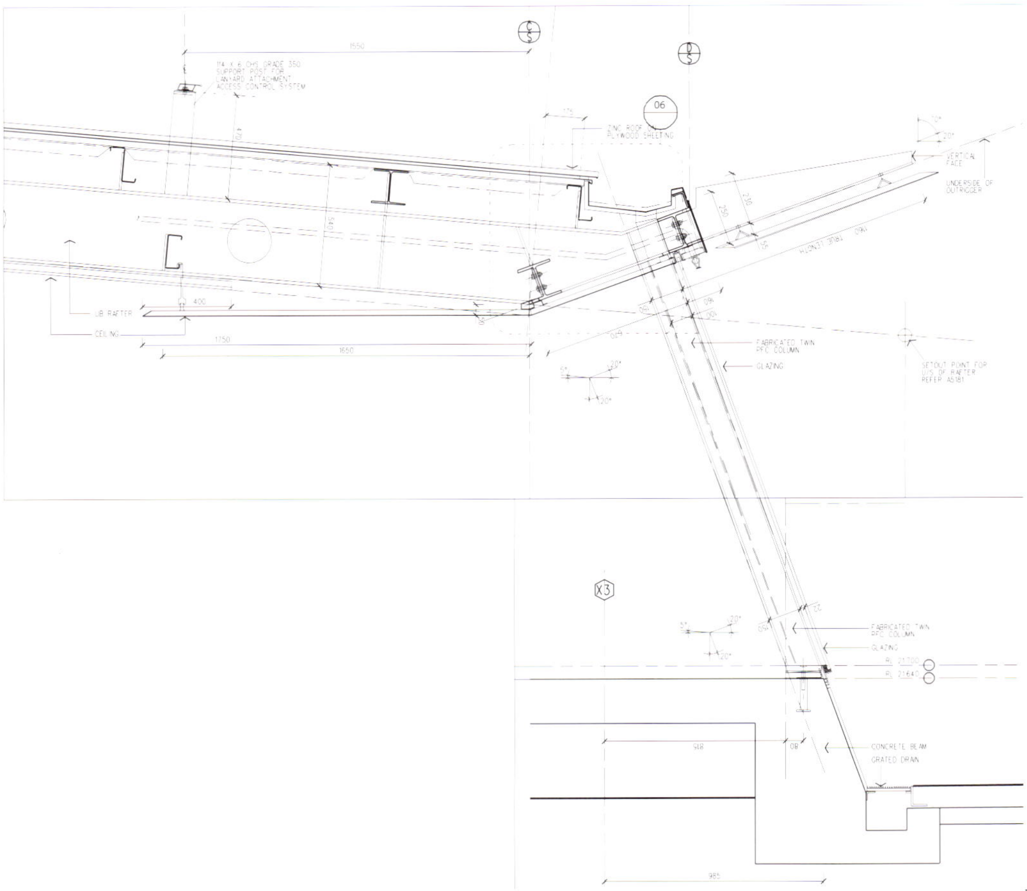

Cutting down into the Sydney sandstone beside the Greenway Stables, some three levels below Macquarie Street, created an archaeological and geological condition which added to the complexity of conservation, architectural, botanical and acoustic demands.

The historical and auditory elements were thoroughly researched and the renewed Concert Hall and new 270-seat music workshop, twin recital halls and some 130 practice rooms now sit beneath the landscaped parterres of a reconstructed section of the Botanic Gardens.

The expression of the new architecture challenges the existing with a light glass and zinc-clad steel structure sleeve cut into and spanning the major drama of the descending entrance stair. The idea of progression and penetration of the earth's crust is enhanced by the interior galleria and the large three-tier central stair. The accelerated perspective of the major entrance hall foyer evidences these interests and interpretations. It focuses the eye towards the Botanical Gardens beyond, at the same time enabling patrons to recognise Greenway's original work, sitting, as it always has, on a column of Sydney sandstone.

Level 3

Mukim Tebrau is a design study for a new mixed-use Malaysian town centre, located on virgin ground adjacent to the border with Singapore.

A cylindrical tower some 100 floors high creates a key symbolic element for a globally oriented, communications-driven business city.

A large, open urban court is deployed to anchor the tower to the ground plane and to house an array of associated conference areas, hotels and theatres.

Set upon the highest section of the site, the centre is embraced by the curve of the main thoroughfare: it is a central point where commerce and government come together.

Other elements of the new town include retail/leisure and sports/recreation facilities, which are distributed throughout a number of residential precincts. A mosque, tropical gardens, a town park and a series of smaller outdoor squares complement the housing layout design, providing a range of variously sized outdoor urban spaces, so often missing in emerging Southeast Asian cities.

A long diagonal broadway cuts through the grid to bring the forms together and distinguish the composition. A highly memorable new form of climatically informed urbanism is the result.

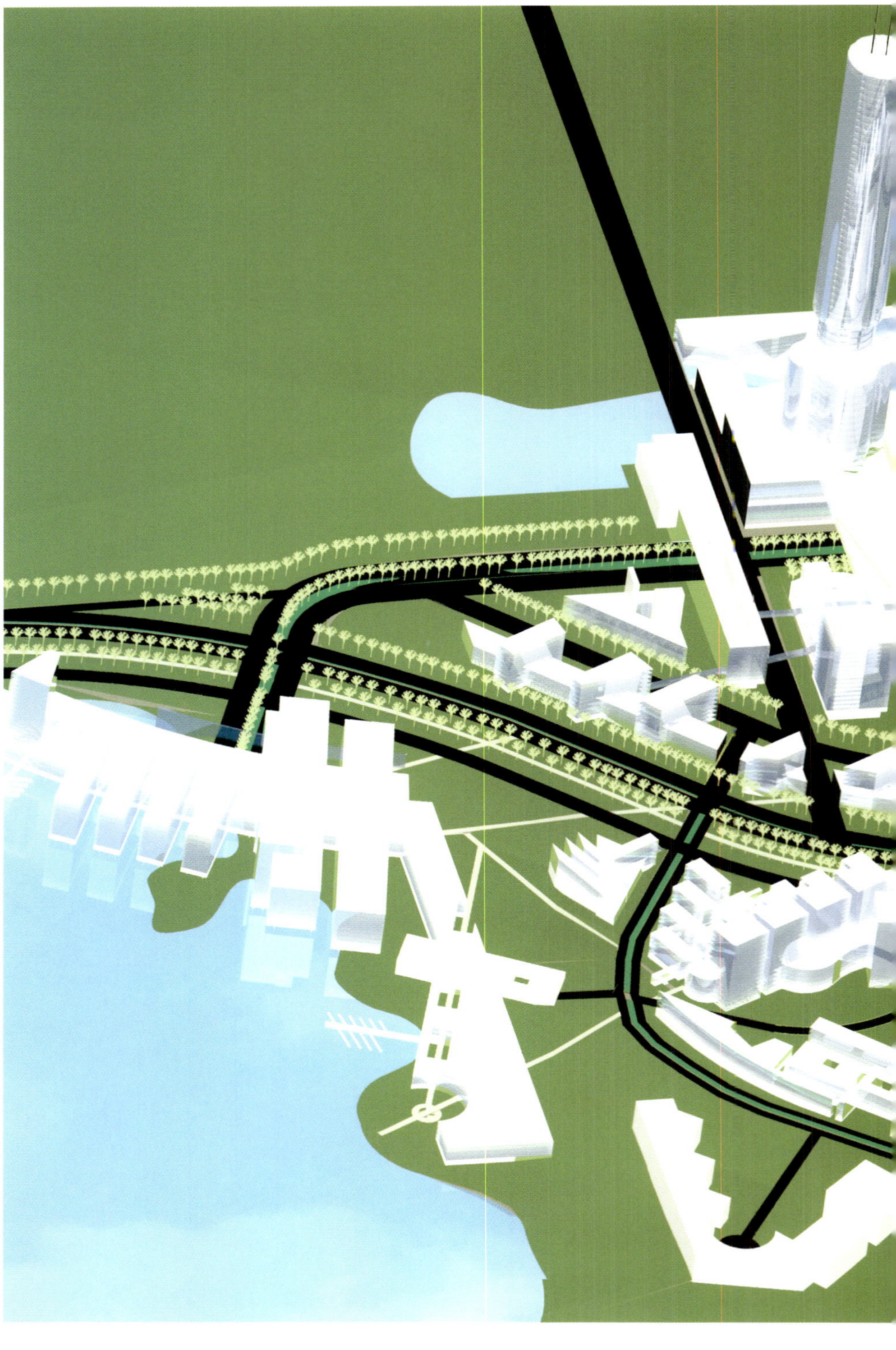

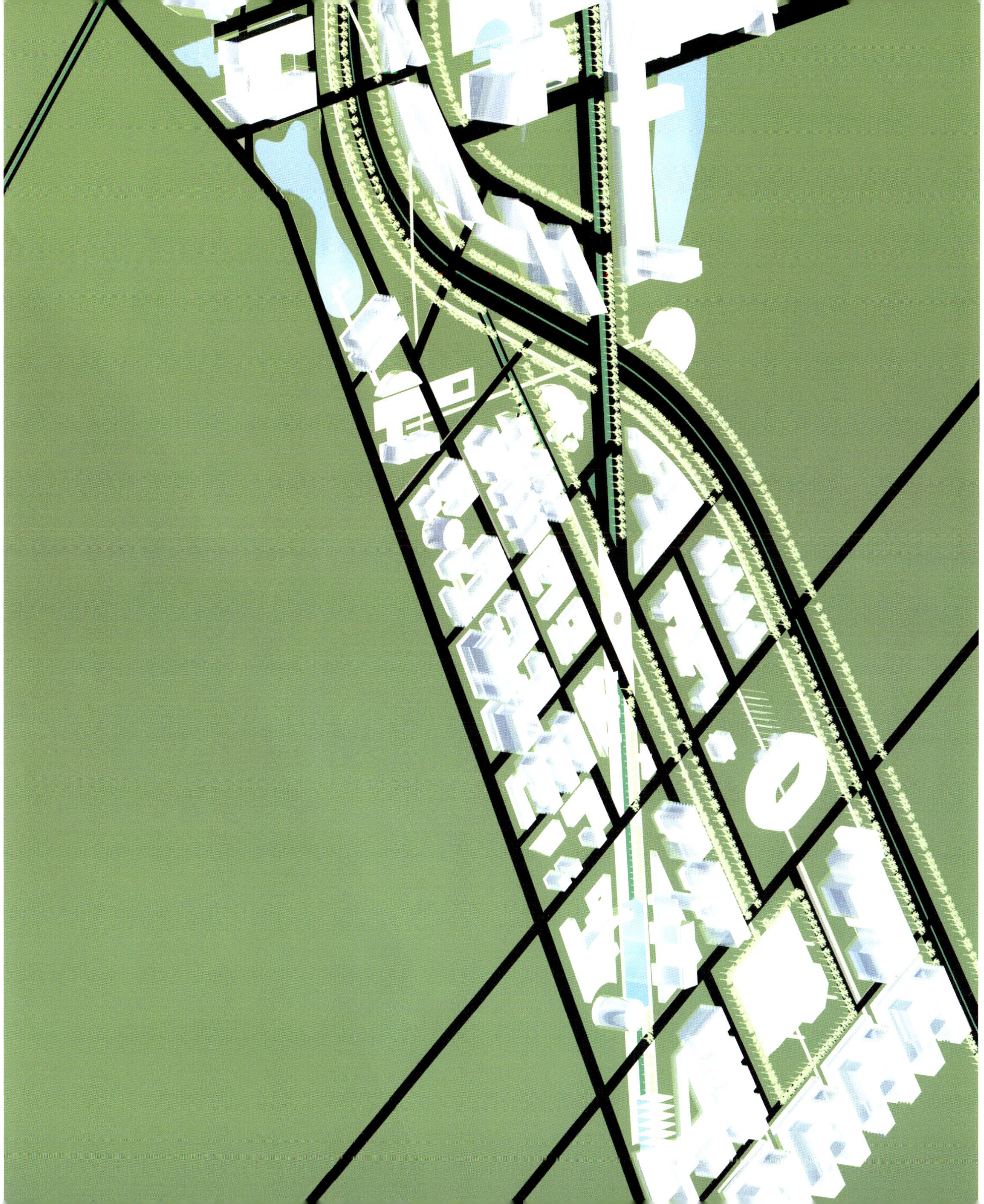

MUKIM TEBRAU

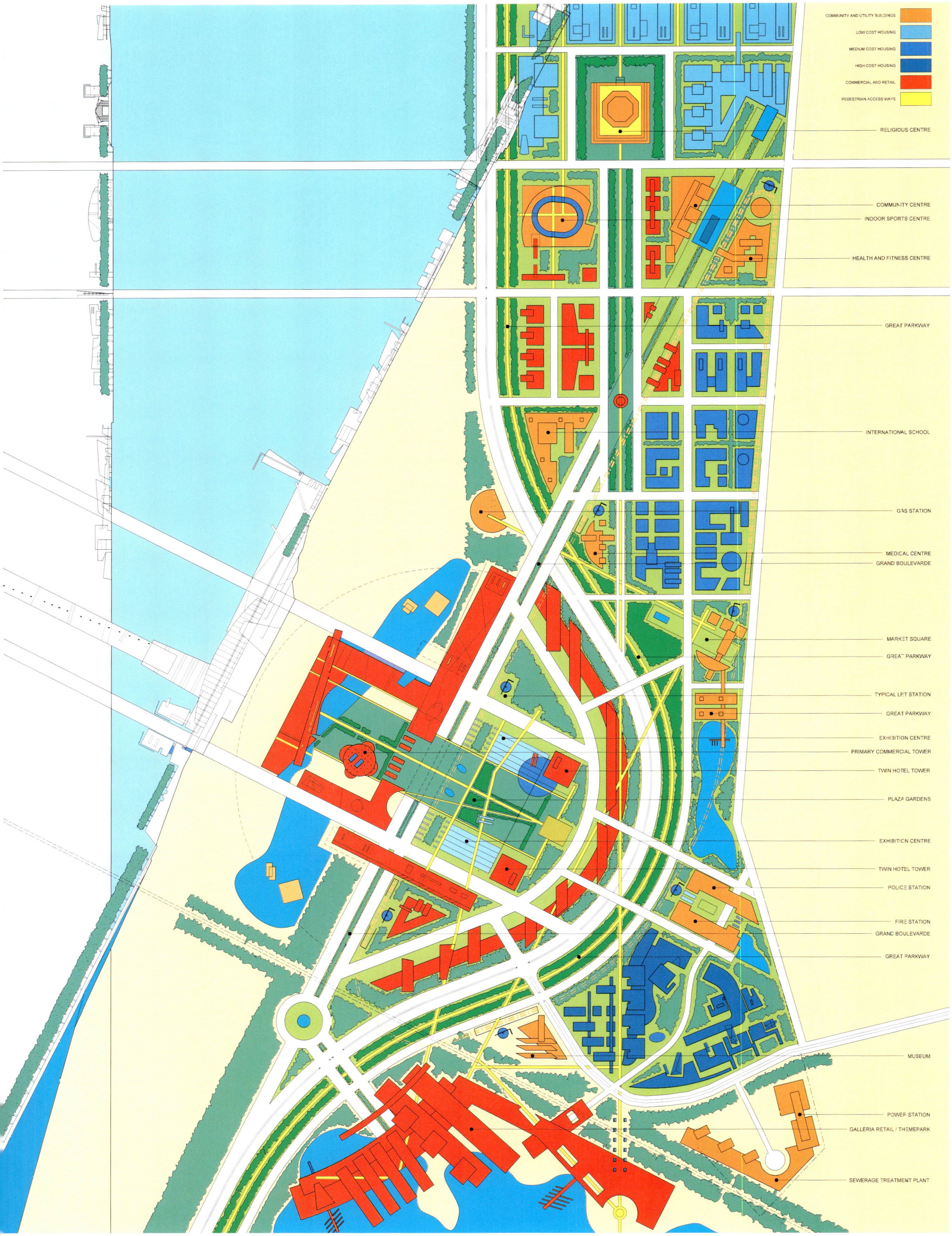
COMMUNITY AND UTILITY BUILDINGS
LOW COST HOUSING
MEDIUM COST HOUSING
HIGH COST HOUSING
COMMERCIAL AND RETAIL
PEDESTRIAN ACCESS WAYS
RELIGIOUS CENTRE
COMMUNITY CENTRE
INDOOR SPORTS CENTRE
HEALTH AND FITNESS CENTRE
GREAT PARKWAY
INTERNATIONAL SCHOOL
GAS STATION
MEDICAL CENTRE
GRAND BOULEVARDE
MARKET SQUARE
GREAT PARKWAY
TYPICAL LRT STATION
GREAT PARKWAY
EXHIBITION CENTRE
PRIMARY COMMERCIAL TOWER
TWIN HOTEL TOWER
PLAZA GARDENS
EXHIBITION CENTRE
TWIN HOTEL TOWER
POLICE STATION
FIRE STATION
GRAND BOULEVARDE
GREAT PARKWAY
MUSEUM
POWER STATION
GALLERIA RETAIL / THEMEPARK
SEWERAGE TREATMENT PLANT

In cities everywhere, worn out areas are being perceived anew; in their renewal, figure and ground, object and subject, similar and mixed uses, all play a role in establishing a newfound syntax.

The aim of this project is to create a network of new connections between separated city elements each side of divisive rail tracks. The mechanism involves an urban intervention to bridge the rail tracks and create a new edge to Wellington Street. An under-loved strip of land is transformed with new enterprise and a renewing presence, around which other urban extensions can occur – a green park forecourt, an elevated pedestrian bridge, a raised urban colonnade and inclined public plateau – all civic ingredients that convey significance. The agenda is the accommodation of 14,000 fans, eager to participate in events that include sport, concerts, public assembly and theatre.

Each edge of the plaza is framed with an elevated bar/restaurant strip building along Wellington Street. A matching sun tube shelter along the north edge closes down views into the rail yard/bus laneway beyond to create an enclosed, distinguished civic plaza. The tree-lined green bridge crossing the tracks makes an inclined entry into the composition; a ramp zigzag allows an easy gradient between street and rail overpass.

"…a green park forecourt, an elevated pedestrian bridge, a raised urban colonnade and inclined plateau – all civic ingredients that convey significance".

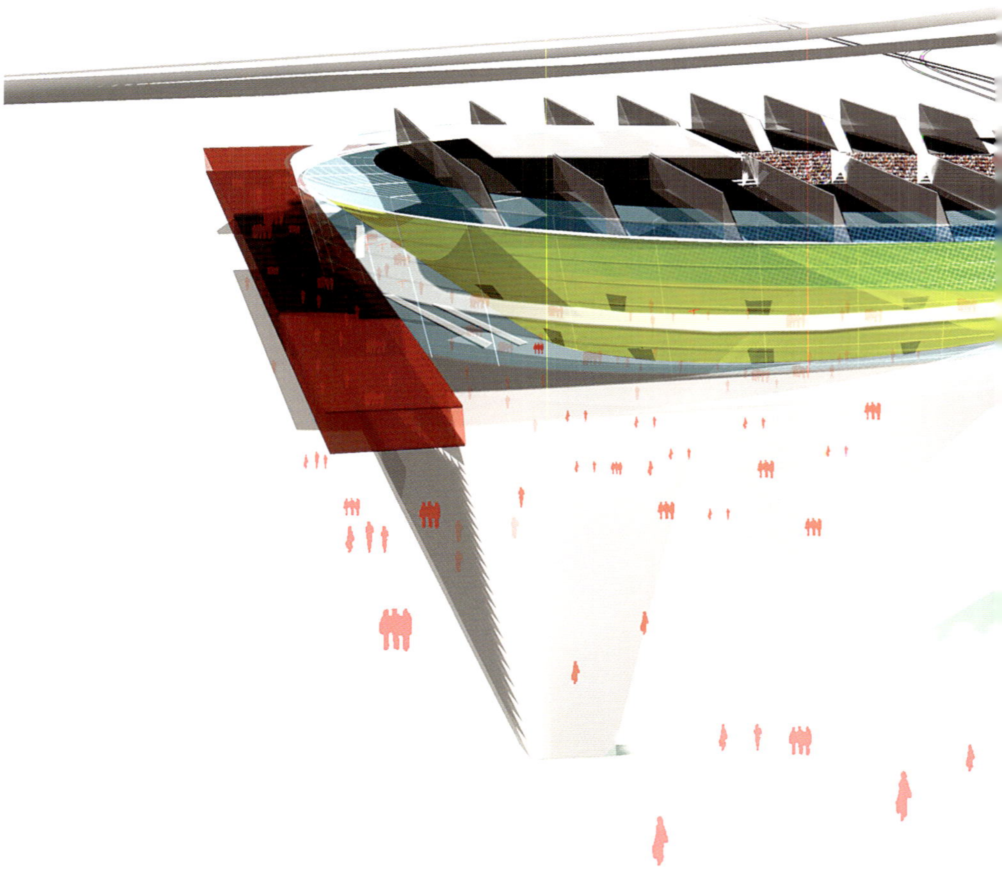

PERTH ARENA

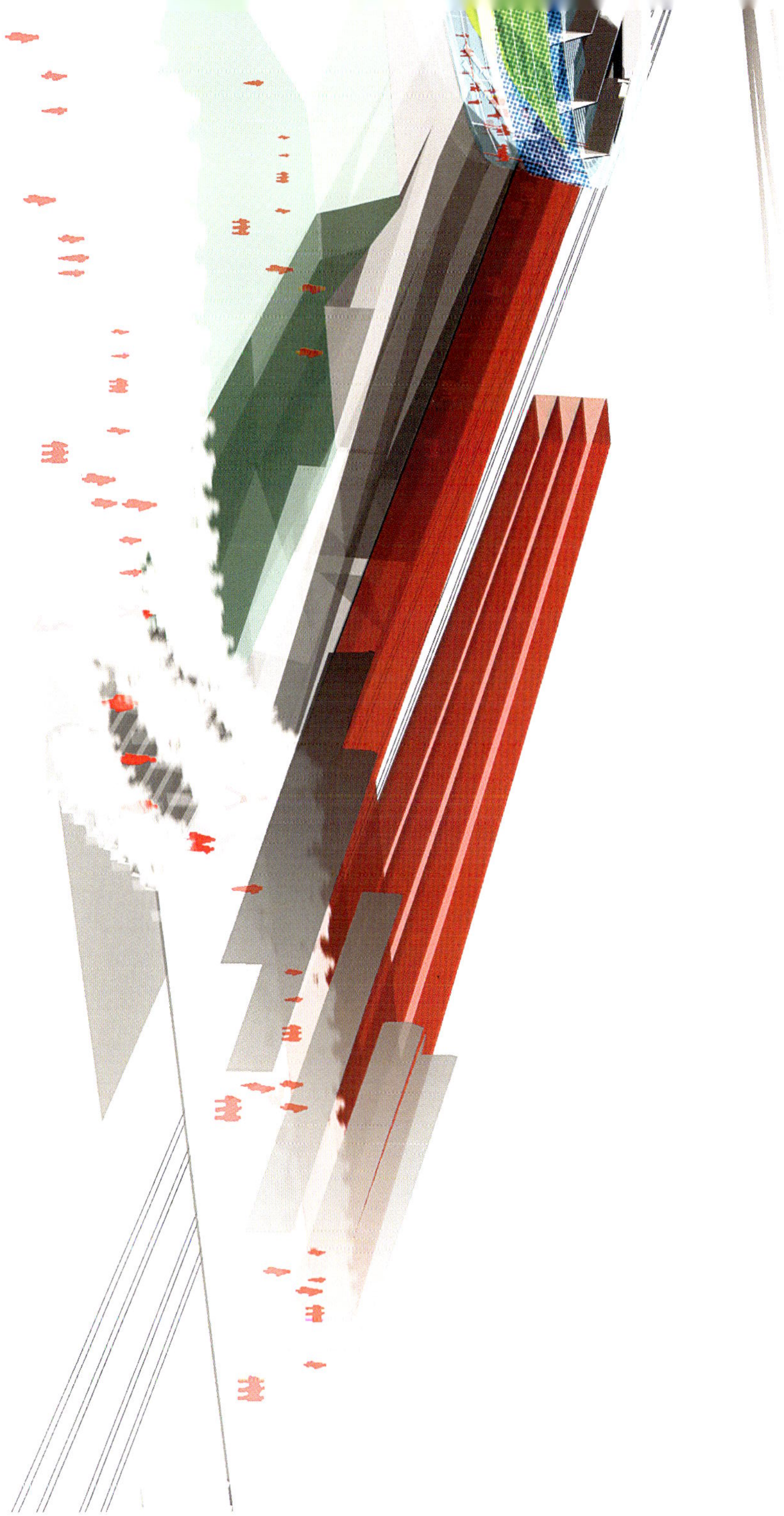

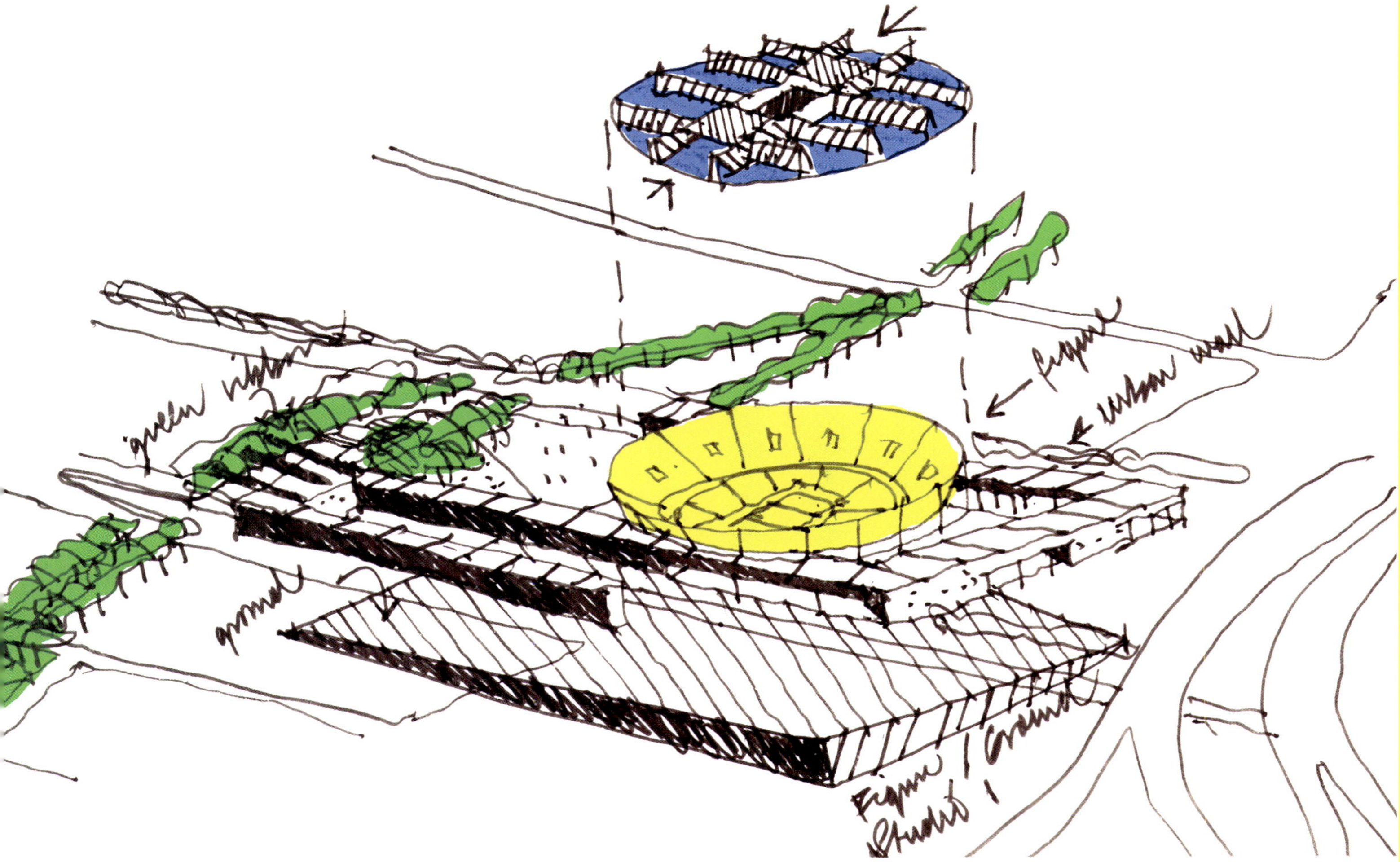
green ribbon
ground
figure
urban wall
Figure / Ground
Studio 1

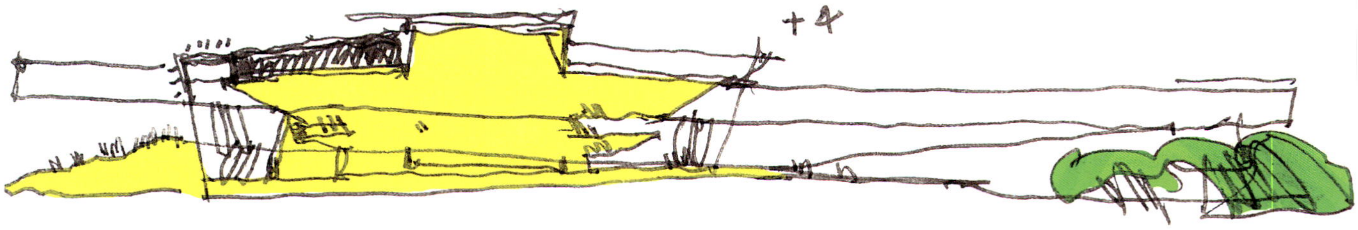
+4

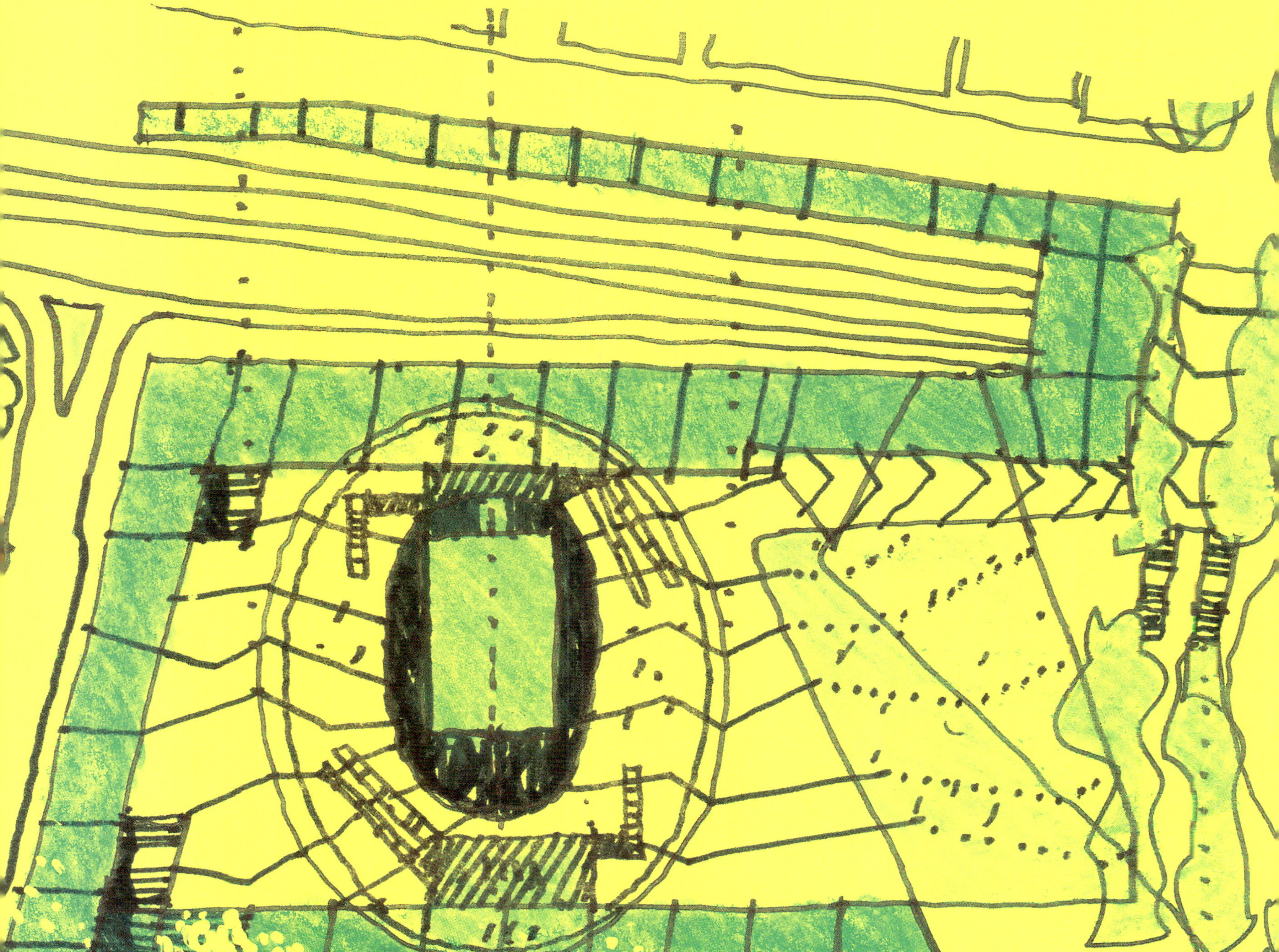

As a set is to a play, the Stadium bowl is a platform for its highly technical interior; connecting previously separated elements, the audiences and performers now encounter each other.

Externally, the skin is transparent, allowing the dramatic upturned conical form of the bowl, the drama of the curving ends, and the tapered walls that move out to meet the keyed-in structure of tensioned steel columns. To establish a further lightness to the image the glass skin is frameless, utilising cables and spider connectors to create a diaphanous skin.

At night the scene changes with theatrical up lighting; by day, the edges of the roof are glazed to allow filtered sunlight to enter and highlight the forms from above.

The final gesture is the roof plane, tautly covering the top of the bowl with a diaphragm-like structural skin. Above the roof a grid of beams spans the roof to provide a corrugated lid. The trusses are zinc-clad on their south face; on the north face, photovoltaic solar panels add energy to the grid.

Rainwater is collected, filtered and stored in a tank below the plaza. Aerated by a water basin, the idea is to use water/ice as a heat sink coolant.

The roof of the bowl provides a specific urban quality with its city-like metallic form; it is a highly machined, computer-controlled piece of industrial design. Sitting above the roof trusses, the roof opens north and south from the centre point; a shade screen underlay moves independently across the opening to reduce glare or heat.

The idea is founded upon a proposition of form and counter form – a light, visually open exterior and a heavy interior enclosure offer a material contrast. The transparent glass skin embraces the city beyond, while an acoustically tuned and isolated body, the bowl, sustains the experience within.

In architectural function and style, content and symbol progress in an interpretative state of intention and invention, transformation, imagination and idea-making.

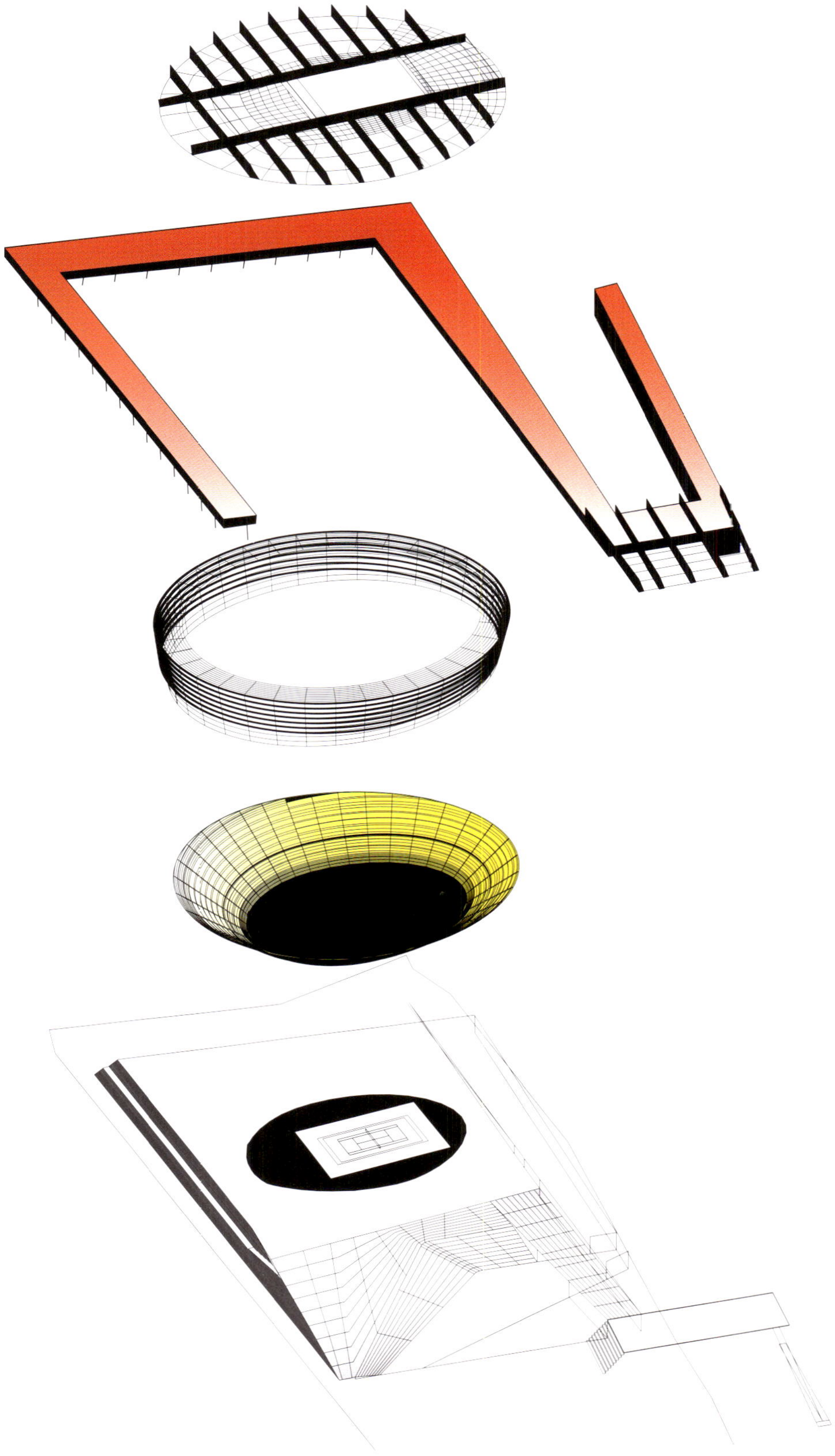

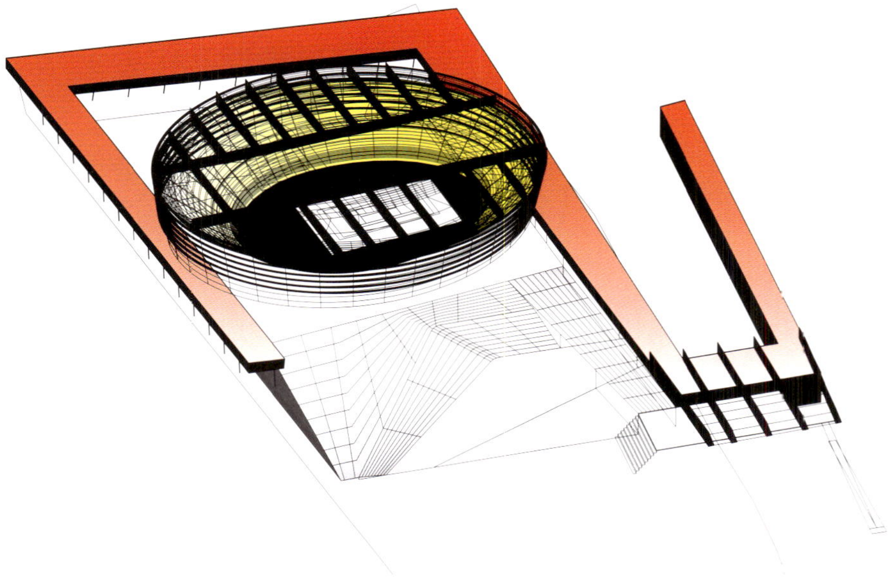

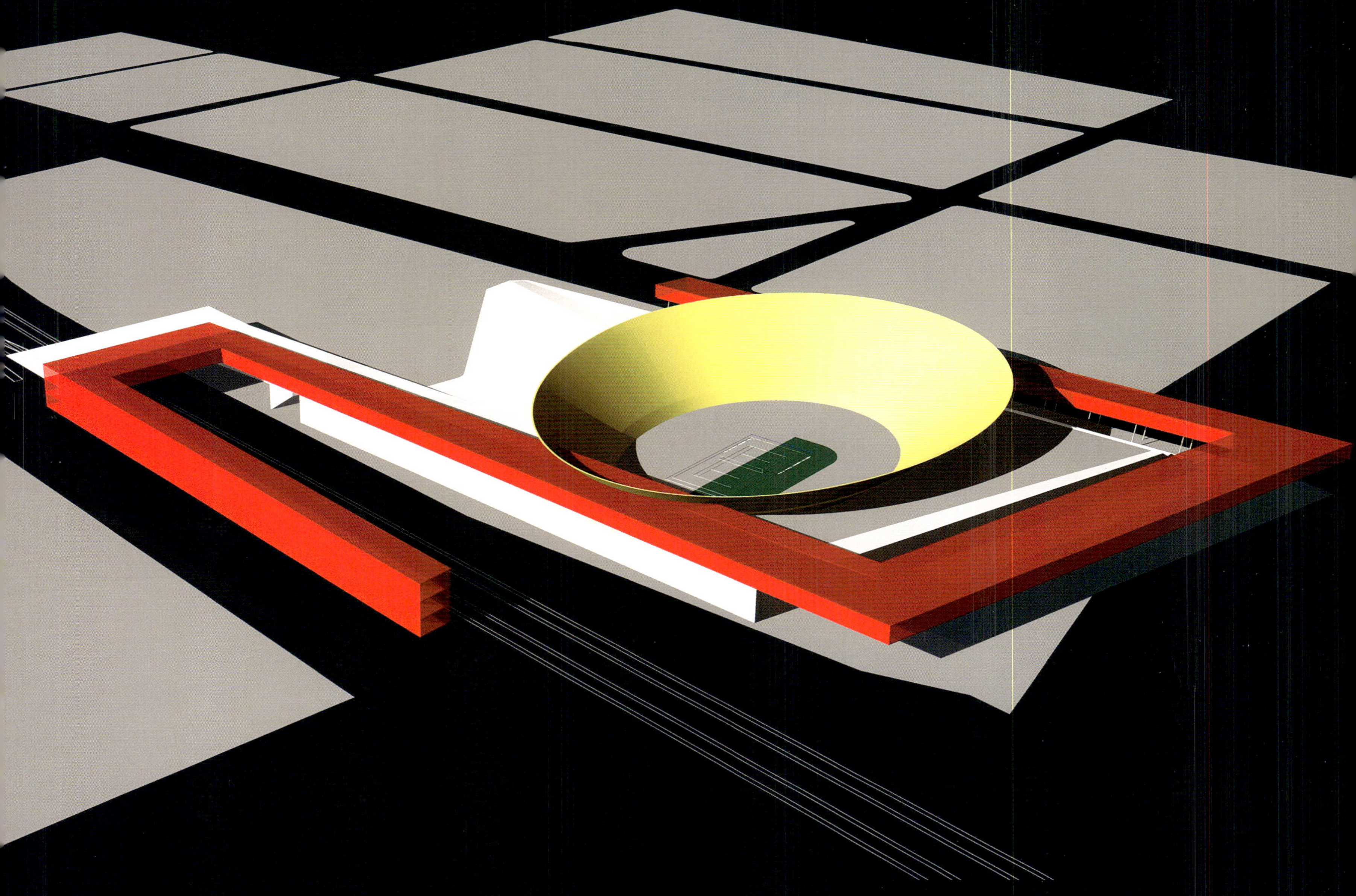

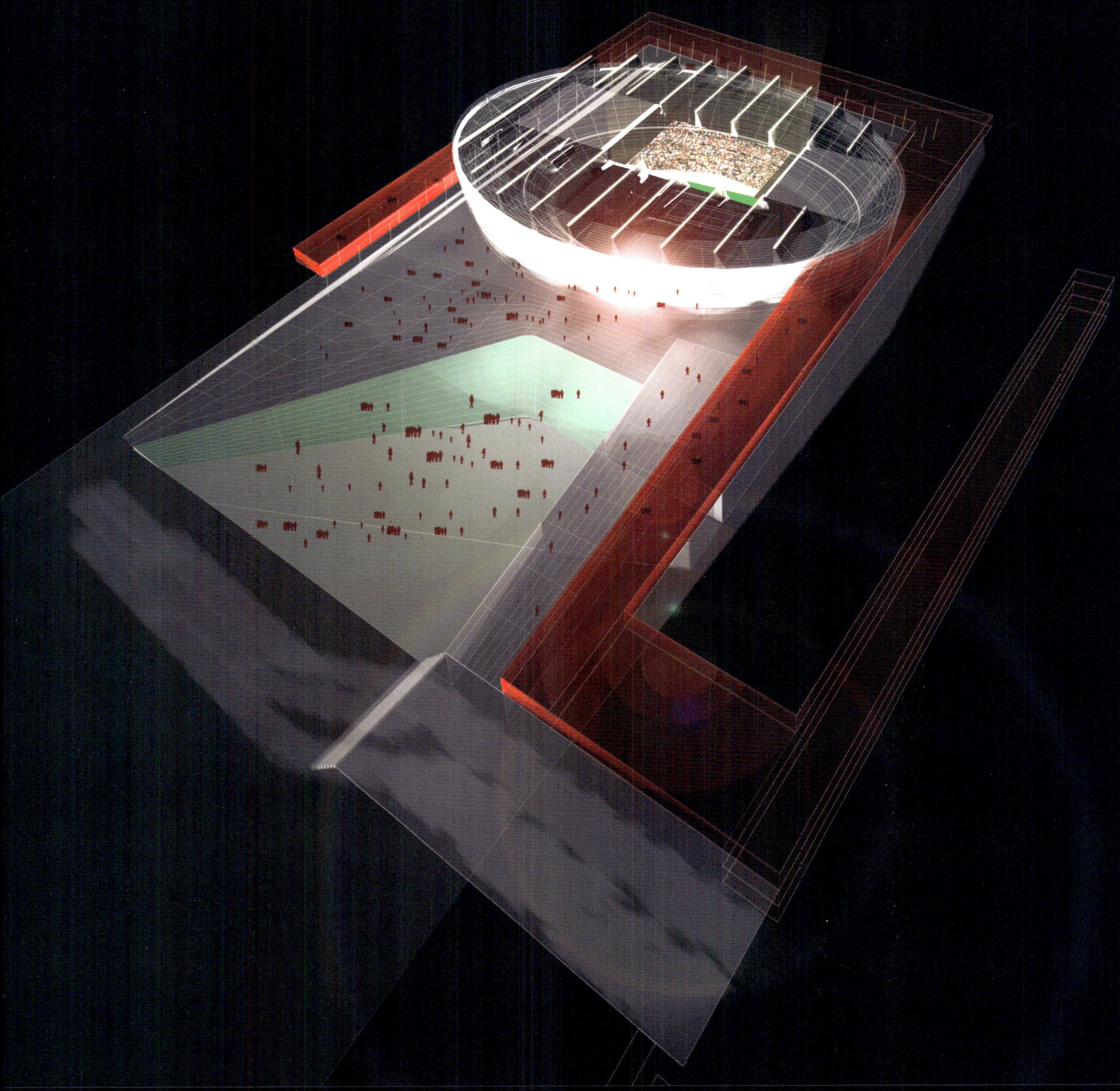

Daryl Jackson AO

B.Arch. (Melb), Dip.Arch. (RMIT)

LFRAIA, Hon FAIA, ARIBA

Honorary Doctorate, University of Ballarat

Honorary Fellowship, AIA (1990)

Conferred upon Daryl Jackson in 1990, in recognition of his esteemed character and distinguished world-class achievements in the field of architecture.

RAIA Gold Medal (1987)

Royal Australian Institute of Architects' highest award to an architect who has made a significant contribution to the development of architecture in Australia.

Daryl Jackson was born in Clunes, Victoria in 1937. He graduated from the Royal Melbourne Institute of Technology and the University of Melbourne in 1958.

Jackson commenced an architectural practice (with Evan Walker) in 1965, having spent four years working in the UK and the USA between 1960–64.

Jackson has taught architecture part-time at RMIT, has written a regular column on housing for *The Age* newspaper (1966–1969), has been principal lecturer at RAIA conventions and was Visiting Professor of Architecture (Design) at the University of New South Wales in 1982.

Currently Daryl Jackson is the Principal Director of Jackson Architecture and its constituent practices. In this capacity he provides the lead in establishing the design philosophy and management principles for the professional development of the practice.

The practice has undertaken a wide range of projects from housing, education and institutional projects to commercial developments and larger scale urban planning and design, including master planning.

Under his leadership, the Australian-based practice operates through offices in Brisbane, Canberra, Melbourne and Sydney, producing architecture of high quality and consistency.

BIOGRAPHY

Daryl Jackson's offices have acquired a national reputation for architecture of excellence, as demonstrated by their consistent receipt of distinguished national and state architecture awards. Subjects of these awards have included such projects as the Great Southern Stand at the Melbourne Cricket Ground; 120 Collins Street, Melbourne; the Walter and Eliza Hall Institute in Melbourne; the Royal Melbourne Hospital redevelopment; the Australian Film, Television and Radio School and Conservatorium of Music in Sydney; the CSIRO Discovery Centre in Canberra, and the Australian Embassy in Riyadh, Saudi Arabia.

The extensive range of educational design and briefing experience includes master planning for the University of the Northern Territory, Griffith and Bond universities in Queensland, and Swinburne and Melbourne universities in Victoria. In addition, a considerable array of sports architecture is now completed at the Australian Institute of Sport in the Australian Capital Territory and at the Melbourne Cricket Ground. The new stadia for Woolloongabba in Brisbane and Subiaco in Perth are further testimony to the diversity of the practice.

For the past 35 years, Daryl Jackson has been involved in a number of diverse, large-scale architectural planning and urban design projects in Australia, the United Kingdom, China and the Middle East. A separate practice, Daryl Jackson International, has offices in London, and Berlin to undertake work in the UK and Eastern Europe.

Daryl Jackson's built works, together with his considerable teaching, writing and lecturing have had a significant influence on the course of Australian architectural development. He is an Associate Professor of the University of Melbourne and an Associate Professor of Deakin University. He is a Life Fellow member of the RAIA and an RAIA Gold Medallist.

In 1990, public recognition of the quality of his services to architecture resulted in the conferring of an Order of Australia and an Honorary Fellowship of the American Institute of Architects.

With his extensive participation in various significant cultural organisations, including formerly held positions as Chairman of the Australian Film Institute, Trustee of the National Gallery of Victoria, Member of the Victorian Council of the Arts, President of Wesley College and Vice President of the Melbourne Cricket Club, Jackson continues to contribute to a heterogeneous notion of Australian culture.

David Trott
Dip.Arch. (RMIT)

Daryl Jackson
Brisbane

Directors
Daryl Jackson
David Trott

Associate Director
Gary Carter

Associate
Mark Craig

Robin Dyke
B.Arch. (Hons) (UTS)
Associate RAIA

Daryl Jackson Robin Dyke
Sydney

Directors
Robin Dyke
Daryl Jackson

Associates
Andrew Hipwell
Alex Kibble
Daniel Beekwilder

Alastair Swayn
Dip.Arch., Dip.CABD

Daryl Jackson Alastair Swayn
Canberra

Directors
Alastair Swayn
Daryl Jackson

Associates
James Andrews
Melinda Dodson

FIRM PROFILE

Melbourne
Daryl Jackson Pty Ltd
Daryl Jackson Interiors Pty Ltd

Sydney
Daryl Jackson Robin Dyke Pty Ltd

Brisbane
Daryl Jackson Pty Ltd

Canberra
Daryl Jackson Alastair Swayn Pty Ltd

Perth
Daryl Jackson and Peter Hunt

Shenyang
Daryl Jackson Pty Ltd

Shanghai
Daryl Jackson Pty Ltd

Hanoi
Daryl Jackson Pty Ltd

London
Daryl Jackson International
with John Lyall Architects

Berlin
Daryl Jackson International

Jackson Architecture is an interdisciplinary design practice of professional architects, urban planners and interior designers led by Daryl Jackson, one of Australia's most influential contemporary architects.

Established in 1964, Jackson Architecture now has significant architectural practices in each eastern seaboard capital city, as well as in Perth with Peter Hunt, and in London with John Lyall. Each practice is a substantial organisation in its own right, committed to regional resources and delivery. Project offices exist in Hanoi, Berlin, Shanghai and Shenyang.

The quality of Jackson Architecture's work is reflected in the significant number of awards received from the Royal Australian Institute of Architects and from organisations such as the Master Builders' Association and the Property Council of Australia. Jackson Architecture is one of the most highly awarded architectural offices in Australia.

The practice has gained both a national and international reputation for high quality consultation based on an ability to synthesise the conflicting demands of creativity, community planning and sustainability, cost effectiveness and quality design.

This reputation is based on an ability to lead, explore, conciliate and resolve the critical issues of urban projects; only through comprehensive and interactive client and consultant dialogue can a project's objectives be refined and met. All work is undertaken by a director or a senior designer, with teams assembled to enable these leaders to remain with the project to completion, thus guiding the client through the complex path of briefing, planning, design and procurement. Architecture is seen as a visionary design medium with problem-solving of an array of differing architectural properties – philosophical and technical, caring and sensible, imaginative and operational – always being necessary

Design is a process of exploration and resolution. The working method is propositional; formal ideas are developed for discussion with clients and relevant authorities. Evaluation and testing are welcomed as fundamental parts of the process. Other ideas may also emerge before real synthesis can occur. This method of working ensures that a particular identity is established for each individual project.

As an international practice, Jackson Architecture understands the need to pursue local objectives in cultural, legal, technical, heritage and planning matters. Requisite specialist local talents and architects are engaged wherever a project is to be constructed, to ensure a smooth passage into the field. Frequently this involves estate management and feasibility; cost planning (capital and recurrent); and understanding environmental content and context. The practice has managed projects ranging in scale from refurbishments and redevelopment of existing buildings, to individual houses, multi-level apartments and major sporting stadiums. Specialist skills exist to generate research laboratories and hospitals, universities and pre-school centres, retail and commercial office buildings, luxury hotels and tourist resorts.

In parallel with such building typologies, are urban renewal and master-planning projects, including major town centre developments and community design.

The architects that comprise Jackson Architecture remain passionate about architecture and the attention to detail at all project stages to ensure a consistent and highly valued result.

YARRA EDGE
1999, Melbourne, Australia
Submission
Client: Mirvac
Office: Daryl Jackson Architects Pty Ltd (Melbourne)

GEORGES
1997, Melbourne, Australia
Client: Georges Melbourne Pty Ltd
Office: Daryl Jackson Architects Pty Ltd (Melbourne) & Daryl Jackson Interiors (Melbourne) in association with Conran Design Partnership
Photography: Trevor Mein

STADIUM IRELAND
2000, Ireland
Competition
Client: Sports Campus Ireland
Office: Daryl Jackson International Pty Ltd (London) and Daryl Jackson Architects Pty Ltd (Melbourne) in association with RKD Architects (Ireland)

CANNONS GYMNASIUM
1995, London, England
Client: Cannons
Office: Daryl Jackson International Pty Ltd (London)
Photography: Dennis Gilbert

PENANG BATU MAUNG
1997, Penang, Malaysia
Submission
Office: Daryl Jackson Architects Pty Ltd (Melbourne) in association with Razak Aziz Architects, Malaysia

WORKS AND CREDITS

COURAN COVE RESORT
1999, South Stradbroke Island, Australia
Client: Interpacific Resorts Australia Pty Ltd
Office: Daryl Jackson Architects Pty Ltd (Melbourne and Brisbane)
Photography: David Sandison

BRISBANE CRICKET GROUND
1999, Brisbane, Australia
Client: Brisbane Cricket Ground Trust
Office: Daryl Jackson Architects Pty Ltd (Brisbane)
Photography: Tim Griffiths

UNIVERSITY OF BALLARAT
2001, Ballarat, Australia
Client: University of Ballarat
Office: Daryl Jackson Architects Pty Ltd (Melbourne)
Photography: Dianna Snape

DOCKLANDS STADIUM
2000, Melbourne, Australia
Client: Docklands Authority
Office: Daryl Jackson Architects Pty Ltd (Melbourne) in association with Bligh Lobb Sports Architects Pty Ltd and HOK Sport
Photography: John Gollings

WESLEY PREPARATORY SCHOOL
1998, Melbourne, Australia
Client: Wesley College
Office: Daryl Jackson Architects Pty Ltd (Melbourne) & Daryl Jackson Interiors (Melbourne)
Photography: Tim Griffiths

CSIRO DISCOVERY CENTRE
2001, Canberra, Australia
Client: CSIRO
Office: Daryl Jackson Alistair Swayn Architects Pty Ltd (Canberra)
Photography: John Gollings

UNIVERSITY OF QUEENSLAND BIOSCIENCES
1999, Brisbane, Australia
Client: University of Queensland/CSIRO
Office: Daryl Jackson Architects Pty Ltd
(Brisbane)
Photography: Graham Meltzer

SINGAPORE LIBRARY
2000, Singapore
Competition
Client: National Library Board, Singapore
Office: Daryl Jackson Architects Pty Ltd
(Melbourne)

VICTORIAN COUNTY COURT
2000, Melbourne, Australia
Client: Department of Justice,
Victorian County Court
Office: Daryl Jackson Sinclair Knight
Mertz Lyons Pty Ltd
Photography: Trevor Mein

UNITED NATIONS INTERNATIONAL SCHOOL
2000, Hanoi, Vietnam
Client: United Nations International School
Office: Daryl Jackson Architects Pty Ltd
(Melbourne) in association with
VNCC Hanoi

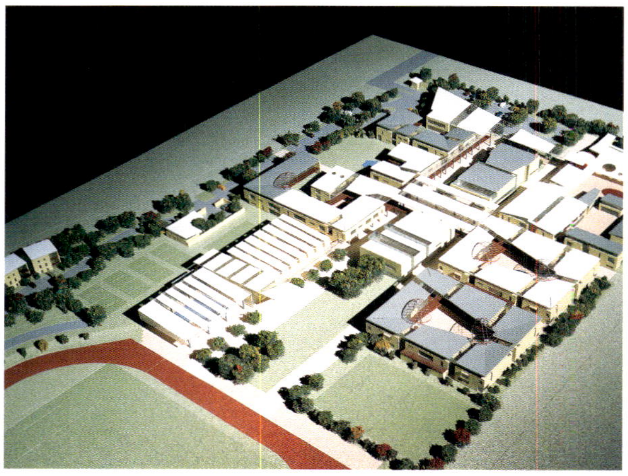

XAVIER PREPARATORY SCHOOL
2000, Melbourne, Australia
Submission
Client: Xavier College
Office: Daryl Jackson Architects Pty Ltd
(Melbourne)

SWINBURNE UNIVERSITY
GRADUATE SCHOOL OF MANAGEMENT
2000, Melbourne, Australia
Client: Swinburne University of Technology
Office: Daryl Jackson Architects Pty Ltd
(Melbourne)
Photography: John Gollings

BRINDABELLA BUSINESS PARK
2001 – ongoing, Canberra, Australia
Client: Capital Airport Group
Office: Daryl Jackson Alistair Swayn Architects Pty Ltd (Canberra)
Photography: John Gollings

AUSTRALIAN AMBASSADOR'S RESIDENCE
1997, Berlin, Germany
Client: Australian Federal Government, Department of Foreign Affairs
Office: Daryl Jackson Architects Pty Ltd (Melbourne and Berlin)

MUSEUM OF IMMIGRATION
1999, Melbourne, Australia
Client: Museum of Victoria
Office: Daryl Jackson Architects Pty Ltd (Melbourne), with Allom Lovell Conservation Architects Pty Ltd
Photography: Ben Wrigley

AOSHAN HOUSING RESORT
2002, Aoshan, China
Competition
Client: Etsong
Office: Daryl Jackson Architects Pty Ltd (Melbourne)

CONSERVATORIUM OF MUSIC
2001, Sydney, Australia
Client: NSW Department of Education and Training
Office: Daryl Jackson Robin Dyke Architects Pty Ltd (Sydney) and NSW Government Architects
Photography: John Gollings, Eric Sierins

MUKIM TEBRAU
1997, Mukim Tebrau, Malaysia
Submission
Office: Daryl Jackson Architects Pty Ltd (Melbourne) in association with Razak Aziz Architects, Malaysia

PERTH ARENA
2005, Perth, Australia
Short-listed competition entry
Client: Western Australian Government
Office: Daryl Jackson and Peter Hunt (Perth)

The practice that began as Daryl Jackson Evan Walker in 1964 now exists as five offices throughout Australia, with project offices in Hanoi, China, London and Berlin. During the period 1965–69, Evan Walker conducted a separate practice in Toronto, Canada. He returned to Melbourne to work with Daryl Jackson, and did so until he entered the Victorian State Parliament in 1979. The partnership was disbanded and Daryl Jackson Pty Ltd was established. Under the leadership of Daryl Jackson, projects are undertaken in Asia and the Pacific, as well as in Europe and the Middle East.

For their continued commitment to the standard of excellence achieved in this practice, special acknowledgement is given to the skills of the current directors, associates and all staff members.

Principal Daryl Jackson

All practices work within the framework of JACKSON ARCHITECTURE in the following cities:

Melbourne

Daryl Jackson Pty Ltd
Directors: Daryl Jackson, Bill Ryan, Peter Cole, Timothy Jackson
Associates: Lincoln Barker, Paul Katz, Geraldine Maher
Daryl Jackson Interiors Pty Ltd
Directors: Geraldine Maher, Jane Mackay, Olivia Jackson

ACKNOWLEDGMENTS

Sydney

Daryl Jackson Robin Dyke Pty Ltd
Directors: Robin Dyke, Daryl Jackson
Associates: Andrew Hipwell, Alex Kibble, Daniel Beekwilder

Brisbane

Daryl Jackson Pty Ltd
Directors: Daryl Jackson, David Trott,
Associate Director: Gary Carter

Canberra

Daryl Jackson Alastair Swayn Pty Ltd
Directors: Alastair Swayn, Daryl Jackson
Associates: James Andrews, Melinda Dodson

Perth

Peter Hunt and Daryl Jackson

Shenyang

Daryl Jackson Pty Ltd
Director: Daryl Jackson

Shanghai

Daryl Jackson Pty Ltd
Director: Daryl Jackson
Associate: Lincoln Barker

Hanoi

Daryl Jackson International
Director: Daryl Jackson

London

Daryl Jackson International
in association with John Lyall
Director: Daryl Jackson
Associate Director: Lincoln Barker

Berlin

Daryl Jackson International
Director: Daryl Jackson
Associate: Katherina Muller-Stuler

We appreciate our clients' trust and vision in commissioning or selecting us. In addition, we thank all consultants and contractors who have applied their talents to get the projects built.

Many photographers have contributed to the work in this book. Special thanks go to John Gollings, Tim Griffith, David Sandison, Dianna Snape, Eric Sierins, Ben Wrigley, Dennis Gilbert and Trevor Mein.

Appreciation also to Demie Manolas and David Fantini, who began working with The Images Publishing Group during the initial stages of this project, sourcing the images presented in this monograph. The practice also thanks The Images Publishing Group for its invitation to participate in the series.

It is the work of these people and all the other architects, interior designers and secretarial staff in the firm that has given the practice a national and international reputation for high quality consultation and performance.

ARTICLES

'120 Collins Street', *Constructional Review*, vol. 65, no. 1, February 1992, pp. 20–27 (Photographs by John Gollings).

'Aerodynamic', *Houses*, Issue 33, 2003, pp. 16–22 (Abraham's House. Photographs by Shannon Pawsey).

Andrews, John, 'Building Australia', *Design World*, no. 19k, 1990, pp. 56–52 (Bond University; Australian Chancery, Riyadh Saudi Arabia; Hyatt Hotel, Canberra).

'Anzac Parade Urban Design Competition', *Landscape Australia*, February 1992, pp. 48–49.

'Architecture Awards: Interior Architecture', *Architect Victoria*, Awards 2003, pp. 22, 23 (Victorian County Court. Photographs by Trevor Mein).

'Australia's Bicentennial Exhibition', *Lightweight Structures*, Connell Group, 1988.

'Australian Chancery Complex, Riyadh', *Architecture Australia*, November 1991, pp. 54–56 (Winner of RAIA International Award. Photographs by John Gollings).

'Australian Chancery Complex, Riyadh', *Tasarim*, Turkey, no. 26, August 1992, pp. 58–67 (Photographs by John Gollings).

'Australian Film, Television and Radio School', *Construction Review*, vol. 62, no. 4, November 1989, pp. 46–53 (Photographs by Tom Balfour of Max Dupain and Associates).

'Australian Institute of Sport, ACT, Athletics Field Grandstand, Canberra', *Innovative Building*, vol. 7, no. 3, March 1992, pp. 1,16.

Bagnall, Diana, 'Diplomatic Unity', *Vogue Living*, vol. 14, no 7, September 1990, pp. 96–105, 158 (Australian Chancery, Riyadh, Saud Arabia. Photographs by John Gollings).

Bagnall, Diana. 'Architecture in Living', *Vogue Living*, vol. XXXIII, no. 1, February 1990, p. 18 (Cox House, Portsea).

'Bank College', *Constructional Review*, vol. 5, no. 3, August 1978, pp. 40–45 (Photographs by John Gollings).

'Baths', *Architecture in Australia*, vol. 58, no. 5, October 1969, pp. 813–818 (Harold Holt Memorial Swimming Pool. Photographs by Ian McKenzie).

Beck, Haig and Jackie Cooper, 'Daryl Jackson: 1987 Gold Medallist', *Architect*, Victoria, April 1987, pp. 8–9.

Biagi, Marco, 'Ville Moderne: Tradizione Liberata', *Ville Giardini*, no. 287, December 1993, pp. 14–21 (Jackson House, Bermagui).

'Bond University Library, Humanities and Administration Buildings', *The Japan Architect*, Japan, no. 402, October 1990, pp. 45–51.

'Bond University', *Constructional Review*, vol. 63, no. 3, August 1990, pp. 10–23 (Photographs by John Gollings).

'Bond University', *Nikkei Architecture*, Japan, 1:20, 1992, pp. 224–231.

Brennan, Betsy, 'Capital Conversion', *Vogue Living*, October 1988, pp. 134–139 (Hyatt Hotel, Canberra. Photographs by John Hay).

Brennan Betsy. 'Romancing the Dune', *Vogue Living*, no. 10, December/January 1990/91, pp. 96–103 (Carter House, Mission Beach, Queensland. Photographs by Scott Frances).

Britt, Brian. 'The Australian Film, Television and Radio School', *Profiles in Building*, James Hardie & Co Pty. Ltd, 1989, pp. 10–14.

Buchanan, Peter, 'Big Top Down Under', *Architectural Review*, London, vol. 177, no. 1059, May 1985, pp. 64–67 (Australian Bicentennial Touring Exhibition).

'Canberra School of Art', *Architecture Australia*, vol. 70, no. 6, December 1981, pp. 4, 6–8 (Winner of the Sir Zelman Cowen Award 1981. Photographs by Max Dupain).

'Canberra School of Art', *Architecture Australia*, vol. 70, no. 6, December 1981, pp. 46–47.

'Canberra School of Music', *Architecture Australia*, vol. 65, no. 6, January 1977, pp. 15–20 (Photographs by Max Dupain).

'Canberra's Architecture', *Architecture Australia*, vol. 72, no. 5, September 1983, pp. 47–48 (Canberra School of Art; National Swimming Training Centre).

'Centenary House', *Constructional Review*, vol. 67, no. 1, February 1994, pp. 26–31 (Photographs by Eric Sierins).

'Commercial Union Assurance', *Corporate and Office Design*, Autumn/Winter 1989, pp. 40–43 (Commercial Union, Melbourne).

Cooper, Jackie, 'Architecture Ergonomics', *Vogue Living*, no. 8, October 1991, pp. 138–139 (Gollings Studio, Richmond. Photographs by John Gollings).

'Daryl Jackson International Limited: Penguin Parade', *Architectural Review*, London, vol. CLXXXIX, no. 1130, April 1991, p. 73.

'Daryl Jackson International Limited: Welsh Walk', *Architectural Review*, London, vol. CLXXXIX, no. 1130, April 1991, pp. 71–72.

'Daryl Jackson Pty Ltd', *Design Ink*, no. 8, March 1992, pp. 22–25.

'Daryl Jackson Pty Ltd: Two Projects', *Architecture Australia*, vol. 78, no. 2 March 1989, pp. 48–55 (Hyatt, Hotel Canberra; Australian Bicentennial Exhibition. Photographs by John Gollings).

'Daryl Jackson', ('Australian Interior Design 1991: A Survey',) *Design World*, no. 20, 1991, pp. 64–68.

'Daryl Jackson', *Space Design*, Japan, no. 293, February 1989, pp. 26–27.

'Daryl Jackson: RAIA Gold Medal 1987', *Architecture Australia* (special) commemorative issue, vol. 76, no. 7, November 1987, pp. 51–82. (Articles by Haig Beck and Daryl Jackson: 12 early buildings; Lake Ginninderra College, Belconnen; Monash Gallery Building, Monash University, Clayton; the Walter and Eliza Hall Institute of Medical Research, Parkville; Australian Defence Force Academy Indoor Sports Centre, Canberra; Bond University, Gold Coast; Cape Schanck Golf Club; Ringwood Pool, Melbourne; Carey Grammar Sports Hall, Melbourne; 120 Collins Street Office Tower, Melbourne; Commercial Union Office Building, Melbourne).

Deas, Greg, 'Public Sector Architecture', *Architecture Australia*, July 1990, pp. 42–44 (Belconnen College, Canberra).

Dickinson, Michael, 'Downtown Looks Up: the Missing Ingredient', *Bulletin*, June 30, 1987 (Daryl Jackson's personal view for the City Perfect).

Drew, Philip, 'Complementing the Best of Sport', *Business Review Weekly*, January 15, 1993, pp. 68–69 (MCG Southern Stand. Photographs by John Gollings).

Duncan, Jenepher and Conrad Hamann, 'Seven in the Seventies', *Architecture Australia*, vol. 71, no. 1, January 1982, pp. 51–59 (Review of an exhibition).

'Emu Ridge Government Housing', *Constructional Review*, vol. 53, no. 1, February 1980, pp. 40–45.

'Financial Management Consulting Group', *Corporate and Office Design*, Autumn/Winter 1989, pp. 146–149 (Financial Management Consulting Group, Melbourne. Photographs by Mark Chow).

'Food Technology Building', *Constructional Review*, vol. 66, no. 2, May 1993, pp. 48–51 (Photographs by Richard Stringer).

Friss-Clark, Anny, 'Stonier's Merricks Vineyard', *Corporate and Office Design*, Spring/Summer 1991, pp. 94–97 (Stonier's Winery, Merricks. Photographs by Tim Griffith).

Gardner, Carl, 'Australian Converts', *RIBA Journal*, London, vol. 98, no. 6, June 1991, pp. 64–66 (Cannons Sports Club and Seymour Powell Studio, London. Photographs by Rory Carnegie).

Gardner, Johnthan, '120 Collins Street, Melbourne', *Architecture: Middle East*, no. 001, 1997, pp. 26–29.

Georgiev, Peter, 'Great Southern Stand Wins Victorian Architecture Medal', *Architect*, Victoria, June 1992, p. 4.

'Grandstand in a Bush Setting', *Architecture Australia*, December 1990, p. 10 (Athletics Field Grandstand, Australian Institute of Sport, ACT).

Green, Louise, 'The National Golf Club', *Corporate and Office Design*, Spring/Summer 1990, pp. 216–218 (National Golf Club, Cape Schanck. Photographs by John Gollings).

Greenwood, Helen, 'The Hide-Art', *Plenty*, vol. 5, November/January 1990, pp. 42–44 (Abrahams House, Brighton. Photographs by Ashley Evans).

Griffiths, Anna, 'Stonier's Winery', *Design Ink*, no. 7, December 1991, pp. 24–31 (Photographs by Tim Griffith).

Grose, James, 'National Sports Centre Swimming Halls, Bruce', *Architecture Australia*, December 1984.

'Ground Control', *Australian Design Trends*, vol. 18 no. 14, 2003, pp. 65–83.

'High School', *Constructional Review*, vol. 47, no. 2, June 1974, pp. 24–26 (Princes Hill High School, Carlton).

'Hit or Miss', *Architect*, Victoria, vol. 3, no. 36, January/February 1975, pp. 4–8 (Royal Melbourne Tennis Club, Richmond).

Holder, Christopher, 'Melbourne Cricket Ground', *Venue*, Issue 8, February 2006, pp. 90–95 (Photographs by Heath McCurdy).

'Housing City Edge', *Constructional Review*, vol. 50, no. 3, May 1977, pp. 26–33.

'Hover Craft', *Steel Profile*, no. 91, July 2005, pp. 10–17 (Station Pier Restaurant. Photographs by Peter Hyatt).

Hutson, Andrew, 'The MCG: The Games we Play', *Artichoke*, vol. 15, pp. 76–85 (Photographs by Trevor Mein).

'Hyatt Hotel, Canberra: Daryl Jackson Pty Ltd', *Architecture Australia*, vol. 78, no. 11, December 1989, pp. 28–30 (Winner, President's Award for Recycled Buildings; Winner, Belle Interiors Award in Association with Hirsch Bedner Incorporated. Photographs by John Gollings).

Hyatt, Peter, 'Pool Hall Operators', *Steel Profile*, no. 38, December 1991, pp. 26–31 (Dandenong Pool. Photographs by Peter Hyatt).

Hyatt, Peter, 'Shrines of Remembrance', *Steel Profile*, no. 41, September, 1992, pp. 16–23 (MCG Southern Stand. Photographs by Peter Hyatt).

Hyatt, Peter, 'Wild Colonial Boy', *Steel Profile*, pp. 11–16 (Colonial Stadium. Photographs by Peter Hyatt).

'I.T.E.E. Building', *Constructional Review*, vol. 67, no. 2, May 1994, pp. 50–55 (Information Technology & Electrical Engineering Building, University of Melbourne. Photographs by John Gollings).

Jackson, Daryl and Geoff Nairn, 'Adelaide 2000 Competition', *Architecture Australia*, vol. 75, no. 6, September 1986, pp. 45–49.

Jackson, Daryl and Patrick McCaughey, 'Daryl Jackson: Architecture, Drawings and Photographs', *Architect*, Victoria, vol. 8, no. 2, June/July 1984, pp. 18–23.

Jackson, Daryl, 'Daryl Jackson: Four Projects', *Architecture Australia*, vol. 79, no. 2, March 1990, pp. 27–42 (Australian Film, Television and Radio School, Sydney; Bond University, Queensland; Penguin Parade, Phillip Island; Australian Chancery, Riyadh, Saudi Arabia. Photographs by John Gollings).

Jackson, Daryl, 'Desert Diplomat', *World Architecture*, London, issue no. 13, 1991, pp. 58–61 (Australian Chancery, Riyadh, Saudi Arabia).

Jackson, Daryl, 'Design in the Eighties: The Search for an Urban Australia', *Architect*, Victoria, September 1988, pp. 4–5.

Jackson, Daryl, 'Extract', *Edge Magazine*, no. 2, 1991 (Review of firm).

Jackson, Daryl, 'From Edge to Centre: Sense and Stylism in Current Australian Architecture', *UIA International Architect*, Japan, no. 4, 1984, pp. 4–5.

Jackson, Daryl, 'Response to Philip Drew's Paper by Daryl Jackson', *Architecture Australia*, vol. 73, no. 4, June 1984, pp. 80–84 (following the article 'Terra Australis Nondum Cognita' by Philip Drew).

Jackson, Daryl, 'Two New Buildings', *Architecture Australia*, vol. 69, no. 5, November 1980, pp. 48–57 (AME School, Canberra and Collingwood Pool, Melbourne. Photographs by John Gollings).

Jackson, Daryl, 'Urban Frontiers', *Melbourne Lygon Arts Festival*, vol. 1, no. 2, 1989, pp. 62–65.

Jackson, Davina, 'Dynamic Recycling', *Vogue Living*, vol. XXVII, no. 2, April/May 1994, pp. 138–141 (Boiler House Lecture Theatre, University of Canberra. Photographs by John Gollings).

Jahn, Graham, 'Far East, Down Under', *Architectural Record*, USA, May 1991, pp. 58–65 (Library Administration Building, Bond University, Queensland).

Keens, Leta, 'St Monica's Church', *Corporate Office Design*, Autumn/Winter 1991, pp. 215–217 (Photographs by John Gollings).

Kerr Forster, Pannell, 'Building a Name – Client Profile: Daryl Jackson Pty Ltd', *Current Affairs*, vol. 12, October 1990, p. 8.

'Lake Ginninderra College, ACT', *Constructional Review*, vol. 61, no. 2, May 1988 (Photographs by John Gollings).

'Latchford Barracks', *Constructional Review*, vol. 57, no. 2, May 1984, pp. 10–19 (Photographs by Max Dupain).

'Lauriston Girls School', *Architecture in Australia*, vol. 59, no. 4, August 1970, pp. 657–658.

Laurence, Fleur, 'Conservatorium of Music, Sydney', *Monument*, December/January 2001–2002, p. 45 (Photographs courtesy Walter Construction Group).

Liston, Jo, 'Making a Stand', *Panorama*, December 1998, pp. 54–61 (MCG Great Southern Stand).

Logan, Stephan, 'Under the One Roof', *Scope*, June 2000.

Lovell, Peter, 'Chateau Yering A Yarra Valley Winery Re-established', *Architect: Tourism*, April 1995, pp. 8, 9 (Stonier's Winery).

Luker, Paul, 'Business Builds its Future Leaders', *Business Review Weekly*, vol. 9, no. 26, July 3, 1987, pp. 88–90 (Melbourne University Graduate School of Management. Photographs by John Hay).

MacMahon, William, 'The Bare Minimum', *Interior Architecture*, issue 32, 1991, pp. 88–99 (Gollings Studio, Richmond. Photographs by John Gollings).

'MCG Southern Stand: Sir Zelman Cowen Award Winner', *Architecture Australia*, December, 1992, pp. 38–40.

'McLachlan Office', *Constructional Review*, vol. 54, no. 2, May 1981, pp. 12–19 (Photographs by Max Dupain).

'Medical Research Building: The Walter and Eliza Hall Institute of Medical Research, Parkville', *Trends*, James Hardie & Co. Pty Ltd, vol. 2, no. 3, November 1987, pp. 14–15.

Menary, Steve, 'Best of Breed?' *Sport Business International*, no. 90, April 2004, p. 45 (Telstra Dome).

Menary, Steve, 'Ground Force', *Panstadia*, vol. 12, no. 4, May 2006, pp. 14–19 (MCG).

Missingham, Greg and Norman Day, 'Daryl Jackson Architecture: Two Reviews Prompted by the Exhibition', *Transition*, vol 3, April/June 1984, pp. 77–82.

'Modern Australian Architecture', *Process Architecture*, Tokyo, no. 22, March 1981 (St Paul's Woodleigh; Jackson Walker Offices, Fitzroy; Collingwood Pool).

'Mt Scopus College', *Constructional Review*, vol. 50, no. 3, August 1977, pp. 38–41 (Photographs by Ian McKenzie).

'Murray House, Templestowe', *Architecture in Australia*, vol. 62, no. 5, October 1973, pp. 78–79.

Murray, P, 'Architecture in the Antipodes', *RIBA Journal*, London, no. 91, February 1984, pp. 23–24.

'Music and Museology', *Trends Ideas*, pp. 66–75 (Sydney Conservatorium of Music, Sydney. Photographs by John Gollings and Eric Sierins).

'Music School, Canberra', *Architectural Review*, London, vol. 164, no. 979, September 1978, p. 152.

'New Educational Buildings: Menindee Central School', *Architecture Australia*, July 1990, p. 48.

'New Medical Research Building', *Constructional Review*, vol. 59, no. 2, May 1986, pp. 12–19 (Photographs by John Gollings).

'Oasis Recreational Centre', *Constructional Review*, vol. 64, no. 4, November 1991, pp. 36–41 (Dandenong Pool. Photographs by John Gollings).

'Old Physics Courtyard and Art Gallery', *Architecture in Australia*, vol. 64, no. 4, August 1975, p. 93 (Old Physics Building, University of Melbourne).

'On Your Marks', *Commercial Design Trend*, vol. 22, no. 4, pp. 124–160 (MCG. Photographs by Jamie Cobeldick).

Osborne, Catherine, 'Bond University', *Corporate and Office Design*, Spring/Summer 1990, pp. 52–55 (Photographs by John Gollings).

'Penguins on Parade', *Steel Profile*, no. 27, March 1989, pp. 10–17 (Penguin Parade, Phillip Island. Photographs by Peter Hyatt).

'Pleasures in Architecture: Engehurst', *Architecture Australia*, vol. 69, no. 2, May 1980, pp. 46–47 (Design competition entries for the 'Pleasures of Architecture' RAIA Conference).

'Pluralism Down Under: The Work of Daryl Jackson', *Building*, London, vol 245, no. 7314 (42), October 21, 1983, p. 22.

'Pooling Resources', RIBA Journal, February 1996, pp. 47–51.

'Premiated Parliament House Entry', *Transition*, no. 3, March 1980, pp. 23–25.

Raftopoulos, Andrew and Michael Bialek, 'Princes Hill High School', *Architect*, Victoria, vol. 3, no. 31, March/April 1974, pp. 13–16.

'Raise the Roof', *Steel Profile*, no. 94, March 2006, pp. 2–9 (Photographs by Peter Hyatt).

Rasch, Horst, 'A Large House for Long Holidays', *Hauser*, no. 2, 1994, pp. 26–33 (Jackson House, Bermagui. Photographs by Reiner Blunck).

'Redevelopment of Royal Melbourne Hospital', *Constructional Review*, vol. 65, no. 4, November 1992, p. 8.

Remington, Kay, 'Design for Designers', *Interior Design*, issue 7, 1987, pp. 104–112 (Daryl Jackson Offices, Melbourne. Photographs by William Rethmeier).

'Residential Wing, St. Hilda's College', *Architect*, Victoria, vol 3, no. 25, March/April 1973, pp. 14–17.

'Resource Centre', *Construction Review*, vol. 47, no. 2, June 1974, pp. 30–33 (Methodist Ladies College Resource Centre, Kew).

'Ringwood Swimming Centre, Ringwood, Victoria', *Trends*, James Hardie & Co. Pty Ltd, vol. 2, no. 3, November 1987, pp. 6–7.

'Riyadh Chancery Complex', *Constructional Review*, vol. 63, no. 1, February 1990, pp. 22–29 (Photographs by John Gollings).

Rollo, Joe, 'Under the Big Top', *The Weekend Australian Magazine*, April 1–2, 2006, pp. 16–20 (Southern Cross Station. Photographs by Nick Cubbin).

'Royal Tennis Club', *Constructional Review*, vol. 50, no. 3, August 1977, pp. 32–37 (Photographs by Ian McKenzie).

Ryder, Terry, 'The New Stadium: Not just for footy fans', *Property Australia*, June 1998, pp. 38.

Scheiling, Samantha, 'Seven Up: Melbourne Harbour's Transformation', *Stadium & Arena Management*, vol. 4, no. 1, February 2000, pp. 10–14 (Colonial Stadium).

'School of Art', *Constructional Review*, vol. 50, no. 3, August 1981, pp. 20–27 (Canberra School of Art).

'Scuola in Australia', *Domus*, Italy, no. 564, November 1976, pp. 36–40 (Yooralla Hospital School for Crippled Children, Glenroy).

'Set to Shine', *Panstadia International: Quarterly Report*, vol. 9, no. 4, May 2003, p. 28 (Telstra Dome).

'Shelter for Bandsmen', *Architecture Australia*, vol. 65, no. 4, August/September 1971, pp. 70–71 (Collingwood Bandstand, Melbourne).

Sinclair, Bob, 'Budapest Business Centre', *Architect*, Victoria, March 1993, p. 8.

Sinclair, Bob, 'Commercial Union', *Architect*, Victoria, April 1992, p. 13.

'Singapore High Commission', *Constructional Review*, vol. 59, no. 1, February 1986, pp. 28–33 (Photographs by John Gollings).

Smith, Brian, 'New Southern Stand for MCG', *Innovative Building*, vol. 6, no. 11, November 1991, p. 10.

'Southern Stand, Melbourne Cricket Ground', *Constructional Review*, vol. 65, no. 2, May 1992, pp. 16–23 (Photographs by John Gollings).

Spence, Rory and Peter Davey, 'Australia: Sydney/Melbourne', *Architectural Review*, London, special issue, vol. 178, no. 1066, December 1985, pp. 22–95 (Esprit de Corps Offices and Warehouse, Abbotsford).

Spence, Rory, 'Three Australian Houses', *Architectural Review*, London, vol. 176, no. 1052, October 1984, pp. 26–31 (Jackson Houses, East Melbourne and Shoreham).

'St Paul's Woodleigh, Baxter', *Architectural Review*, London, vol. 164, no. 979, September 1978, p. 167.

'State Bank Staff College', *Architecture Australia*, vol. 67, no. 5 October/November 1978, pp. 69–70 (Photographs by John Gollings).

'State of the Art Stadium', *Business Link*, Quarterly issue, November 1998, pp. 16, 17.

Styant-Brown, Anthony, 'Dynamic Order', *Architecture Australia*, March/April 1995, pp. 56–61 (IBM tenancy, Southgate, Melbourne. Photographs by John Gollings).

Sudjic, D, 'Australia: The Great Indoors', *Blueprint*, London, September 1988.

'The Australian Film, Television and Radio School', *Profiles in the Building*, pp. 10–14.

'The Bond University, Queensland – A Study of Style with Steel', *Metal Building News*, vol. 5, no. 8, August 1990, pp. 1, 16–17.

'The Graduate School of Management', *Constructional Review*, vol. 60, no. 2, May 1987, pp. 30–37 (Photographs by John Gollings).

'The Head Office for the Digital Equipment Corporation, Rhodes, Sydney', *Innovative Building*, vol. 7, no. 1, January 1992, p. 11–12.

'The Law of Courts', *Architectural Review*, Spring 2002, pp. 52–55 (Photographs by Trevor Mein).

'The Music of Construction', *Building Australia*, November 2000, pp. 14–16 (Sydney Conservatorium).

'The Search for Identity', *Steel Profile*, no. 19, March 1987, pp. 10–15 (Profile/interview with Daryl Jackson. Photographs by Peter Hyatt and John Gollings).

'The Singapore High Commission in Canberra by Daryl Jackson, Alastair Swayn and Peter Rees', *Architecture Australia*, vol. 74, no. 8, December 1985, p. 24 (The Sir Zelman Cowen Award Finalists).

Tombesi, Paolo, 'Australian Architecture', *Casabella 550*, Italy, anno LII, October 1988, pp. 54–62 (Monash Gallery Building, Melbourne).

Towndrow, Jennifer, 'Making Waves in the New World', *RIBA Journal*, London, vol. 97, no. 7, July 1990, pp. 10–23 (Review of current work).

'Training Centre and Special School', *Constructional Review*, vol. 50, no. 2, May 1977, pp. 18–25 (Yooralla Hospital for Crippled Children, Glenroy. Photographs by Ian McKenzie).

'Tribune in Canberra', *Baumeister*, Germany, October 1991, pp. 30–31 (Athletics Field Grandstand, Australian Institute of Sports, ACT).

Trimble, Judith, 'Images and Function', *Architecture Australia*, July 1991, pp. 20–25 (Dandenong Pool. Photographs by John Gollings).

Turnball, Jeff, 'Style and Repose: Unity in Plurality', *Architecture Australia*, vol. 75, no. 5, July 1986, pp. 55–62 (Swimming Training Halls, Canberra; Catholic Diocesan Offices, Ballarat; Esprit de Corp, Abbotsford. Photographs by Jeff Turnball and John Gollings).

'Two Recent Projects by Jackson/Walker', *Architect*, Victoria, vol. 3, no. 42, July 1976, pp. 22–23 (Raiwaga Youth Centre; Ballarat Student Union and Student Housing).

'University Complex', *Constructional Review*, vol. 5, no. 3, August 1980, pp. 28–33 (Deakin University Administration and Lecture Theatre Building. Photographs by John Gollings).

'Up and Under', *Designers' Journal*, London, May 1991, p. 4 (Cannons Sports Club and Seymour Powell Studio, London).

Van Schaik, Leon, 'Daryl Jackson Pty Ltd: Reflections on the Role of the Designer in the Corporate Firm', *Transition*, no. 22/23, Summer 1987, pp. 56–58.

'Warehouse Architectural Office', *Architecture in Australia*, vol. 62, no. 4, August 1973, pp. 76–78 (Jackson Walker Offices, Fitzroy).

Welsh, John, 'Coastal Orders', *Building Design*, London, no. 1112, February 19, 1993, pp. 16–17 (Jackson House, Bermagui).

'Wesley Senior College', *Constructional Review*, vol. 65, no. 4, November 1992, pp. 36–41 (Photographs by Tim Griffiths).

Wheeler, Tony, 'Pool', *Architecture Australia*, September/October, 1993, pp. 47–51 (Tuggeranong Pool. Photographs by John Gollings).

'YWCA Community Resource Centre, Suva, Fiji', *Architecture in Australia*, vol. 63, no. 6, December 1974, pp. 50–51.

'YWCA, Suva', *Constructional Review*, vol. 47, no. 3, September 1974, pp. 28–33.

MONOGRAPHS

Bartlett Works: Architecture Buildings Projects, August Projects in association with the Bartlett School of Architecture, UCL, England, 2004.

Bingham-Hall, Patrick, *Austral Eden: 200 years of Australian architecture*, The Watermark Press, Sydney, 1999.

Butten, John Norman, *Look Here: Considering the Australian environment*, based on a series of lectures of the Victorian Fabian Society, Cheshire, Melbourne, 1968.

Clarke, Ron, *Never say never: Couran Cove from dream to reality*, Banyan Tree Creative Services, Avalon, NSW, 1999.

Day, Norman, *Modern Houses Melbourne*, Brian Zouch Publications, Melbourne, 1976 (Murray House, Boyle House, Parson House).

Dunstan, Keith, *The People's Ground: The MCG, 2000*, fourth edition, Arcadia/Australian Scholarly Publishing Pty Ltd, Sydney, 2000.

Goad, Philip, *Judging Architecture: Issues Divisions Triumphs*, Victorian Architecture Awards 1929–2003, Royal Australian Institute of Architects, Melbourne, 2003.

Griggs, Michael and Leon Paroissien (eds), *Old Continent New Buildings: Contemporary Australian Architecture*, David Ell Press, Sydney, 1983 (Jackson House, East Melbourne; Canberra School of Art; Southport Nursing Home).

Jackson, Daryl, *Architecture: Drawings and Photographs*, Macmillan Company of Australia, Melbourne, 1984.

Jackson, Daryl, *Daryl Jackson Selected and Current Work*, The Master Architect Series II, The Images Publishing Group Pty Ltd, Melbourne, 1996.

Judd, Bruce and John Dean (eds), *Medium Density Housing in Australia*, RAIA Education Division, Canberra, 1985 (City Edge Housing, South Melbourne; Royal Melbourne Hospital Staff Housing, Melbourne; Emu Ridge Housing, Canberra).

Leonard, Mike, *The Making of Colonial Stadium Melbourne Docklands*, Mercedes Waratah Press, Melbourne, 2002.

Pegrum, Roger, *Details in Australian Architecture*, Volume 1, RAIA Education Division, Canberra, 1984, pp. 108–109 (Abrahams House, Brighton).

Pegrum, Roger, *Details in Australian Architecture*, Volume 2, RAIA Education Division, Canberra, 1987, pp. 72–76 (Swimming Training Halls, Canberra).

Walter, Betsy, *Australian Style*, New Holland Publishers, 2000.

Waterfront Spectacular: creating Melbourne Docklands the people's waterfront, ETNCOM Pty Ltd, Sydney, 2005.

Zimmer, Jenny, *Anthony Pryor: Sculptures & Drawings 1974 – 1991*, Macmillan, Melbourne, 1999 (Chapter 1).